OUR VOICES:
Essays in Culture, Ethnicity, and Communication

An Intercultural Anthology

Alberto González
Bowling Green State University

Marsha Houston
Tulane University

Victoria Chen
Denison University

Foreword by Molefi K. Asante

ROXBURY PUBLISHING COMPANY

Library of Congress Cataloging-in-Publication Data

Our voices: essays in culture, ethnicity, and communication: an intercultural anthology/
edited by Alberto González, Marsha Houston, Victoria Chen.
    p. cm
    Includes bibliographical references and index.
    ISBN 0-935732-45-4
    1. Intercultural Communication
      I. González, Alberto, 1954-
      II. Houston, Marsha
      III. Chen, Victoria
GN345.6.0927 1993   93-24049
303.48'2—dc20   CIP

**OUR VOICES: ESSAYS IN CULTURE, ETHNICITY,
AND COMMUNICATION**

Publisher: Claude Teweles
Editors: Claude Teweles and Dawn VanDercreek
Assistant Editor: Anton Diether
Cover Design: Allan Miller (based on a poster by Otl Archer)
Typesetting and Design: Ingrid Herman Reese and Christy Canary

Printed on acid-free paper

Printed in the United States of America

10 9 8 7 6 5 4 3 2 1

ISBN 0-935732-45-4

ROXBURY PUBLISHING COMPANY
P.O. Box 491044
Los Angeles, California 90049
(213) 653-1068

TABLE OF CONTENTS

Part III: Representing Cultural Knowledge in Interpersonal and Mass Media Contexts

Part IV: Traversing Cultural Paths

Appendices

To those who spoke unheard before us.

To those who make mathematics...

ACKNOWLEDGEMENTS

We wish to acknowledge that this book represents the efforts of more than just the editors, publication staff, and contributors. An anthology of this nature and scope requires extraordinary patience, encouragement, latitude, and commitment from a publisher. Claude Teweles, the publisher at Roxbury Publishing Company, possesses each.

Thanks to the following reviewers for their helpful suggestions: Benjamin J. Broome, Donal Carbaugh, Kristine L. Fitch, Dennis S. Gouran, Lyndrey A. Niles, Gerry Philipsen, Robert Shuter, and William J. Starosta, as well as those unknown to us. Special thanks to Terrence L. Albrecht for steering us to Roxbury.

Gratitude is also extended to Department Chairs John J. Makay (Bowling Green State University) and Robert L. Ivie (formerly at Texas A&M University) for providing support for this project. Deep thanks to all our students who gave us inspiration and encouragement, and to the following for their various contributions, often on very short notice: Pamela Bachman, Alice Crume, Donna Dudgeon, James Fry, J.B. González, Esteban Mariscal, and Vilma Matos-Ortiz.

FOREWORD

Molefe Kete Asante

The appearance of the book, *Our Voices: Essays in Culture, Ethnicity, and Communication*, is a remarkable achievement in the field of communication. It reflects the evolution of a field that has too long marginalized the voices of African, Asian, Latino, Native, Jewish, and Arab Americans. Because the field of communication has demonstrated a tendency to represent the hegemonic position of white Anglo-Saxon Protestants, the voices of scholars from other traditions have not been heard as often as they might. Indeed, the field has lacked the sustained cultural insights of these intellectuals in any meaningful way.

Our Voices is an innovative contribution to the current dialogue about the nature of communication and a refreshing addition to multicultural studies. It presents an array of original essays by outstanding scholars from various cultures that have been under-represented in the literature of the field.

Several years ago a friend of mine, a well-known professor in an influential communication department, told me that he felt the field of communication was too narrowly focused. When I inquired about the meaning of his statement, he explained that it needed more scholars who were interested in cultural themes from many perspectives. I believe that the many authors who have produced this volume have applied a pluralistic, non-hegemonic idea to the production of their work. The book comes to us as a projection into the future, to the extent that it broadens the way we see ourselves as communication researchers and as human beings.

Communication is the defining characteristic of contemporary life. We are engaged in communication both as producers and consumers of messages and images. In writing these essays, the contributors have begun the process of providing the basis for a new perspective. The fact that we now have this volume of essays from scholars trained in the field means that we are well on our way toward a new chorus of human voices in communication.

ABOUT THE CONTRIBUTORS

Ling Chen (Ph.D., Ohio State University) is an assistant professor at the University of Oklahoma. She has been published in *Gazette*, *Asian Journal of Communication*, *Howard Journal of Communications*, and *Speech Communication Association International and Intercultural Communication Annuals*. Her major areas of interest include interpersonal communication, intercultural communication, cross-cultural communication, particularly of Chinese culture, and discourse analysis.

Victoria Chen (Ph.D., University of Massachusetts) is an assistant professor of Communication at Denison University. Her work has appeared in *Research on Language and Social Interaction* and *International and Intercultural Communication Annual*. Her research interests include analyses of ethnic autobiographies and of cultural experiences in multicultural realities.

Gloria Flores (M.S., Southern Illinois University) is coordinator of Student Development and Multicultural Programs at Texas A&M University, a member of the Texas Association for Chicanos in Higher Education, and serves as placement commission chair on the executive board of the Texas Association of College and University Student Personnel Administrators. She has presented programs on ethnic student retention, cultural diversity, and student development at local, state, and national conferences.

Margarita Gangotena (Ph.D., University of Minnesota) is an assistant professor of Speech Communication at Texas A&M University. Her selected areas of teaching and research are health communication, intercultural communication, and rhetorical criticism.

Thurmon Garner (Ph.D., Northwestern University) is an associate professor of Rhetorical Criticism and African American Communication in the Department of Speech Communication at the University of Georgia. He has been published in *The Quarterly Journal of Speech*, *Journal of Language and Social Psychology*, *Communication Quarterly*, *The Western Journal of Black Studies*, *The Journal of Black Studies*, and other journals. His interests include cultural communication, African American discourse, and popular criticism.

Gwendolyn Gong (Ph.D., Purdue University) is an associate professor at Texas A&M University and has served as director of Freshman English Studies and as a writing consultant for The Center for Executive Development, Texas A&M University, and for various colleges and universities. Her book *Editing: The Design of Rhetoric* (co-authored with Sam Dragga) received the 1990 NCTE Achievement Award as "Best Book of the Year." Gong and Dragga are currently completing *A Writer's Repertoire* and *A Reader's Repertoire*, to be published by HarperCollins.

Alberto González (Ph.D., Ohio State University) is an associate professor of Interpersonal Communication at Bowling Green State University. He has been published in *The Quarterly Journal of Speech*, *Western Journal of Communication*, *Southern Communication Journal*, and elsewhere. He co-edited (with M.J. Medhurst and T.R. Peterson) *Communication and the Culture of Technology* (1990, Washington State University Press).

Janice D. Hamlet (Ph.D., Ohio State University) is an assistant professor in the Department of Speech and Theater Arts at Shippensburg University of Pennsylvania. She teaches courses in African American communication, rhetorical criticism and women's rhetoric. Her research interests include African American rhetoric, African American women in society, rhetorical studies in speech communication and journalism, and religious rhetoric.

Marsha Houston (Ph.D., University of Massachusetts) is an associate professor of Communication and Women's Studies at Tulane University. She has been published in *Women's Studies in Communication*, *Howard Journal of Communications*, and several anthologies, and has co-edited (with Cheris Kramerae) a special issue of *Discourse and Society*, "Women: Speaking from Silence." Her forthcoming book on African American middle-class women as a community of speakers will be published by Temple University Press.

Navita Cummings James (Ph.D., Ohio State University) is an associate professor of Communication at the University of South Florida in Tampa and currently serves as director of African Studies. She is also president of the Southern States Communication Association and vice-chair of the Florida Commission on the Status of Women. Her teaching and research interests include cultural diversity, gender and communication, and media, technology and communication.

Elizabeth Lozano (Ph.D., Ohio University) is an assistant professor in the Department of Communication at Loyola University in Chicago. Her articles have been published in *Communication Theory*, *Dia-logos de la Comunicación*, *Media Development*, *Communications*, and other journals on the topics of communication and Pan-American cultures, postmodern literature, aesthetics, and television.

Casey Man Kong Lum (Ph.D., New York University) is an assistant professor of Communication at Adelphi University and currently serves as founding vice-chair of the Asian/Pacific Islanders Caucus of the Speech Communication Association. His articles have been published in *Critical Studies in Mass Communication*, *ETC: A Review of General Semantics*, *The Speech Communication*

Annual, and other journals. His research interests include media and culture, history of communication research, and human interactions in the social context of electronic media.

Bishetta D. Merritt (Ph.D., Ohio State University) is the chairperson of the Department of Radio, Television and Film in the School of Communications at Howard University. She has served on various committees in the Speech Communication Association. Her articles have been published in the *Journal of Black Studies*, *Howard Journal of Communications*, *Journal of Popular Culture*, and *Perspectives of Black Popular Culture*. She is also a member of the editorial board of the *Journal of Applied Communication*.

Thomas Nakayama (Ph.D., University of Iowa) is an assistant professor of Rhetoric and Public Communication in the Department of Communication at Arizona State University. He is currently serving as vice-chair of the Asian/Pacific Islander caucus of the Speech Communication Association. His research interests include rhetorical studies, cultural studies, and intercultural communication.

Charles I. Nero (Ph.D., Indiana University) is an assistant professor of Rhetoric and serves as chair of African American Studies at Bates College. His articles have been published in the *Howard Journal of Communications*, *Journal of Counseling and Development*, *Brother to Brother: New Writings by Black Gay Men*, and *Law and Sexuality: A Review of Gay and Lesbian Legal Issues*. He has received fellowships from the Ford and Rockefeller foundations and is currently in residency at the Center for Lesbian and Gay Studies of the City University of New York.

Hana S. Noor Al-Deen (Ph.D., SUNY, Buffalo) is an associate professor of Mass Communication and International/Intercultural Communication at the University of North Carolina in Wilmington. She is currently serving as Chair of the Intercultural Communication Division and as vice-chair of the Mass Communication Division of the Southern States Communication Association. Her work has appeared in books, national and international journals, and regional conventions.

Sheryl Perlmutter Bowen (Ph.D., University of Massachusetts) is an assistant professor of Communication Arts and Women's Studies at Villanova University and is currently vice-chair of the Speech Communication Association's Commission on Health Communication. She has co-edited *Transforming Visions: Feminist Critiques in Communication Studies* (Hampton Press, 1993) and has worked extensively in the area of AIDS education and prevention among college students and urban African Americans.

Sidney A. Ribeau (Ph.D., University of Illinois) is a professor of Communication and currently serves as vice-president for Academic Affairs at California State Polytechnic University in Pomona. He has published articles and chapters in a number of journals and books, and has recently co-authored a book entitled *African American Communication*. He has taught courses in intercultural communication, African American culture, and media criticism.

Patricia Riley (Ph.D. candidate, University of California, Berkeley) is a poet and writer who has taught courses in Native American Literature in the Native American Studies program. She has been published in *Understanding Others: Cultural and Crosscultural Studies and the Teaching of Literature* and *Earth Song, Sky Spirit: An Anthology of Native American Fiction*, and is the editor of *Growing Up Native American*. Her research interests include Native American cultural criticism, post-colonial theory, and feminism.

Diana I. Ríos (Ph.D., University of Texas) is an assistant professor of Intercultural and Mass Communication at the University of New Mexico in Albuquerque. Her interests include mass communication research on Chicano audiences, ethnic studies, women's studies, and field research methods.

Charmaine Shutiva (Ph.D., Texas A&M University) is a teacher and coordinator at Isleta Elementary School in Isleta Pueblo, New Mexico. She has been published in several journals and chapters on the topic of Native American gifted and talented education and multicultural education, and was the principal writer for Project Northstar, a 1992 national study investigating the current status of gifted and talented Native American education.

Dolores V. Tanno (Ph.D., University of Southern California) is an associate professor of Communication Ethics and Contemporary Rhetorical Theory at California State University in San Bernardino. She has been published in the *International Journal of Intercultural Relations* and *Proceedings* of the Communication Ethics Conference, and has contributed chapters to several anthologies. Her research interests include rhetorical, ethical, and intercultural issues.

Changsheng Xi (Ph.D., University of Massachusetts) is a temporary assistant professor of Interpersonal Communication, Intercultural Communication, Small Group Communication, and Fundamentals of Public Speaking at Iowa State University. He has been published in the 1989/90 journal issue of *Research on Language and Social Interaction*.

INTRODUCTION

Beginning in the 1960s, and continuing well into the 1980s, the mission of intercultural studies was largely to prepare students for travel abroad, which usually meant Europe. Studies of cultural communities in the United States were considered "intracultural," just as America was thought to represent one culture. At best, non-mainstream cultures, like radioactive elements, were assumed to possess a half-life due to the process of assimilation. At worst, such cultures were deemed nonstandard, irrelevant, and inferior.

But today, a different reality challenges the presumption that a passport is required for intercultural experience. There is a continuous flow of immigration to the United States, especially from Asian and Latin American countries; demographic trends indicate that ethnic populations are increasing more rapidly than Euro-American populations; accessible air travel allows first- and second-generation U.S. citizens to visit their ancestral lands with relative ease; racial and ethnic populations, unlike their European predecessors, are reluctant to relinquish their cultural origins; and increasingly interdependent and volatile world economies and politics bring awareness of the world's people into our everyday lives. The metaphor of the melting pot has been challenged by a social movement that not only celebrates cultural pluralism, but also engages a critique of the assimilationist tradition. *Our Voices* was inspired by this dynamic reality. It is intended as a resource for exploring the relationships between culture and communication.

Origin, Purposes, and Goals of This Anthology

In April, 1991, at the Southern States Speech Communication Association Convention, a panel convened that was titled "Cultural Diversity and Communication: Exploring the Curriculum." Its moderator was Navita Cummings James; the presenters were the future editors of this book: Victoria Chen, Alberto González, and Marsha Houston (along with Bishetta Merritt and Hana S. Noor Al-Deen). The members of this panel were familiar to the presenters and many of the observers. We were frequently called upon to address issues pertaining to culture and communication. We were the few "cultural voices" in a sea of whiteness.

During the panel, a note made its way down the table from Marsha Houston. It proposed that we put our voices, and the voices of others we knew who were not being sufficiently heard, into a single volume of essays. The book would serve as a point of departure for those interested in exploring how the *telling* of experience constructs and informs about a culture and its participants. We enthusiastically embraced the idea and ultimately supplied our selected contributors with a goal to answer the question: "What cultural knowledge do you most wish to share?"

The resulting essays examine communication in a variety of settings and from a variety of cultural perspectives. "Our Voices" signifies that each contributor is writing from the perspective of his or her cultural experience instead of writing to accommodate the voice that is culturally desirable by the mainstream Anglo standard. This collected work offers an alternative for people who are interested in learning something about culture, ethnicity, and communication from ethnic scholars' points of view. Our premise is that communication has much to do with specific individuals' perspectives in social interaction, and that one person's unique descriptions and interpretations of his or her experience will contribute to a better understanding of one's cultural group as a whole.

One purpose of this book is to provide a discussion of the communication styles and practices of cultural groups from these writers' points of view. Currently in American intercultural studies, writers from the dominant culture, and some ethnic writers who represent and reproduce the interests of the dominant culture, often "speak for" cultural communities to which they are unrelated. Through the privileged form of scientific inquiry, these scholars often display unfamiliarity with the specific practices that lend significance to the general cultural categories or dimensions that are created. Further, we rarely hear any single cultural participant's voice in the abundant intercultural work that has been produced by various researchers. Surely, research by the cultural outsider is legitimate and can be useful, but the literature does not yet reflect a *balance* between the voices of the dominant perspective and our voices—the voices in this volume.

Many of the contributors to this book teach courses in intercultural communication. They report that students and instructors alike complain of one ironic fact: the lack of a truly intercultural perspective in intercultural literature. In a field that has traditionally adopted a Eurocentric theoretical and methodological approach, this book offers the first collection of so-called "minority" scholars' works, addressing cultural and intercultural issues in what we hope are accessible, helpful, and intriguing essays.

A second purpose of this volume is to maintain a consistent focus on communication and culture. Each essay applies concepts and ideas from areas of the communication field such as rhetoric, mass communication, and interpersonal communication in examining how culture influences the creation and sharing of meaning, and how various meanings and symbols constitute what we call cultural reality. Our goal, then, is to place communication practices within specific cultural contexts. Each essay addresses the question: "What is a cultural explanation and interpretation for this communication phenomenon from the ethnic scholar's perspective?"

A third purpose is to invite *experience* into our understanding and studying of cultural communication. Shuter (1990) notes that most intercultural research is essentially directed toward "theory validation" and fails to describe how people actually live and interact. He argues, "The challenge for intercultural communication in the 1990s. . . is to develop a research direction and teaching agenda that returns culture to preeminence. . . ." (p. 238). The notion that theory is developed solely through the traditionally defined scientific paradigm is ethnocentric. As Christian (1988) observes, "People of color have always theorized—but in forms quite different from the Western form of abstract logic . . . . [O]ur theorizing (and I intentionally use the verb rather than the noun) is often in narrative forms, in the stories we create, in riddle and proverbs, in the play with language, because dynamic rather than fixed ideas seem more to our liking" (p. 68). What Marsha Houston writes of feminist research also applies to intercultural research. She states that as students of human communication, we should be open to "research methods that free communication scholars to emphasize the experiential rather than the experimental, the specific case as much as the general tendency" (Houston Stanback, 1989, p. 190).

Some readers may not recognize this anthology as a product of "typical" intercultural research. It is one of our goals to expand and recreate the notion and scope of "scholarly work," providing an alternative form to learn about cultural practices and to engage in intellectual conversations. We take the anthropologists' idea of "experience-near understanding" very seriously, believing that we can be better enlightened by the rich stories and experiences told and lived by real people than by scientific findings reported by researchers. We view this experience-driven approach as a complement to theory-driven approaches in intercultural communication research. We believe that being human is being able to tell stories and to actively interpret our social activities and cultural experiences. As Rabinow and Sullivan (1987) state, "This interpretive turn refocuses attention on the concrete varieties of cultural meaning, in their particularity and complex texture . . . ." (pp. 5-6).

A fourth purpose of this anthology is to demonstrate the vast cultural diversity within any given racial, ethnic, and national category. In much of the intercultural literature, studies of African American, Asian, Asian American, Native American, Latino/a, and Semitic communication tend to treat our cultures monolithically; that is, reducing each category to one type. Our premise is that there is not "one" style of any particular ethnic group any more than there is "one" style of Anglo-American communication. Collectively, our essays explore the rich variety of communication practices within a broad cultural spectrum.

Approaching Cultural Intersections: Our Influences

On the whole, we do not turn to the academic world for intellectual emancipation. After centuries of exclusion from and misrepresentation in academic literature, we derive our warrants from sources that we trust and appreciate, knowing that they are perhaps unfamiliar or may not be credible to mainstream interculturalists.

The pressure is great to put aside our cultural selves in order to gain scholarly credibility. We are led to think that the two cannot coexist. In *Talking Back: Thinking Feminist, Thinking Black*, bell hooks recounts her experience as a graduate student in English. She concludes that "The academic setting, the academic discourse I work in, is not a known site for truthtelling" (hooks, 1989, p. 29). Her professors and peers, women and men alike, required of hooks a transformation out of her cultural self and into someone *they* recognized. With such recognition came the possibility of control. "Within the educational institutions," she continues, "where we learn to develop and strengthen our writing and analytical skills, we also learn to think, write, and talk in a manner that shifts attention away from personal experience" (p. 77).

Inventing Landmarks

Our influences are interdisciplinary, contradictory, and often contentious. They are noted in the supplementary reading lists following each unit in this volume. We do not include them for any purpose other than to indicate those sources that resonate with our own experiences as members of cultural groups. In the field of communication, we invent and celebrate our own landmarks. The early work of Turner (1949), for example, remains a point of reference that exemplifies the merging of scholarship and the exploration of one's own cultural present.

Landmarks also include studies that assume and represent the "naturalness" of our everyday interaction and issues that concern us. Ramos and Ramos (1979) write that "the more I read and do research, the more I realize that there is a contradiction between my own self-image and what others have written about how I am supposed to be" (pp. 49-50). Therefore, the publication of articles by scholars such as Sedano (1980), Garner (1983), and Nakagawa (1990) and of books such as *Talkin and Testifyin: The Language of Black America* (Smitherman, 1977) and *The Afrocentric Idea*

(Asante, 1987) is important because the analyses of communication grew out of a social context we could recognize. What was always vital and visible to us suddenly became visible to the field of communication. The ordinary and extraordinary communicative practices and patterns of meaning among people of color began to inform the field's understanding of human communication.

The theoretical position of this anthology is couched within a broad social constructionist and interpretive framework. As Berger and Luckmann (1967) state, "[T]he sociology of knowledge must concern itself with whatever passes for 'knowledge' in a society, regardless of the ultimate validity or invalidity (by whatever criteria) of such 'knowledge.' And . . . the sociology of knowledge must seek to understand the processes by which this is done in such a way that the taken-for-granted 'reality' congeals for the [hu]man in the street" (p. 3). Within this social constructionist approach, we see both culture and communication as human creations and as ongoing processes of making history and meanings. The strength of this perspective is that it takes communication to be the primary social process by which we create meanings and engage in cultural practices. We recognize and welcome the reflexive connection between social structure and an individual's action, between communication and culture (Cronen, Chen, & Pearce, 1988). Furthermore, the social constructionist approach also highlights the fluid nature of studying communication and culture. It draws our attention to the specificity, uniqueness, and richness of individual cases.

An interpretive framework allows the introduction of the ethnography of communication in our field, which we consider to be akin to our approach to understanding cultural communication. Almost two decades ago, Philipsen (1975) concluded his study of the cultural talk of a Chicago neighborhood by stating, "We have barely any information on what groups in the United States view speaking as an effective means of social influence and what alternatives they envision. Such a deficit in the fund of information should be remedied by descriptive and comparative studies of American speech communities" (p. 22). More recently, Carbaugh's (1988a, 1988b, 1990) work examined various forms of cultural talking with the assumption that communication must be studied in a specifically situated cultural setting. Whereas the ethnography of communication examines shared cultural meanings and rules that render the individual's action intelligible, this book explores personal voices that contribute to shared cultural meanings.

Playing with Conceptualization

A brief introduction of our conceptualization of culture and intercultural communication may be useful to the reader.

First, we want to emphasize the importance of regarding culture as a dynamic, communication-based idea. Humans are organizing beings, and culture is an organizing term. Culture is an idea for recognizing and understanding how groups create communities and participate in social activities. Geertz (1973) insists that "culture is public because meaning is" (p. 12) and notes that "[I]t is through the flow of behavior—or more precisely, social action—that cultural forms find articulation" (p. 17). As an ordering term, "culture" renders coherent the values held and the actions performed in a community. At the same time, cultural participants engage in communication that constantly defines and redefines the community.

We are concerned with the production of cultural knowledge. As Geertz (1983) points out in *Local Knowledge*, we often treat our cultural knowledge as common sense, as something "natural" beyond question. We take our acculturation for granted without realizing that our experience is accumulative and always historically based. In the study of cultures we attempt to learn as much as we can about this natural side to the patterns of everyday life. Culture, then, can be said to refer to a community of meaning and a shared body of local knowledge rather than a region or a nation. Charmaine Shutiva is Native American, but this does not describe her culturally. Her cultural community is the Acoma of New Mexico. Gwendolyn Gong is Chinese American, but her cultural community is the Chinese of the Mississippi Delta. Both are American citizens, but their dialogue is intercultural.

Second, we see culture as an idea that is creating and being recreated symbolically. For example, one day, Alberto González had a meeting with Charmaine Shutiva. When the meeting was over, both had to walk to a classroom in a nearby building. During the walk, a thunderstorm began. González offered his umbrella to Shutiva, but she declined. "We pray for rain in the desert," she said, laughing in the storm. "It's against my teachings to shield myself from something so sacred." The two walked on. González ignored the glares of passersby who judged him selfish for not sharing his umbrella. Shutiva turned to him and said, "But that doesn't mean we can't run!"

Langer (1942) writes that language transforms experience. For the Acoma, the desire for rain in the desert was transformed into solemn prayer. Moving beyond language, for Shutiva, the prayer's meaning was transformed into a nonverbal act (e.g., refusing the umbrella and exposing herself to rain). In this episode, one cultural belief of the Acomas was enacted and reconstructed through verbal and nonverbal symbols. Access to symbols becomes access to the shared meanings of a people. For Geertz (1973), cultural analysis is "sorting out the structures of signification" (p. 9). And as Carbaugh (1988b) states, "[I]f one wants to understand the action persons do, from their point of view, one should listen for the terms they use to discuss it" (p. 217). Both statements suggest that cultural meanings are constructed through people's use of symbols, both verbal and nonverbal. Communication, then, is an ongoing process of reconstructing the meanings of the symbols through social interaction.

Our experience-driven view of intercultural communication allows a reevaluation of previous literature. For example, Hall (1976) writes, "[T]he natural act of thinking is greatly modified by culture; . . . there are many different and legitimate ways of thinking; we in the West value one of these ways above all others—the one we call 'logic,' a linear system that has been with us since Socrates" (p. 9). From our perspective, Hall is only partially

right. Western societies *have* privileged logical demonstration and scientific reasoning as "ways of knowing." "The West," however, is not one culture. Hall cannot contemplate that various cultural communities exist *within* the West which privilege epistemologies other than logic and linear reasoning. Further, in Hall's influential work, we miss the voices of real cultural participants who can narrate their personal stories and cultural experiences to shed light on the ways of knowing as described by the scholar.

A useful conception of culture allows a critique of power in society. We believe communication and social power to be interdependent. Kramerae, Schulz, and O'Barr (1984) note that "Speech functions in different ways for different cultures as well as for different individuals and groups within a culture" (p. 13). In a hierarchically stratified society, the communication styles and practices of every individual are not accorded equal prestige. Members of privileged social groups have the material resources and social position to define their ways of speaking and acting as "standard" and to define other groups as "deviant," "incompetent," or "powerless." Yet as individuals and groups negotiate their relationships with one another, ways of speaking are redefined or recoded according to culture-specific criteria.

For example, Marsha Houston remembers an African American woman who had been a top debater at a predominately white high school. During her first year at a traditionally black women's college, this student ran for class president. Her campaign speech, a model of the low-keyed Anglo American rhetorical style taught in her high school public-speaking class, was greeted by her classmates with polite applause. Her opponent's speech, enlivened by the high-keyed Afrocentric delivery style characteristic of such African American orators as Jesse Jackson, received an enthusiastic ovation. The student confided, "When I heard the audience reaction to my opponent, I knew I'd lost."

The contributors to this volume demonstrate how socially privileged speakers use communication to diminish the voices of those less privileged and how cultural communities are empowered by a recreation and reinvention of historical/traditional communication forms, styles, and strategies. Admittedly, in a North American society that tends to value the universal over the particular, attention to cultural community can be both emancipatory and awkward. Yet if human experiences are indeed characterized by storytelling and the creation of meanings, we offer this volume as an invitation to a form of intercultural communication inquiry in which ethnic scholars create their own research agenda and contribute to a truly polyphonic cultural melody.

The Essays in this Book

Each essay in this book represents what each contributor feels is most significant to share about his or her culture. Some contributors respond to what they perceive as gaps in the knowledge we have about their cultures. Others acknowledge "the central role that narrative structure plays in the formation of the self and in the construction, transmission, and transformation of cultures" (Witherell & Noddings, 1991, p. 3) and employ narrative to express their cultural knowledge.

We organized the essays not by approach, but by overlapping concerns centering around (1) an examination of the language of self-identification and construction of "others"; (2) an exploration of the intersection of culture, sexuality, and gender; (3) a description of the cultural knowledge imbedded in various communication contexts; and (4) the experience of crossing into and through multiple cultural systems of meaning.

Part I: Naming Ourselves

Victoria Chen's essay begins with the assumption that ethnic Americans' autobiographies provide the most intriguing and useful sources for learning about the construction of cultural experience. By examining one Chinese American woman's writing, Chen explores the double voice in Maxine Hong Kingston's *The Woman Warrior*. She argues that the hyphen commonly used to designate ethnic Americans marginalizes their position.

Thomas Nakayama's essay poses the question: What does being an American mean? As a fourth-generation Japanese American who has never visited Japan, Nakayama is still constructed as the "other" due to his Asian heritage and physical characteristics. He tells us what it is like to be a "perpetual foreigner" in one's native country and asks the reader to redefine Japanese American experience as central, instead of peripheral, to the making of American culture and history.

Hana S. Noor Al-Deen problematizes the cultural naming of "Arab" and offers a diverse outlook of Arab Americans' rich heritage and communication practices. She traces the histories of Arab Americans and examines the stereotypes of their communication as portrayed by the mainstream media. Noor Al-Deen's deep commitment to challenging the monolithic conception of "Arab culture" connects back to a major purpose of this volume.

Sydney A. Ribeau recounts his struggle to unite his personal and intellectual identities as an African American and a communication scholar. He highlights the importance of the articulation of African American experience and its conspicuous absence in intercultural literature. Ribeau uses Afrocentricity as an example of how historically marginalized Americans and ethnic scholars can recreate their identity through communication.

Dolores V. Tanno, echoing Victoria Chen's discussion of double vision for Chinese Americans, provides a response to the central concern of this section: What do we call ourselves as ethnic Americans? She argues that each ethnic self-reference is a rhetorical device insofar as it communicates a particular story. Tanno then offers the possibility of multiple names that allow the historical and cultural continuity of identity.

Part II: Negotiating Sexuality and Gender

Alberto González and Gloria Flores examine *Tejana* music as cultural rhetoric; that is, how *Tejana* singers and songwriters use song to renegotiate cultural constructions of gender. They argue that *Tejana* artists, through song, both respect their

Mexican roots and reflect contemporary North American feminism.

Both Navita Cummings James and Charles Nero offer meditations on their personal/gendered communicative lives. James traces her own meanings for blackness and black womanhood, as a "baby boomer, middle-class African American woman who grew up in the integrated North," to the personal narratives of her extended family. Nero charts key moments in his life by interweaving poetry, popular song lyrics, feminist and gay/lesbian theory, and personal experience to probe the meanings of home, family, and community for African American gay men.

Bishetta Merritt discusses the persistent illusions beneath the apparent changes in African American female characters on primetime television. She argues that television's portrayal of black women has not advanced far beyond traditional images of "the oversized, sexless mammy [and] the yellow gal of unbridled passion."

Sheryl Perlmutter Bowen reflects upon the particular intersection of her Jewish upbringing and the feminism she has adopted as an adult. Yet even her Judaism is specific to her position as a woman since, "Jewish women and men have traditionally lived in different worlds." Perlmutter Bowen describes how cultural roles are open to transformation in traditional ways and reinterpreted on the basis of new values and perspectives.

Part III: Representing Cultural Knowledge in Interpersonal and Mass Media Contexts

Margarita Gangotena describes Mexican American family communication. Through a review of several critiques of previous social science research on Mexican Americans, she states that research on *la familia* has been biased, leaning toward an assimilationist agenda. That is, a family is assessed as "normal" only if it conforms to Eurocentric models of family structure and communication. Gangotena argues that the distinctive rhetorical devices Mexican Americans use to show family affiliation should not be seen as rejections of Eurocentric values but as enactments of values informed by Mexican heritage.

Thurmon Garner's essay examines the "culture logic" underlying the rhetoric of everyday talk among African Americans. Drawing upon a variety of previous communication scholarship, he isolates indirection, improvisation, and playfulness as three practices that African Americans value.

Gwendolyn Gong writes about the conversational strategies of the Chinese from the Mississippi Delta, based on her experience growing up in that part of the United States. She presents an intriguing combination of Chinese Confucianism and Southern Genteelism that influences Mississippi Chinese when they talk. In a personal narrative, Gong provides us with insightful analyses of how these conversational features play out in communication practices. Like Thomas Nakayama, she also experienced others' construction of her "Chineseness."

Concentrating on the traditional black church, the central institution in most African American communities, Janice D. Hamlet analyzes traditional black preaching as "the careful orchestration of the biblical scriptures interpreted in view of the people's history and experiences." Her study reinforces the notion that, in addition to worshipping, the rhetorical action of preachers powerfully preserves the cultural identity of black communities.

Patricia Riley considers cultural knowledge in Louise Erdrich's novel *Love Medicine*. She encourages us to probe the symbolic world of Native American authors so that we might better appreciate "mythologically subtle" works. Without knowledge of the meaning of the oral tradition and the Midewiwin ceremony among the Chippewa, she argues, *Love Medicine* has been given a naive reception. As the novel demands from the serious reader an investigation of its cultural premises, it creates an intercultural dialogue that leads one to new knowledge.

Diana I. Ríos discusses how mass communication functions in two seemingly contradictory ways. Among Mexican Americans in Texas, Riós argues, media messages serve to acculturate audiences to mainstream values *and* to preserve and strengthen ethnic identity. Interestingly, the latter is not achieved simply by the existence of Mexican American-owned media outlets or through Spanish language messages. These forms of communication quite often serve the goal of assimilation. Ríos suggests that media outlets open to audience involvement in the development of media content are more directly connected to the function of cultural self-preservation.

Charmaine Shutiva contradicts a popular notion that Native Americans are a "stoic, quiet people." She argues that, as an element of interpersonal talk, humor often functions pedagogically as it is used to maintain traditional values of respect for nature, humility, and care for the group.

Part IV: Traversing Cultural Paths

If making sense and creating meaning are inherent features of communication, Ling Chen's essay offers a detailed description of how Chinese students in the U.S interpret the various facets of American culture. The value of Chen's work lies in the specific, detailed accounts given by native Chinese at different stages of their acculturation into American society. As she points out, things can "go wrong" in intercultural communication if we impose our own cultural knowledge when trying to make sense of interaction that has a totally different logic from another cultural perspective.

Marsha Houston explores some of the barriers African American women perceive as preventing them from having satisfying conversations with white women. The communication climate is such that "blacks can never take for granted that whites will respect them, treat them with courtesy, judge them fairly, or take them seriously." Houston concludes by describing attributes of a positive communication environment.

Elizabeth Lozano describes "the particular tensions and differences that appear when the posited 'standard' voice—the Anglo-Saxon American— confronts a 'marginal' voice—such as the Latino— with the consequent noise and mutual inflection of accents." She shows how an entire range of perceptions and behaviors reveals contrasting Latin American and Anglo cultural concepts of "public space." As a bicultural participant observer, Lozano articulates an insider's assumptions in both Anglo and Latin American settings.

Casey Man Kong Lum's essay begins with an anecdote highlighting the fact that various dialects and practices exist and can create confusion and difficulties when two Chinese persons communicate. He examines three dominant groups of Chinese immigrants in New York City and discusses how they maintain their own ethnicity through specific forms of interaction.

Finally, Changsheng Xi challenges the well-known and often cited cultural dimensions of individualism/collectivism by discussing these terms as they relate to American and Chinese cultures. He argues that these semantic categories, widely used to describe different cultures, perpetuate a false dichotomy of communication and culture. By offering examples of social interaction, Xi shows how both aspects of this dimension apply to Chinese and American cultural practices, but in different forms and with different consequences.

* * *

These essays merely scratch the surface of the social and cultural knowledge that inform our symbolic creations of, and responses to, the experience of living in the United States. We hope that the reader is inspired to explore this experience further.

REFERENCES

Asante, M. K. (1987). *The Afrocentric idea*. Philadelphia: Temple University Press.

Berger, P. L., & Luckmann, T. (1967). *The social construction of reality: A treatise in the sociology of knowledge*. New York: Doubleday Anchor.

Carbaugh, D. (1988a). Talking American: Cultural discourses on 'Donahue.' Norwood, NJ: Ablex.

Carbaugh, D. (1988b). Cultural terms and tensions in the speech at a television station. *The Western Journal of Speech Communication, 52*, 216-237.

Carbaugh, D. (Ed.). (1990). *Cultural communication and intercultural contact*. Hillsdale, NJ: Lawrence Erlbaum Associates.

Christian, B. (1988). The race for theory. *Feminist Studies, 14,* 67-79.

Cronen V. E., Chen, V., & Pearce, W. B. (1988). Coordinated management of meaning: A critical theory. In Y. Y. Kim & W. B. Gudykunst (Eds.), *International and intercultural communication annual, XII: Theories in intercultural communication* (pp. 66-98). Newbury Park, CA: Sage.

Garner, T. (1983). Playing the dozens: Folklore as strategies for living. *The Quarterly Journal of Speech, 69,* 47-57.

Geertz, C. (1973). *The interpretation of cultures.* New York: Basic Books.

Geertz, C. (1983). *Local knowledge.* New York: Basic Books.

Hall, E.T. (1976). *Beyond culture.* New York: Anchor Press.

hooks, b. (1989). *Talking back: Thinking feminist, thinking black.* Boston: South End Press.

Houston Stanback, M. (1989). Feminist theory and black women's talk. *The Howard Journal of Communications, 1,* 187-194.

Kramerae, C., Schulz, M., & O'Barr, W. (1984). *Language and power.* Beverly Hills: Sage.

Langer, S. K. (1942). *Philosophy in a new key: A study in the symbolism of reason, rite, and art* (3rd ed.). Cambridge, MA: Harvard University Press.

Nakagawa, G. (1990). 'What are we doing here with all these Japanese?': Subject-constitution and strategies of discursive closure represented in stories of Japanese American internment. *Communication Quarterly, 38,* 388-402.

Philipsen, G. (1975). Speaking 'like a man' in Teamsterville: Culture patterns of role enactment in an urban neighborhood. *The Quarterly Journal of Speech, 61,* 13-22.

Rabinow, P., & Sullivan, W.M. (Eds.). (1987). *Interpretive social science: A second look.* Berkeley: University of California Press.

Ramos, R., & Ramos, M. (1979). The Mexican American: Am I who they say I am? In A. D. Trejo (Ed.), *The Chicanos: As we see ourselves* (pp. 49-66). Tucson: University of Arizona Press.

Sedano, M. V. (1980). Chicanismo: A rhetorical analysis of themes and images of selected poetry from the Chicano movement. *The Western Journal of Speech Communication, 44,* 170-190.

Shuter, R. (1990). The centrality of culture. *The Southern Communication Journal, 55,* 237-249.

Smitherman, G. (1977). *Talkin and testifyin: The language of black America.* Boston: Houghton Mifflin. Reissued, Detroit: Wayne State University, 1986.

Turner, L. D. (1949). *Africanisms in the Gullah dialect.* Chicago: University of Chicago Press.

Witherell, C., & Noddings, N. (Eds.). (1991). *Stories lives tell: Narrative and dialogue in education.* New York: Teachers College Press.

PART I

NAMING OURSELVES

1

(De)hyphenated Identity: The Double Voice in *The Woman Warrior*

Victoria Chen
Denison University

> It's difficult to hear the songs of more than one world at any one time. And yet sometimes it's necessary to forget the songs of one world and learn the songs of another, especially if you're a Chinese American.
>
> —*Laurence Yep*

Maxine Hong Kingston's (1976) *The Woman Warrior: Memoirs of a Girlhood among Ghosts* tells the story of an American-born Chinese woman. In her nostalgic and yet critical voice, Kingston narrates her experience of growing up in Stockton, California, in the late 1940s as a second-generation Chinese American daughter. In her dramatic autobiographical style, she describes the ambiguity of living on the interface between two cultural traditions, the pain of defying some elements of her Chinese heritage, and the struggle to find a legitimate private and public voice in American society. In the process of trying to maintain a bittersweet relationship with her cultural heritage and with her Chinese mother, the champion storyteller, Kingston has herself become a powerful storyteller and one of America's most prominent writers. *The Woman Warrior* is one of the most widely studied works in American literature on college campuses.

I have chosen to write on the issue of bicultural experience through Kingston's autobiography, which over the years has provided me not only with comic and therapeutic relief (through our shared mother-daughter experience) but with strength and hope (through her vision of a woman warrior). When I recently had the opportunity to meet her, we both discovered that our mothers grew up in the same small village in the Kwantung Province of China! The ineffable connection that I have felt with this warrior woman storyteller on meeting her has become indeed real. I hope that, through my interpretation and discussion of Kingston's "talk-stories" in *The Woman Warrior*, readers will gain new insights into Chinese American women's experiences and a more positive appreciation of the dual enmeshment of ethnic Americans.

There has been little work done in intercultural communication that has emphasized the importance of learning from literature produced by ethnic Americans. While mainstream research has by and large adopted a "scientific" approach to comparing different cultures within a quantitative framework, we rarely learn how bicultural participants make sense of their experiences in their own words.

I begin with the assumption that ethnic American literature provides us with valuable knowledge of and insights into culture and communication from the point of view of those who have lived the experience. Writings by these Americans illuminate us with fresh, different perspectives and interpretations of their cultural experience within the broader cultural milieu. Autobiographies are particularly enlightening about how authors construct their own cultural identities in response to changing family structures, traditional narratives, and social and historical contexts. As Fischer (1986) discussed, an autobiography is predicated on a vibrant yet ambiguous relation between a sense of self and community: "What thus seem initially to be individualistic autobiographical searchings turn out to be revelations of traditions, re-collections of disseminated identities and of the divine sparks from the breaking of the vessels" (p. 198). Fischer also interpreted *The Woman Warrior* as "an archetypical text for displaying ethnicity processes analogous to translations of dreams" (p. 208).

Autobiographical works such as *The Woman Warrior* present both intrigue and confusion to the reader. Kingston had to cross the boundaries of both ethnicity and gender to reach a mainstream audience. We can learn about a writer's work from the response that it generates. A look at some of the critiques of Kingston's widely celebrated book helps us to focus on the issues of cultural identity and bicultural voices. In this essay I use *The Woman Warrior* as my primary source of data to explore the marginalization of Chinese Americans and the possibilities of transcending hyphenated identity. I will first outline three critical views of Kingston's work, from "general" Americans, from Chinese, and from Chinese Americans. I will then discuss the notion of hyphenated identity and explain why I believe the expression "Chinese American" should be dehyphenated as a means to empower a double vision for individuals who are simultaneously enmeshed in disparate cultural traditions.

Critiques of *The Woman Warrior*

Three broad critical viewpoints of *The Woman Warrior* can be identified. The first comes from the "general" American audience, readers who are not familiar with Chinese or Chinese American culture, as well as those who hope to find the "truth" about Kingston's life and cultural heritage. A typical response from these readers has been that the book is interesting but confusing: Kingston does not write clearly, and it is difficult to tell where her fantasies end and reality begins. While praising the charming, exotic myths and customs described in the work, these critics insist that clarity and certainty are the most important criteria by which to judge the quality of Kingston's autobiography. Furthermore, they feel that the real contribution of Kingston's work lies in how she reveals Chinese culture through her and her mother's storytelling.

One response to these comments would be that writing is a symbolic activity. It is not necessarily intended to reflect "the truth," even in the genre of autobiography. There are multiple ways to be an ethnic American, as Fischer (1986) stated: "Being Chinese American exists only as an exploratory project, a matter of finding a voice and style" (p. 210). Kingston found a new way to construct her life stories with a bicultural voice that is imbued with her imagination and dreams. The fictionalization of her autobiography conveys the idea that all cultural discourse is made up, fabricated, and reconstructed, always engaging the reader in an ongoing dialogue.

If these critics would be willing to suspend their disbeliefs long enough to fathom Kingston's talk-story, they might discover that Kingston herself, in her double voice, could not sort out which part of her childhood consisted of stories, which part was dreams, and which part was the real historical events that involved her family. As she said, "Chinese Americans, when you try to understand what things in you are Chinese, how do you separate what is peculiar to childhood, to poverty, insanities, one family, your mother who marked your growing with stories, from what is Chinese? What is Chinese tradition and what is in the movies?" (Kingston, 1976, p. 215). What these readers forget is that Kingston is not Chinese, but a Chinese American who comes from a specific family background and a lifelong struggle between disparate cultural traditions. It is no surprise to the Western eye that Kingston is inevitably "Chinese"; the customs and practices vividly depicted in her book are inexorably alien. Her "Chineseness" tends to overshadow the "Americanness" that she shares with "general" Americans.

The second critique comes from the "real" Chinese such as scholars or readers from China, Hong Kong, and Taiwan, who have mastered Chinese language(s) and grown up in Chinese societies. Although some of these critics highly praise Kingston's book, a typical response has been that, being Chinese American, she has somehow "misrepresented" Chinese culture by relating only the "negative" and "shameful" aspects of an ancient, laudable civilization which has eluded the American-born, culturally disadvantaged author. They contend that Kingston has rendered descriptions of exotic foods, Chinese superstitions, values, and customs that are not really practiced by many Chinese. They quickly dismiss *The Woman Warrior* as a "poor," "inaccurate," and "degrading" depiction of high Chinese culture in an attempt to pander to mainstream American taste. In some versions of the Chinese translation of *The Woman Warrior*, a few of Kingston's myths and stories were "corrected" by the translators in order to conform to the "Chinese" way of storytelling.

These Chinese scholars further warn readers that not all Chinese women are like Kingston's mother, who displayed all the "virtueless" behaviors of Chinese women—dominant, controlling, strong, and stubborn. American readers, they argue, should realize that, though her family is from a Chinese village, the American-born writer really does not know that much about Chinese culture; that, in fact, she is not even fluent in her Cantonese dialect, let alone Mandarin, the official Chinese language. These critics question Kingston's cultural credibility, despite the obvious fact that her autobiography is not about Chinese culture, nor is it intended to reflect any experiences other than her own.

The third critique comes from other Chinese American writers. Interestingly enough, it stems primarily from Chinese American male writers such as Frank Chin, Benjamin Tang, and Paul Chan. Though they are pleased that this enchanting work has finally made its way into mainstream America, they believe that *The Woman Warrior* does not speak for other Chinese Americans' experiences. Further, these critics scrutinize Kingston's ideology as an ethnic American writer. Kingston grew up in a very peculiar family and community, they contend; many Chinese American girls growing up in this country do not think or behave like her. Despite its widely acclaimed success, they argue that *The Woman Warrior* represents a distorted view of the Chinese American experience—a "fake" Chinese American culture. They further ignore the feminist ideas, insights, and practices found throughout the book and accuse Kingston of buying into the dominant American ideology, "whitewashing" her prose to seek out white acceptance. In

their minds, she does not directly challenge the issue of racism that Chinese Americans experience in this society. In other words, she is simply not radical enough.

There is some irony in these accusations, given that, as Kim (1982) pointed out, "Among some contemporary Asian American male writers. . . a strident anti-female attitude can be discerned" (p. 197). In an interview during a visit to the University of California, Santa Barbara, Kingston countered by saying, "The content of this book is overtly feminist, although it is not the feminist's typically political rhetoric. The feminist side of this work is couched in a dramatic writing style. And the title *The Woman Warrior* was chosen to denote that throughout Chinese literature, there have always been knights and fighters who are women." The most gratifying responses to *The Woman Warrior*, she claimed, have come from Chinese American women who not only have experienced Kingston's stories in their own life, but whose appreciation of her work is not mediated by the expectation of exoticism and foreign sensibility.

If all of us are indeed cultural interpreters, we should realize that the attempt to inscribe one's family life is no more or less than the multi-layered reconstruction of what we call cultural experience. The insights into Kingston's work is derived neither from a "scientific" assessment of the veracity of Kingston's and her mother's narratives, nor by generalized comparisons of her personal life experience with that of other Chinese Americans. Rather, her relevations rely on the specificity, uniqueness, richness, ambiguity, playfulness, and sense of irony that characterize Kingston's talk-story. It is through her array of conversations, imageries, and communication practices that we learn about Kingston's bicultural experience and her ongoing struggle for a coherent cultural identity.

Despite all the controversy surrounding *The Woman Warrior*, the real issue of all these critiques is, "What is this cultural construct that we call 'Chinese American'?" Who defines these ethnic Americans? Who describes, articulates, and represents their experiences? In our effort to understand the wide array of such diverse experiences, whose voices are heard, and at the expense of what other voices? Even more significantly, how do we even attempt to understand a Chinese American woman's autobiography when she is constantly weaving her stories (and "lies") from a hyphenated cultural world in which she is simultaneously enmeshed and marginalized?

As for any other ethnic group, there is no single, overall Chinese American perspective from which we can decipher the myths, dreams, and fantasies in Kingston's storytelling. Nor is she attempting to present a coherent set of Chinese American cultural narratives to the reader. Many Asian Americans' experiences can often be characterized by a kind of discontinuity and incoherence, combined with a sense of jarring reality and fragmentation, as depicted by such authors as Wong (1989), Tan (1989), Kingston (1989), Ng (1993), Sone (1979), Okada (1979), and Kadohata (1989). Mixing fictional characters with autobiographical accounts, these writers probe into immigrant family histories and the precarious nature of riding on the hyphen commonly used to describe their identity as ethnic Americans. While the term "hyphenated identity" may seem appropriate to describe the bicultural experience that Chinese Americans grow up with, I would argue that the hyphen marginalizes these individuals in American society and would strongly advocate the dehyphenation of Asian Americans.

Hyphenated Identity and Marginalization

. . . the paradoxical sense that ethnicity is something reinvented and reinterpreted in each generation by each individual and that it is often something quite puzzling to the individual, something over which he or she lacks control. Ethnicity is not something that is simply passed on from generation to generation, taught and learned; it is something dynamic, often unsuccessfully repressed or avoided.
—*Michael M. J. Fischer*

One way to conceptualize the term "identity" is not by trying merely to define who we are, but by contextualizing the term within our relationships,

practices, actions, and experiences. Because our identity is inexorably bound with what we do and how we make sense of what we do, and the significance of our activities is interpretable only within the context of communication, identity can be viewed as "the actual experience of self in a particular social situation," as explained in *The Homeless Mind* (Berger, Berger, & Kellner, 1973, p. 76). The authors described a phenomenon of the modern era: the pluralization or segmentation of lifeworlds, whereby the condition of modernity is characterized by the plurality and fragmentation of our identity. Berman (1982) made a similar point: Western cultural history virtually compels modernists to go through life experiences feeling groundless, centerless, and filled with a sense of loss.

It is certainly not unusual that our ideas and cultural endeavors do not always coexist well together; we may even face a sense of contradiction, incoherence, struggle, loss, and unbelonging in our social relationships. Surely all individuals, regardless of ethnicity, may have experienced the crossing of boundaries between lifeworlds at various stages. However, Chinese Americans' bicultural experiences are especially characterized by this pluralization of lifeworlds. It can be argued that these homeless characteristics are accentuated or exacerbated by the fact that Chinese Americans are simultaneously enmeshed between two powerful cultural traditions.

One feature of this phenomenon of pluralized lifeworlds is manifested in the commonly adopted hyphenated designation. For Asian Americans, dual cultural traditions are separated *and* connected by the hyphen that is used to describe their identity. On the one hand, the hyphen reminds them that they have a distinct ethnic heritage and are somehow different from other immigrant Americans who descended from European ancestry but are referred to simply as Americans. On the other hand, the hyphen also draws attention to the fact that they are not Asian foreigners but Americans by birthright, born and raised in this country just like other Anglo Americans.

The hyphen used to designate different Asian American groups thus functions as a paradoxical boundary continuously mediating between the two disparate cultural baggages that these individuals carry, or sometimes abandon. In a larger context, the hyphenated identity of these Americans is also mediated by the "Others," the constraints in the social and historical system, the dominant American cultural institutions, and the powerful persons in their life. This muti-levelled and multi-directional mediation creates an important part of the context by which we can meaningfully address the issue of bicultural identity.

Feminist writer Rey Chow argued that ethnicity in America is not "voluntary" in character, and that "the consciousness of ethnicity for Asian and other non-white groups is inevitable—a matter of history rather than of choice" (Chow, 1990, p. 45). We also learn from Richard Rodriguez' (1982) autobiography that one's ethnicity cannot be chosen, just as Rodriguez, an American of Mexican ancestry, did not consciously choose to end his "private" childhood to enter the "public" American life. "The day I raised my hand in class and spoke loudly to an entire roomful of faces," he wrote, "my childhood started to end" (p. 28).

The hyphen lets us assume that the two cultures on either side of the hyphen are somehow connected, that Asian Americans somehow must think and act like Asians in some ways simply because their ethnicity is visually communicated. In *The Woman Warrior*, Kingston, living in the interface between her mother's Chinese myths and her American dreams, poignantly articulated the ambiguous identity of Chinese Americans. Blessed with the warrior woman's courage, Kingston demythologized the assumed continuity between the great culture of China and the American-born Chinese. In her double voice, Kingston told us that there is no such continuity, and that "even now China wraps double binds around my feet" (Kingston, 1976, p. 57). Therefore, she must bridge the gap between China and America. Of course, we see the irony in Kingston's denial of cultural continuity, as the whole book is devoted to the memories of her mother's talk-stories.

Kingston's writing points out that the hyphen used to describe her "apparent" cultural identity only provides some connection that is taken for granted, yet is remote and ambiguous in relation to her ethnic heritage. What she and her siblings actually experienced in their childhood was their inability to penetrate Chinese wisdom and their frustration over their Chinese relatives' unwillingness to explain Chinese folklores and customs. She wrote, "I don't see how they kept up a continuous culture for five thousand years. Maybe they didn't; maybe everyone makes it up as they go along" (Kingston, 1976, p. 216).

One characteristic of hyphenated identity is a sense of being marginalized as one strives for a coherent life script and legitimate Chinese and American voices. In her many stories, Kingston shares such experience with us. For example, her mother often referred to her children as "You American children." She would reprimand them, "Stop being silly. You Americans don't take life seriously" (Kingston, 1976, p. 174). Later, the mother would scold her children, "What do you know about Chinese business? Do as I say" (p. 175). This, of course, requires that children realize they are perceived as Americans who lack knowledge of Chinese culture; but at the same time they are also expected to act like good Chinese children, obeying the parents with total deference. Indeed, this double bind is a common feature of ethnic Americans' dual cultural enmeshment, and many do not fit comfortably in either world.

Kingston complained, "They would not tell us children because we had been born among ghosts, were taught by ghosts, and were ourselves ghost-like. They called us a kind of ghost" (Kingston, 1976, pp. 213-214). Non-Chinese are referred to as ghosts in the Chinese way of thinking. Kingston wrote, "But America has been full of machines and ghosts—Taxi Ghosts, Bus Ghosts, Police Ghosts. . . Once upon a time the world was so thick with ghosts, I could hardly breathe; I could hardly walk, limping my way around the White Ghosts and their cars" (p. 113). To the Chinese, ghosts symbolize the alien, the strange, the incomprehensible, all with a pejorative overtone. Kingston's parents were often puzzled by their American-born and American-educated children's "foreign" behavior. The mother would complain in exasperation, "You children never tell me what you're really up to. How else am I going to find out what you're really up to?" (p. 118). What is interesting about Kingston's case, as in other Chinese Americans' experiences, is that the "otherness" in their identity is being constructed by their family members, to whom they are ethnically related, as much as by Americans outside their families. In their own Chinese families, Kingston and her siblings were always the "other ghosts," the hopelessly ignorant and Americanized second-generation offspring. For many Chinese American children, however, ghosts are the residue of the fragmentary past, the family history, and the old tradition that seems so foreign to them, all of which must be exorcised and externalized. As Kingston wrote, "Whenever my parents said 'home,' they suspended America. They suspended enjoyment, but I did not want to go to China. In China my parents would sell my sisters and me" (p. 116).

Being marginal also means being without a community. Just like the mythical Chinese warrior woman Fa Mu Lan, who felt that she must fight the battle away from home until her task and duty were fulfilled, Kingston found it ambivalent, difficult, and at times painful to be a Chinese American: "I've stopped checking 'bilingual' on job applications. I could not understand any of the dialects the interviewer at China Airlines tried on me, and he didn't understand me either" (Kingston, 1976, p. 239). And "when I visit the family now, I wrap my American successes around me like a private shawl; I *am* worthy of eating the food. From afar I can believe my family loves me fundamentally. . . I refuse to shy my way anymore through our China-town, which tasks me with the old sayings and the stories" (p. 62).

While Kingston's lack of Chineseness is ridiculed by her parents and relatives, in the larger society Chinese Americans are often portrayed as the "others" as well, the inassimilable Asians who are still sometimes told to go back to their own country after generations of settlement in America. Mainstream white America insists that Kingston writes from an exotic Eastern perspective. In response to

her critics, Kingston countered in exasperation, "*The Woman Warrior* is an American book. Yet many reviewers do not see the American-ness of it, nor the fact of my own American-ness" (Kingston, 1982, p. 58). Chinese American women indeed experience a double alienation, from the mainstream American culture due to their race, gender, and ethnic heritage, and from their own Chinese communities because of both their inevitable Americanization and the traditional Chinese marginalization of women. This double-edged social displacement can leave them homeless; Kingston found that she had to escape to survive. Even though the children told one another, "Chinese people are very weird" (Kingston, 1976, p. 183), she still pleaded, "The swordswoman and I are not so dissimilar. May my people understand the resemblance soon so that I can return to them" (p. 62). Where is home for individuals like Kingston? And how do they build a new route to "return" home?

Dehyphenated Double Vision

Postmodern knowledge. . . refines our sensitivity to differences and reinforces our ability to tolerate the incommensurable.

— *Jean-François Lyotard*

Like many others, I have argued that the identity of Asian Americans is not an *either/or* choice, but a *both/and* transformation; a new kind of integration, or sometimes a lack of integration, of two cultural lifeworlds. One reason that the use of the hyphen to designate Asian Americans has been challenged is that even the third or fourth generations of Asian Americans have a difficult time being accepted as "full-fledged" Americans in white America. Toni Morrison (1992) in *Playing in the Dark* argues that "Deep within the word 'American' is its association with race. . . American means white, and Africanist people struggle to make the term applicable to themselves with ethnicity and hyphen after hyphen after hyphen" (p. 47). Although Asian Americans' physical characteristics may remind others that their ancestry is indeed from a remote land, a significant part of their cultural history and knowledge is at the same time deeply rooted in American tradition. The hyphen may give the false impression that there is some middle point along the Asian American continuum that poses the ultimate triumph for these ethnic Americans—to find that golden mean which bridges the gap between Asian wisdom and American dreams, allowing any individual to be fully integrated into and accepted by both worlds.

In reality, many Asian Americans would find it indeed an American dream to conflate the hierarchical structure of the two cultural impositions. The reality is that there is a qualitative disjunction between Asian and American cultural experiences and practices. The imaginary balancing point wrongly assumes the possibility of converging the two cultural worlds into the same sphere of discourse. I have suggested that some of the intergenerational conflicts between the American-born Chinese and their immigrant parents are incommensurate, that there is no shared discourse upon which the conflicting ways of life can be adjudicated or even discussed (Chen, 1992). The hyphen thus serves not only as a political boundary between Asian American and white American, but more as the illusion of an imaginary bicultural ideal than as a connective means to a perfectly blended and integrated bicultural reality.

While I am not presuming that the simple elimination of the hyphen in describing Asian Americans would solve all the issues involved, I do believe that the hyphen is a metaphor which highlights the boundary between minority Americans and white Americans. The hyphen often provides the locus for homelessness while marginalizing the social position of Asian Americans. To dehyphenate Asian Americans would enable us to recognize and accept their ambiguous, unequal, and often imbalanced cultural worlds, to survive the lack of continuity in their ethnic heritage with a sense of irony, and to invent new, creative ways to experience and appropriate from different cultural traditions. As Fischer (1986) pointed out, the struggle for a sense of ethnic identity is the reinvention and discovery of a vision for the future.

Kingston chose to write her autobiography as a way to sort out her childhood memories. An irony in *The Woman Warrior* is that she opens it with the chapter "No Name Woman" wherein her mother warned her to forget about a disgraceful aunt, whose name should remain unspeakable in the family history: "You must not tell anyone what I am about to tell you" (Kingston, 1976, p. 3). Kingston, however, rebelled against her mother's wish and gave this woman's life back: "My aunt haunts me—her ghost drawn to me because now, after fifty years of neglect, I alone devote pages of paper to her. . . " (p. 19). "They want me to participate in her punishment. And I have" (p. 18).

The end of *The Woman Warrior* realized the making of a storytelling Chinese American daughter. Despite all the "lies" that Kingston accused her mother of telling, she let the lying go on by retelling us her mother's lies and recounting to us her own stories, which in a sense are lies themselves. "Here is a story my mother told me, not when I was young, but recently, when I told her I also talk-story. The beginning is hers, the ending, mine" (Kingston, 1976, p. 240). The family tradition is not only "passed down" but also reinvented and made real: "Hong Kingston grows up a warrior woman and a warrior-woman-storyteller herself. She is the woman warrior who continues to fight in America the fight her mothers fought in China" (Trinh, 1989, p. 134). Kingston transformed the cultural myths and family stories through her fascinating double voice: "And I have so many words—" (Kingston, p. 63).

Dreams, imagination, ambiguities, and visions pervade Kingston's storytelling. The entire book is full of ironies and paradoxes beyond the simple contradictions between so-called Eastern and Western philosophies. What makes Kingston's feminist work so intriguing and powerful is the array of rich, specific, intimate, and personal stories that are characterized by intense conflict between the loved ones, ambivalence toward one's own family and cultural heritage, and paradoxical choices made through a double identity, which ultimately refer back to the choices that were left out. As Kingston said, "If one lives long enough with contradictions, they will form a larger vision" (Kingston, 1976, p. 35).

Living on the fault line between cultures and trying to hold them together is like oscillating between choices in a double bind. But if indeed "modern man (sic) has suffered from a deepening condition of 'homelessness'" (Berger, Berger, & Kellner, 1973, p. 82), all of us then share this sense of living on the margin at one time or another in a culture that is rapidly changing. Perhaps real people *are* hyphenated people after all.

One way to transcend the double bind that traps Chinese Americans is to build a community in which dehyphenation and double vision are the central practices. The notion of double vision for bicultural individuals points to their ability to see things from multiple perspectives, to live in these paradoxes without being entrapped by them, to appreciate the ambiguity of their bicultural world, and to create new possibilities from these paradoxes. As Kingston explained during an interview, "Even in America there's still some heritage of mythical women. Women must find a new way of being a knight in the U.S." Accompanying this double vision is what W.E.B. Dubois called "double consciousness," multiple cultural insights to construct meanings out of chaos, to deepen our awareness of the plurality of our cultural interpretations and practices. To deny this characterization of ethnic Americans is to neglect an opportunity to transcend their marginal status in this society. Perhaps the celebration of marginality is the beginning of a joint effort by all ethnic Americans to once and for all center their social marginality.

The idea of double vision takes a critical look at the cultural construction of the metaphorical hyphen. It empowers ethnic Americans to use their marginality to create a new community, a community where their double voice is articulated and heard, a community where one is steeped in several cultural traditions and discourses, and a community where multiple subjectivities are encouraged and even celebrated. One of the important messages in *The Woman Warrior* is that a marginal person derives power and vision from living with paradoxes. As Kingston put it, "I learned to make my mind large, as the universe is large, so that there is room for paradoxes" (Kingston, 1976, p. 35).

Reconceptualizing one's hyphenated identity is the ultimate act of self-affirmation and cultural continuation. Kingston emphasized the importance of Asian Americans recognizing themselves as warriors instead of victims. Being a true warrior requires wisdom and courage. Even Kingston's act of writing *The Woman Warrior* rode on the precarious and marginalizing hyphen, risking "misinterpretation" and criticism from both sides of the hyphen, thus rendering her vulnerable in both Chinese and American communities. Nonetheless, she was determined to make public the memoirs of her girlhood among ghosts. Writing her stories thus became a powerful source of Kingston's strength as a woman warrior. In presenting her private words and feelings to the American public, Kingston also immortalized the No Name Woman, giving new meaning to her life. Fischer (1986) insisted that ethnic memory is and ought to be oriented toward the future, not the past. Writing *The Woman Warrior* dehyphenated Kingston and empowered her with a futuristic vision to transform the alienation and marginalization imposed by the hyphen. Kingston not only continued but even surpassed her mother's talk-story tradition; she found a home in America. As she told her mother, "We belong to the planet now, Mama. Does it make sense to you that if we're no longer attached to one piece of land, we belong to the planet? Wherever we happen to be standing, why, that spot belongs to us as much as any other spot" (Kingston, 1976, p. 125).

Inherent in Kingston's writing is the uncertainty and ambiguity of her bicultural identity, as well as the ongoing, at times turbulent process of trying to make sense of the confusion created by the hyphen. As readers, we feel the pain in her talk-story; but we also taste her triumph. Although Kingston's creative style of writing presents a challenge for the reader to decipher multi-faceted cultural imageries, she also found some stories difficult. As she wrote, "To make my waking life American-normal . . . I push the deformed into my dreams, which are in Chinese, the language of impossible stories" (Kingston, 1976, p. 102). How do we recognize what is American-normal to Chinese American women? What are their dreams? What are Chinese dreams? How do we enter their impossible stories, written in such incommensurate language? How do they do it themselves, being enmeshed in and marginalized by two disparate narratives?

Even Kingston herself was confused: "I continue to sort out what's just my childhood, just my imagination, just my family, just the village, just movies, just living" (Kingston, 1976, p. 239). Perhaps once this sorting begins for us as readers and students of other cultural experiences, we can redefine our questions about cultural identity, ethnicity, marginalization, and America. Without doubt, this is an ongoing effort with no guarantee of ever finding the "correct" realities, just as we never can be sure if Kingston's life stories were not mixed with "lies."

If open-ended ambiguity is an inherent feature of a woman's autobiography, perhaps it is also what empowers Kingston's double-voiced talk-story. *The Woman Warrior* symbolizes a journey of searching for self-realization and self-creation which remains still unfinished at the autobiography's close. The ultimate feminist moment in *The Woman Warrior* comes at the end, when "two powerful woman storytellers meet. . . both working at strengthening the ties among women while commemorating and transmitting the powers of our foremothers. At once a grandmother, a poetess, a storyteller, and a woman warrior" (Trinh, 1989, p. 135). And in Kingston's own words, "She said I would grow up a wife and a slave, but she taught me the song of the warrior woman Fa Mu Lan. I would have to grow up a warrior woman" (Kingston, 1976, p. 24). Maxine Hong Kingston has triumphed as an enchanting storyteller, a true warrior—a Chinese American woman warrior. Her double voice has translated well.

REFERENCES

Berger, P., Berger, B., & Kellner, H. (1973). *The homeless mind.* New York: Vintage Books.

Berman, M. (1982). *All that is solid melts into air.* New York: Simon & Schuster.

Chen, V. (1992). The construction of Chinese American women's identity. In L. F. Rakow (Ed.), *Women making meaning: New feminist directions in communication* (pp. 225-243). New York: Routledge, Chapman & Hall.

Chow, R. (1990). Politics and pedagogy of Asian literatures in American universities. *differences, 2* (3), 29-51.

Fischer, M. M. J. (1986). Ethnicity and the post-modern arts of memory. In J. Clifford & G. E. Marcus (Eds.), *Writing culture: The poetics and politics of ethnicity* (pp. 194-233). Berkeley: University of California Press.

Kadohata, C. (1989). *The floating world.* New York: Viking.

Kim, E. H. (1982). *Asian American literature.* Philadelphia: Temple University Press.

Kim, E. H. (1987). Defining Asian American realities through literature. *Cultural Critique, 6,* Spring, 87-111.

Kingston, M. H. (1976). *The woman warrior: Memoirs of a girlhood among ghosts.* New York: Alfred A. Knopf. Reprint Vintage Books Edition, 1977. (All references are to the Vintage edition.)

Kingston, M. H. (1982). Cultural mis-readings by American reviewers. In G. Amirthanayagam (Ed.), *Asian and Western writers in dialogue: New cultural identities* (pp. 55-65). London: Macmillan.

Kingston, M. H. (1989). *Tripmaster monkey: His fake book.* New York: Alfred A. Knopf.

Morrison, T. (1992). *Play in the dark: Whiteness and literary imagination.* Cambridge, MA: Harvard University Press.

Ng, F. M. (1993). *Bone.* New York: Hyperion.

Okada, J. (1979) (original 1957). *No-no boy.* Seattle: University of Washington Press.

Rodriguez, R. (1982). *Hunger of memory: The education of Richard Rodriguez.* New York: Bantam Books.

Sone, M. (1979) (original 1953). *Nisei daughter.* Seattle: University of Washington Press.

Tan, A. (1989). *The joy luck club.* New York: G.P. Putnam's Sons.

Trinh, T. M. (1989). *Woman, native, other.* Bloomington: Indiana University Press.

Wong, J. S. (1989). *Fifth Chinese daughter* (rev. ed.). Seattle: University of Washington Press.

2

Dis/orienting Identities: Asian Americans, History, and Intercultural Communication

Thomas Nakayama
Arizona State University

> If I'm not who you say I am, then you're not who
> you think you are.
> —*James Baldwin (1990, p. 5)*

One morning while I was walking to the Mouton-Duvernet Métro station in Paris's 14th Arrondissement, where I was renting a room for the summer, a woman came running up to me in an obvious hurry. Out of breath, she blurted out, *"Monsieur! Pardon! Où est le métro, s'il vous plaît?"*[2] I quickly gave her directions and she ran off, disappearing around the corner.

On my way to the Latin Quarter, I thought about how odd that little interaction had been for me. Here was a woman running up to me, assuming that I spoke French. I felt dis/oriented, as if I were called into a position that I do not normally occupy. When in Europe, I have come across many people who assume that, as someone of Asian ancestry, I speak French. Living in the U.S., I rarely encounter people who assume that I speak French.

I begin with this story because I think it contributes to an understanding of the way that various histories influence intercultural communication

practices. France's history with Asia is different from that of other European nations and certainly from that of the United States. These varying histories position me in different ways in different cultural contexts. As an Asian American, my ties to France and French history are distant indeed; yet this past confronts me when, for example, Europeans assume I speak French. My goal in this paper is to explore the cultural and historical constructions of the "Orient" and its relationship to my communication experiences in both domestic and international contexts.

My hope is that this essay will help challenge assumptions that continue to hamper many communication interactions. If James Baldwin is correct, I want to encourage a rethinking of what "American" means as a nationality and as an identity. As Kim (1982, p. 22) points out: "For Asian American writers, the task is to contribute to the total image and identity of America by depicting their own experiences and by defining their own humanity as part of the composite image of the American people." My goal here is not to argue simply that Asian Americans are Americans, but to suggest *why* this definition is a problem for Asian Americans. Unlike European Americans, Asian Americans have long been considered "forever foreign."

I do not wish to confuse the already confusing difference(s) between "Asians" and "Asian Americans." Yet, I believe it is important for Asian Americans to begin seeing their identities in both domestic and international contexts. For example:

> Asian American Studies has been located within the context of American Studies and stripped of its international links. This nationalist interpretation of immigration history has also been a more comfortable discourse for second- and third-generation Americans of Asian ancestry. Tired of being thought of as foreigners, these scholars have been particularly reluctant to identify with Asian Studies and its pronouncements on the distinctiveness of Asian cultures in counterpoint to Euro-American culture. (Mazumdar, 1991, pp. 29-30)

My point is not to reinforce this binary view of "Euro-American culture" versus "Asian cultures" in which Asian Americans are invisible, marginalized, and silenced. Rather, I want to suggest that we cannot understand the experiences and histories of Asian Americans outside of the context of *both* domestic and international contexts.

It is not enough simply to mark the difference between "Asian" and "Asian American." Asian Americans, like Asians, are diverse groups of people that can be categorized under the same discursive label. The cultural backgrounds and histories of Americans of Asian ancestry are at least as diverse as Americans of European ancestry, if not more so. It is important, therefore, to recognize the heterogeneity concealed in the construction of Asian American identity since an essentialized ethnic identity "also inadvertently supports the racist discourse that constructs Asians as a homogeneous group, that implies we are "all alike" and conform to 'types'" (Lowe, 1991, p. 30). The cultural and discursive construction of "Asian American," then, is certainly inadequate to describe the diversity and complexity of the differences between and among us, but it does help us understand how "Orientals" are often categorized as "Other" in U.S. culture, due to histories of discrimination.

The Specter of the 'Orient'

As *yonsei*, a fourth-generation Japanese American, I feel at home in the United States. Like many Americans of European ancestry who have not been to Europe, I have not yet visited Japan. While I would like to visit Japan, the reality of Japan is not part of my experience. Certainly, I have been influenced by Japanese culture, filtered down through the generations and experiences of my forbearers in the U.S. Like many U.S. citizens whose ancestors came from overseas, my relation to the "Orient" is similar to those who trace their origins elsewhere.

There is a specter haunting the United States, the specter of the Orient. The cultural image of the Orient invades and structures much of my intercultural communication interactions. My physical features identify my Asian ancestry, and it is this identification that structures my communicationinteractions with others. The phenomenon of being a U.S. citizen without European ancestry is noted by Chan (1991):

> The history of Asians in America can be fully understood only if we regard them as both immigrants and members of nonwhite minority groups. As immigrants, many of their struggles resemble those that European immigrants have faced, but as people of nonwhite origins bearing distinct physical differences, they have been perceived as "perpetual foreigners" who can never be completely absorbed into American society and its body politic. (p. 187)

The question here is one of identity: Who am I perceived to be when I communicate with others? What does it mean to be a "perpetual foreigner" in one's native country? My identity is very much tied to the ways in which others speak to me and the ways in which society represents my interests. In order to begin to answer these questions, we have to understand the complexity of the cultural construction of the Orient.

It is the cultural construction of the Orient that many Asians and Asian Americans find negative. Therefore, the term "oriental" is not the preferred term; it is fraught with stigmatizing ideological meanings. The use of oriental to refer to people, then, should also be avoided.

Where is the Orient?

We can sense the ideological framework that produces the cultural construction of the Orient when we juxtapose European with American visions of this imaginary place. Europeans tend to think of the Near East (Turkey) and the Middle East when they speak of the Orient. However, as Said (1978, p. 1) points out, "Americans will not feel quite the same about the Orient, which for them is much more likely to be associated very differently with the Far East (China and Japan, mainly)." The Orient is not a place with clearly defined boundaries in the way that nations or even continents are demarcated. The Orient crosses continents "from

North Africa and Turkey to China and Japan"[1] (Thomas, 1990, p. 6).

But what do Turkey and Japan share that Italy and Japan do not? How is North Africa like China, but not like France? These are more than analogy questions; they point to an odd system of categorizing, of ordering the world through a discourse in which the Orient becomes the Other, the antithesis of the West. This binary opposition between the Occident and the Orient is reflected in U.S. culture as well.

The cultural construction of the Orient is evident in the innumerable films, television and radio programs, advertisements, and cartoons that depict this "Other" place. This exotic place is occupied by odd people, as evidenced by their bizarre clothes, eyes, and the sounds emanating from "Orientals." This is not a new discovery, as "caricatures of Asians have been part of American popular culture for generations" (Kim, 1981, p. 3).

Even when I was young, I hated seeing media and movie images of martial arts, Fu Manchu types, and other limited and distorted representations of Asians. I longed for images of Asian Americans, rather than Asians. Yet the creation of Asian American images might have upset the binary opposition between East and West. I often wonder if we still need this oppositional force in our culture, but as I watch "Japan-bashing" on television, its continuation seems assured.

How to Become Dis/oriented

Dis/orientation is a dialectical process. The first part of this process, that of Asian Americans, comprises the historical experiences of Asian Americans living in the U.S. The second part, that of non-Asian Americans, is the socially learned expectation that Asians are not American, and can never become Americans. The combination of these processes invariably constructs identity positions that rarely correspond to where we, Asian Americans, think we are; hence, we are left dis/oriented.

In order to be dis/oriented, it seems necessary that Asian Americans had to first be "oriented." The historical process by which dis/orientation

happens may take several generations, but the specific time frame seems to matter little. In my family, dis/orientation began in the 19th century and continues today. It is part of a long struggle to distance oneself from the cultural construction of the Orient.

Obviously, there were tremendous influences that caused a split from cultures, rather than a combination thereof. My mother's family, for example, switched from being a primarily Japanese-speaking household to an English-speaking one during their internment in a U.S. concentration camp during World War II. I think they felt it was better to demonstrate their commitment to the U.S. during a time of crisis in which, based on their ancestry, their loyalty was questioned. This historical experience has been one of the most influential aspects of Japanese American identity, a shared collective memory that has bound Japanese Americans as a group and created a distinct identity. In this way, the collective memory serves an important identity function (Ng, 1991). In fact, it is this historical experience that creates my need to insist that I am American, not Japanese.

For non-Asian Americans, dis/orientation is not a split from the Orient, but the disorienting inability to overcome "Orientalism." I suspect that Orientalism manifests itself in different ways in intercultural communication interactions, but it becomes problematic when distinctions between Asian and Asian Americans are not made, when English is assumed a foreign language for Asian Americans, when Asian and American are split into two unrelated terms.

Reconsidering History

"Do you speak English?" This question always dis/orients me; I am lost when asked this question. Why wouldn't I speak the language of my parents, the language of my country? The simple response "Of course I do" does not usually dis/orient the questioner's assumption that one needs European ancestors to be "American."

I once had a Vietnamese American student whose francophone parents wanted her to learn

French. She steadfastly refused, saying, "French is the language of the colonizers." History has situated her relationship to French quite differently from my own. The other students in class objected, insisting that "French is a beautiful language." Once I had explained a little about the history of France in Indochina, they understood her resistance.

History is a process that has constructed where and how we enter into dialogue, conversation, and communication. It has strongly influenced what languages we speak, how we are perceived and how we perceive ourselves, and what domestic and international conflicts affect us.

On the domestic level, the histories of Asians in the United States are often difficult to find. Ignorance of these histories leads many Americans to assume that Asian Americans are recent immigrants. Although many Asian Americans trace their roots back before the tremendous wave of European immigration in the early 20th century, our histories are hidden and silenced. We know that "the major Asian immigrant groups in the U.S. in the 19th century were the Chinese and Japanese, although there is evidence that Filipinos, for example, had been in Louisiana as early as the 18th century" (Odo, 1993, pp. 118-119). Yet, the experiences of Asian Americans in many regions of the U.S. are often overlooked, hence, "much of our [Asian American] social and cultural histories will never be recovered" (Odo, 1993, p. 120). On the international level, the dynamic nature of international relations between Asian nations and the U.S. continues to influence the ways in which Asian Americans are seen. For example:

> Over 50 years after the bombing of Pearl Harbor, Japanese Americans are again victims of rising tensions between Japan and the United States. This should come as no surprise. The fate of Asian Americans has always been historically shaped by the prevailing state of U.S.-Asia relations. (Omi, 1993, p. 208)

The shifting winds of international relations have driven Asian Americans in many directions in their continual struggles to find a place in the U.S. But these international relations are not limited to the U.S. and Asia; they encompass many international interactions, contemporary as well as historical, in which we find ourselves trapped.

While waiting for the RER train at the Luxembourg station in Paris, I stood on the platform near a group of European American tourists who were examining a map and discussing where to go next. One of the women looked around and complained to her friends, in English, that there were "too many foreigners in Paris." As I *am* a foreigner in France, the comment did not strike me until I realized that the tourist assumed that I did not speak English and felt that she had some claim to France that I did not, since I assume she was not complaining about herself. I have wondered from time to time about the nature of her comment. Did she expect a different Paris? Did she know about our shared history on the other side of the Atlantic? Did she know about France's history in Africa and Asia? Would such knowledge have helped her understand France in other ways?

Our many different histories have much to do with where and how we enter into communication. The complexity of these histories can seem daunting, but they are crucial to the study of intercultural communication. Perhaps it is the absence of historical understanding that is no longer tenable if we are serious about understanding intercultural communication.

Another Country?

I do not know the face of this country.
It is inhabited by strangers
who call me obscene names.
Jap. Go home.
Where is home?
—*Janice Mirikitani* (1987, p. 7)

When I was growing up in Georgia, I began first grade at a "white school." At the time, I do not think I understood why there were two types of schools or any of the other racially segregated practices we engaged in daily. In hindsight, it seems bizarre to have lived in a black and white world when one is neither black nor white. How arbitrary these divisions are! Yet, they construct the ways in which we think about ourselves and others. Even today, when I speak to my students about history and intercultural relations, they look at me as if I am from another country.

Today, I live in Central Arizona. Fifty years ago my mother also lived in Arizona, at Poston III, an internment camp. Although we might like to believe that being an American is not a matter of "a common nationality, language, race, or ancestry" (Lapham, 1992, p. 48), the historical divisiveness of these differences and their importance in our everyday understanding of ourselves and others belies this dream.

Because of the inability of many European Americans to perceive any difference—cultural, linguistic, national, etc.—between Asians and Asian Americans, I can only be wary of recent Japan-bashing in the U.S. media. Although it has been 50 years since the U.S. concentration camps opened, it was because of similar racism that the mass incarceration of U.S. citizens was initiated. Here, then, is the irony: Asian American identities cannot be understood outside of the context of international politics and histories, and Asian American history and politics *are* a part of U.S. history and politics. Hence, my identification as an "American" seems ineffectual and, I feel, in an ongoing struggle with those who wish to identify me otherwise. These dis/orienting identities always leave me somewhere other than where I think I am. Asian Americans are trapped among larger discourses and histories, which constantly disrupt any claim to a stable identity; perhaps we are a paradigmatic example of postmodern racial identity.

I resent being considered a foreigner in the U.S., asked if I speak English, or asked when I came to this country. I am angry that my family has lost what I consider to be the most important part of its cultural heritage: its language. Perhaps this is the price to be paid for living in a society that is more interested in acculturation to "the hegemonic values of white U.S. society" (Escoffier, 1991, p. 64) than to multiculturalism. My hope is that Asian Americans will be able to inscribe their experiences and histories into other groups through "the formation of important political alliances and affiliations. . . across racial and ethnic, gender, sexuality, and class

lines" (Lowe, 1991, p. 31). In large part, this strategy would require letting go of the dominant view of U.S. history as one of European conquest and the assumption that Americans are of European descent.

Unlike James Baldwin, Richard Wright, and many other African American expatriates, I did not find Paris as liberating as they did. They lived in a different Paris, in a different context than I did. They also came from a different U.S. As much as I enjoyed Paris, it was not home.

When the Arizona desert heat becomes oppressive, I think of my mother living in a tar-paper barrack without air conditioning. I doubt that she considered Arizona "home." For me, however, I am home far from Georgia. This is my country and my home, even if I do not look "all-American."

NOTES

[1]"Excuse me, sir, where is the Metro station?"
[2]"de l'Afrique du Nord et de la Turquie à la Chine et au Japon" (my translation)

REFERENCES

Baldwin, J. (1990). Quoted in Introduction: A war of images. In J. L. Dates & W. Barlow (Eds.), *Split image* (pp. 1-21). Washington, DC: Howard University Press.

Chan, S. (1991). *Asian Americans: An interpretive history.* Boston: Twayne.

Escoffier, J. (1991). The limits of multiculturalism. *Socialist Review*, 21/3-4, 61-73.

Kim, E. H. (1982). *Asian American literature.* Philadelphia: Temple University Press.

Lapham, L. H. (1992, January). Who and what is American? *Harper's Magazine*, pp. 43-49.

Lowe, L. (1991). Heterogeneity, hybridity, multiplicity: Marking Asian American differences. *Diaspora*, 1/1, 24-44.

Mazumdar, S. (1991). Asian American Studies and Asian Studies: Rethinking roots. In S. Hune, H.-C. Kin, S. S. Fugita, & A. Ling (Eds.), *Asian Americans: Comparative and global perspectives* (pp. 29-44). Pullman: Washington State University Press.

Mirikitani, J. (1987). Prisons of silence. *Shedding silence* (pp. 5-9). Berkeley: Celestial Arts.

Ng, W. L. (1991). The collective memories of communities. In S. Hune, H.-C. Kim, S. S. Fugita, and A. Ling (Eds.), *Asian

Americans: comparative and global perspectives (pp. 103-112). Pullman: Washington State University Press.

Odo, F. S. (1993). Is there a future for our past? Cultural preservation policy. In *The state of Asian Pacific America, a public policy report: Policy issues to the year 2020* (pp. 113-126). Los Angeles: Leadership Education for Asian Pacifics and UCLA Asian American Studies Center.

Omi, M. (1993). Out of the melting pot and into the fire: Race relations policy. In *The state of Asian Pacific America, a public policy report: Policy issues to the year 2020* (pp. 199 -214). Los Angeles: Leadership Education for Asian Pacifics and UCLA Asian American Studies Center.

Said, E. W. (1978). *Orientalism.* New York: Random House.

Takaki, R. (1989). *Strangers from a different shore: A history of Asian Americans.* New York: Penguin.

Thomas, Y. (1990). Présentation. Special Issue: La Tentation de l'Orient. [Introduction. The temptation of the orient]. *Études françaises,* 26/1, 6-8.

3

Understanding Arab Americans: A Matter of Diversities

Hana S. Noor Al-Deen
University of North Carolina-Wilmington

America is a multi-ethnic society which is composed of more than fifty co-cultures. There is no doubt that cultural diversity exists within each of these co-cultures, and Arab Americans are no exception. While Arab Americans share a common heritage with one another, they do differ culturally. Applying a grand scheme of the "Arab culture" to Arab Americans without due consideration for diversities is, I believe, an inadequate approach.

This paper seeks to discuss some of the diversities that exist among Arab Americans in terms of culture and communication and explore examples of Arab American stereotypes in the United States.

Background

Arab Americans are descendants of the Semites who originated in a vast region of enormous historical and cultural complexity. Today, this region is called the Middle East. It is rich in natural resources as well as in religions; it is where Judaism, Christianity, and Islam began. Geographically, Arabs live in four regions of the Middle East: North Africa, a portion of the African Transition Zone, the East, and the Arabian Peninsula. North Africa consists of Algeria, Egypt, Libya, Morocco, and Tunisia. The portion of the African Transition Zone considered part of the Middle East includes Djibouti, Mauritania, Somalia, and Sudan. The East region is composed of Iraq, Jordan, Lebanon, and Syria. Finally, the Arabian Peninsula is made up of Bahrain, Kuwait, Oman, Qatar, Saudi Arabia, the United Arab Emirates, and Yemen. The Palestinians, meanwhile, are dispersed throughout these regions.

Although there are no exact statistics, it is estimated that approximately 3 million Arab Americans are currently living in the United States. Arabs came to the U.S. in two waves, which occurred before and after World War II. The first wave began during the last quarter of the 19th century. Most of the newcomers were "from the lower social classes and with little education" (Nigem, 1985, p. 631). They were mainly Christian (90 percent), single males, and 75 percent of them were between 15 to 45 years of age (Naff, 1980). Later, Arab women joined the wave of immigration. It has been estimated that females totalled approximately 47 percent of all Arab immigrants between 1899 and 1915 (Naff, 1980). Other religious groups such as Muslims and Druze constituted minorities. About 50 percent of the first wave settled in the South. The other 50 percent split into two groups, each half emigrating to the East Coast and the Midwest respectively (Nigem, 1985; Mehdi; 1975, and Naff, 1980).

The second wave began after World War II and continues to the present time. This migration appears to have been predicated chiefly on a need to escape the political turmoil in the Middle East. This wave has tended to be comprised of highly educated professionals such as doctors, lawyers, and engineers (Elkholy, 1969; Mehdi, 1978; Naff, 1988; and Nigem, 1985). They are predominantly Muslim (60 percent) and married; 50 percent of them range in age between 20 to 49 years old, and females constitute about 45 percent of the total (Naff, 1980).

The recent Arab American demographic characteristics were explained by Nigem (1985). His information was based on data from the 1980

Census of Population and the 1979 Current Population Survey. He concluded that Arab Americans tend to be above the national average with respect to education, occupation, and income but older in comparison to the national average of the general population.

> Over 50 percent of Arab Americans have higher education, in comparison to 34 percent of the U.S. population. About 61 percent of Arab Americans are distributed in white-collar occupations, in comparison to 49.4 percent of the U.S. population. The medium income for Arab Americans is $19,950 in comparison to $15,800 for the U.S. population. (Nigem, 1985, pp. 638-640)

About 72 percent of Arab Americans are between the ages of 14 and 64 in contrast to 67 percent of the U.S. population (Nigem, 1985). He also found that the majority of Arab Americans were born in the U.S., speak English well, and reside in large metropolitan areas of the Northeast, Midwest, South, and West.

Cultural Diversities, Communication, and Stereotyping

Cultural Diversities

Culture can be defined as the "deposit of knowledge, experiences, values, beliefs, attitudes, social structures, relationships, language (both verbal and nonverbal), and material objects and possessions a group of people acquires over time through the efforts of the individuals who make up the group" (Klopf, 1991, p. 31). These components are not static; instead, they are influenced by a variety of forces which lead to cultural diversity.

Historically, the Arab region has been ruled by many outsiders such as the Persians, the Turks, and the Europeans. This domination evolved after the Abbasid Empire began to decline in 945 A.D. (Abboushi, 1974). Conquering nations brought with them elements of their culture, which were gradually integrated into the indigenous culture. The result has been numerous co-cultures existing within the broad scope of "Arab culture."

Some of these co-cultures are more Westernized or Easternized than others. The Westernized co-cultures found in countries such as Lebanon and the Arab nations in Africa are those that were influenced by European cultures. The Easternized co-cultures were affected by cultural components of the Persians and the Turks; they are found in countries such as Iraq, Jordan, Syria, and most of the Arabian Peninsula. However, Easternized co-cultures often contain some Westernized elements, and the reverse situation is true as well.

The degree of adaptation of these co-cultures is also influenced, to some extent, by other elements of culture such as religion. Religions often dictate the way of life in the Middle East. For example, Islam is considered "the totality of culture in both its social and individual aspects; it is a regulator of conduct concerning such diverse matters as. . . family life, the individual's relationship to his fellow citizens, inheritance, sexual discourse, marriage, divorce, clothing. . .and so on" (Almaney & Alwan, 1982, p. 54). Arab Muslims tend to be more receptive to Eastern culture than their Christian counterparts because they share Islamic religion with the East. Islam is the universal submission to God (Allah). It is a monotheistic religion in which Allah, whose Prophet is Muhammad, is The Supreme Power. Arab Muslims follow one of three sects: Sunnites (the largest), Shi'ites, or Ibadites (Azzam, 1964). Arab Druze who broke away from the Shi'ites in the 11th century are divided into two groups: those who call themselves semi-Muslims and those who consider their religion to be entirely different from all other religions (Naff, 1988). Meanwhile, Arab Christians tend to be more receptive to Western culture than Arab Muslims because the former share Christianity with the West. Arab Christians may be categorized as Maronites, Melkites, Jacobites, and Chaldean Catholics who are associated with the Roman Catholic Church, while those of the Eastern Orthodox persuasion choose the Episcopalian Church or the Egyptian Copts (Naff, 1988).

Based on such differences, Arab immigrants tend to reside in the United States near people from their respective homeland and/or who share the same religion. The reason for such proximity is based upon the wish to preserve cultural values, customs, and traditions. For instance, the tradition of arranged marriages still prevails in some Arab American communities, particularly among those descended from cultures that observe Eastern cultural values. In the selection of a future spouse, consideration is given to religious background as well as to the ancestral homeland of the male and female to be wed. The marriage candidates must be from the same religious sect—for example, both Sunnites or both Shi'ites. If it is difficult to match the same sect, both of them should at least be of the same religion (e.g., both Muslims). However, interreligious marriages do exist between Arab Americans and non-Arab Americans. Regarding homeland, consideration is given to the country and region of the marriage candidates. A preference is given to those whose ancestors came from the same country; but if there is no match, the region of the ancestors will be considered. For example, an Iraqi male often prefers to marry an Iraqi female or a female from countries within the eastern region of the Middle East, such as Jordan or Syria. Traditional Arab Americans are trying to maintain such customs. For Arab Americans who descended from cultures that observe Western cultural values, proximity with people from their homeland may not be as crucial because they share cultural values with European Americans and are therefore often better able to adapt to the mainstream American culture. Also, their offspring are given more freedom in selecting a future spouse.

Communication

This section discusses a sample of the variations in verbal and nonverbal communication among Arab Americans.

Verbal Communication. Verbal communication can be illustrated by both the spoken and written forms of a language. Arabic (a Semitic language) was the mother tongue of the ancestors of Arab Americans. Also, most Arabs are conversant in some additional languages such as English, French, Italian, or Spanish, to name a few. These languages were either learned from contact with outsiders or through education. Students in most Arab countries are required to learn at least one additional language at an early age during primary school. Consequently, there are few language barriers for them when communicating with others because they have become adept at handling a number of languages and have disciplined themselves to develop "an ear" for learning new languages.

Arab Americans can be grouped into either monolingual or multilingual groups. The multilingual individuals are those who speak more than one language; Arabic may or may not be included. The monolingual individuals use either Arabic or English. Those who are limited to Arabic may have immigrated at an older age, thereby making it more difficult for them to learn a new language. The individuals who only use English tend to be those American-born Arabs who wish to assimilate into mainstream America. However, the increase of Arab nationalist movements after World War II, accompanied by the second wave of Arab immigrants to the U.S., helped to underscore the significance of the Arabic language. Consequently, more Arab Americans have been teaching their children Arabic. Arab Americans who were born in the United States started to learn the Arabic language and the Arab culture in their churches, mosques, and even in courses at U.S. colleges. This blossoming of interest may be attributed to the fact that "Arabic serves as an important cultural device. . . the Arabs have traditionally used language as their primary medium of artistic and political expression" (Almaney & Alwan, 1982, p. 87).

Nonverbal Communication. Nonverbal communication can be explained as "all those stimuli within a communication setting, both humanly and environmentally generated, with the exception of verbal stimuli, that have potential message value for the sender or receiver" (Samovar, et al., 1981, p. 156). When discussing nonverbal communication, Arab Americans can be divided into three main groups: Americanized, acculturated, and traditional. The

Americanized Arabs are those who have assimilated with other Americans and use mainstream American nonverbal communication. The acculturated individuals are those who have merged some of the traditional Arab ways of nonverbal communication with some of the adopted American ways of nonverbal communication. The outcome is a new flexibility which helps these Arab Americans to adapt to many situations. The traditionalists are those who kept their traditional Arab ways of nonverbal communication.

The nonverbal communication of these three groups may be illustrated by examples of physical touch, such as greeting the opposite sex, as well as examples of appearance. During greeting, the Americanized group may touch by kissing, hugging, or shaking hands with a person of the opposite sex, depending on their relationship. The acculturated people may or may not touch the opposite sex depending on the participants in a communication situation. For example, when the acculturated individuals greet Westerners, they may apply a standard similar to their Americanized counterparts above. When they greet non-Westerners, they apply the appropriate way of greeting for that culture such as no hugging or kissing of the opposite sex. The traditionalists, meanwhile, cannot touch due to either religious values or restrictive customs and traditions; their greetings tend to remain strictly verbal. Appearance, too, varies with perspective. The Americanized women may wear clothes similar to those worn by mainstream American women. The acculturated females may garb themselves in more conservative styles of clothing, to some degree, and they do not appear in swimming suits or shorts in the presence of the general public. Feminine fashion for the acculturated is dictated, to some extent, by religion, restrictive customs, and traditions. The traditionalists may wear the Hijab, a long raincoat-like garment with a scarf placed on the head to cover the hair completely. The Hijab has evolved because women in Islam are suppose to be covered completely with the exception of their faces, hands, and feet.

It is noteworthy that, in the above examples of appearance as a type of nonverbal communication, the focus is on women's behavior. The reason for this select focus is that women's conduct is very significant among Arabs. "No aspect of the Arabs' life is more affected by honor than women's sexual behavior; a family's honor can forever be tarnished by a woman who violates the acceptable norm of conduct" (Almaney & Alwan, 1982, p. 100). For example, most Arab women are not permitted to have premarital sex or even to date males. It is absolutely crucial for the family honor that a female remain a virgin until her wedding day.

Stereotyping

Widespread misconceptions about Arab Americans tend to derive from stereotypes. Stereotyping can be defined as "overgeneralized, oversimplified, or exaggerated beliefs associated with a category or a group of people" (Samovar, et al., 1981, p. 122). Arabs, particularly in the U.S., are often negatively stereotyped. They are routinely classified as Muslim fundamentalists and generally portrayed with distorted images. One of the more common Western misconceptions is that Arab means Muslim fundamentalist. It is important to stress that not all Muslims are Arabs, not all Arabs are Muslims, not all Muslims are religious fanatics, and not all religious fanatics are Muslims. It is erroneous, therefore, to assume that every Muslim is a fundamentalist. In most regions in the world there can be found people who are religious zealots, those who moderately practice their religion, and those who are indifferent about religion.

Equally important, one should not assume that all Muslims are Arabs. There are Muslims in Afghanistan, Germany, Malaysia, Pakistan, republics of the former Soviet Union, Turkey, and many other parts of the world. Moreover, it is a mistake to assume that all the Arabs are Muslims. Arabs observe various religions. So in the interest of accuracy, one should avoid using the words Arabs, Muslims, and fundamentalists interchangeably.

The media has contributed greatly to the distorted image of Arabs. As some scholars have observed, "Americans can hardly turn a blind eye to the way in which politics and public perceptions have produced a dangerously distorted image of the Arab world, distortions made perhaps even worse by well-intentioned but inaccurate earlier romanticized notions of Arabs" (Brown, 1991, p. 3). Shaheen (1990) reported that in a recent study, 293 secondary school teachers from five states, Massachusetts, North Carolina, Arkansas, West Virginia and Wisconsin, were surveyed. They were asked to write down the names of any humane or heroic Arab they had seen in a motion picture. Five cited past portraits of Ali Baba and Sinbad; one mentioned Omar Sharif and "those Arabs" in "Lion of the Desert" and "The Wind and the Lion." The remaining 287 teachers wrote "none."

Stereotyping has led to hostile attitudes towards the Arab American community. For instance, during the 1990-1991 Persian Gulf Conflict, Arab Americans were called "A-rabs," "Camel Jockeys," "Ragheads," "Sand Niggers," "Sandsuckers," "Towelheads," and so on. Hate crimes increased, including harassment, threats, offensive language, physical aggression, religious aggression, discrimination, vandalism, and other hostile acts against this community (Noor Al-Deen, 1991). FBI agents across the country were authorized to interview Arab American business and community leaders. It was stated that one of the reasons for those interviews was "to solicit information from Arab Americans regarding possible terrorist activity by Iraqis or their agents against U.S. targets" (ADC, 1991, Jan. 17). Earlier, Arab American community centers and mosques across the U.S. were attacked after a TWA airplane was hijacked overseas (Lerner, 1986).

Discriminatory outbursts such as these are not uncommon. Immediately following the 1985 hijack of the Italian passenger ship *Achille Lauro*, an American university professor whom I had known for some time encountered me at my place of work. Running towards me in a serious manner and in front of my students, he screamed, "Don't shoot me, don't shoot me," with both hands raised in mock surrender. Such negative attitudes have led some Arab Americans to deny their heritage out of fear of discrimination. A six-year-old Arab American boy asked his mother to "change his name to something that 'sounds more American' and re-quested that she not speak to him in Arabic outside the home or send him to school with pita bread. Classmates call him 'camel jockey' and 'Qaddafi's brother'" (Lerner, 1986, p. 24).

Likewise, Arab Americans sometimes suffer from being treated as aliens by their fellow citizens. This occurs despite the fact that many Arab Americans have been living in the United States for generations, perhaps even longer than some other American ethnics. Yet all too often Arab Americans are a nonexistent, suspect, and disenfranchised segment of the U.S. population. During my research for this project, I sought the assistance of a senior librarian at an American public university in order to help me acquire data about Arab Americans. The librarian said in all sincerity, "Why don't you check with their Embassy?"

Conclusion

Arab Americans are descendants of the Semites who originated in a vast region where early civilization arose. Arab Americans' forefathers made extraordinary contributions to western civilization. They "translated and preserved the manuscripts of the ancient Greek philosophers and the writings of the great thinkers of Christian Byzantium (previously the eastern portion of the Roman Empire)" (Naff, 1988, p. 23). Among the contributors to western philosophy and writing are Ibn-Rushd (known as Averroes) and Ibn-Sina (known as Avicenna); in mathematics, the Arabs developed the decimal system, introduced the zero, Arabic numerals replaced Roman numerals in Europe, and al-Khwarizmi is the acknowledged founder of algebraic theories (Abboushi, 1974). Arabs were also pioneers in other fields such as chemistry, medicine, geography, astronomy, astrology, and trigonometry.

Besides the enormous contributions made by their forefathers, Arab Americans are active in many fields today, including public service. As of this writing, some of these Arab Americans are Donna Shalala (U.S. Secretary of Health and Human Services in the Clinton Administration), George Mitchell (U.S. Senate Majority Leader),

James Abourezk (former U.S. Senator, South Dakota), Mary Rose Oakar (U.S. Representative, Ohio), Nick Joe Rahall (U.S. Representative, West Virginia), John Sununu (former White House Chief-of-Staff), Victor Atiyeh (Governor, Oregon), Philip Habib (U.S. peace negotiator to the Middle East), Ralph Nader (consumer rights advocate), Helen Thomas (known as the dean of White House press correspondents), Doug Flutie (Heisman Trophy winner in 1984), and Casey Kasem (America's Top 40 host since 1970) (Naff, 1988, Sadd, et al., 1985).

As has been shown, Arabs may share a common heritage, but they differ culturally. Knowledge of the cultural values of one group of Arabs may not be applicable to another. Applying a grand scheme of the "Arab culture" without due consideration for the diversities that exist among Arabs is an inadequate approach.

Understanding the diversities among Arab Americans can lead to a better understanding of the Arabs in the Middle East, thereby improving communication between Arab and non-Arab cultures. The communicative benefit from this is one that no country can afford to ignore in this Age of the Global Village.

REFERENCES

Abboushi, W. F. (1974). *The angry Arabs*. Philadelphia: The Westminster Press.

ADC Action Alert. (1991, January 17).

Almaney, A. J., & Alwan, A. J. (1982). *Communicating with the Arabs*. Prospect Heights: Waveland Press.

American television: Arabs in dehumanizing roles. (1981). In S. Abraham & S. Abraham (Eds.), *The Arab world and Arab-Americans*. Detroit: Wayne State University.

Azzam, A. (1964). *The eternal message of Muhammad*. London: The Devin-Adair.

Billionaires, bombers, and belly dancers: The TV Arab. (1987). In J. Ruby & M. Taureg (Eds.), *Visual explorations of the world*. Aachen, Germany: Herodot Rader Verlag.

Brown, L. C. (1991). Empires on the sand [Review of *A history of the Arab peoples*]. *The New York Times*, p. 3.

De Blij, H. J., & Muller, P. O. (1991). *Geography regions and concepts* (6th ed.). New York: John Wiley & Sons.

Esman, M. J., & Rabinovich, I. (1988). *Ethnicity, pluralism and the state in the Middle East*. New York: Cornell University Press.

Ghareeb, E. (Ed.). (1983). *Split vision: The portrayal of Arabs in the American media*. Washington, D.C.: American-Arab Affairs Council.

Hourani, A. H. (1991). *A history of the Arab peoples*. Cambridge, MA: Harvard University Press.

Klopf, D. W. *Intercultural encounters: The fundamentals of intercultural communication* (2nd ed.). Englewood, CO: Morton Publishing.

LaFraniere, S. (1991, January 9). FBI starts interviewing Arab-American leaders. *The Washington Post*.

Landau, R. (1974). *The Arab heritage of western civilization* (3rd ed.). New York: The League of Arab States.

Lerner, S. (1986, July). Terror against Arabs in America. *The New Republic*, pp. 20-25.

Media coverage of the Middle East: Perception and foreign policy. (1985). In T. Naff & M. E. Wolfgang (Eds.), *The annals of the American Academy of Political and Social Science: Changing patterns of power in the Middle East*. Beverly Hills: Sage Publications.

Naff, A. (1988). Arabs. In S. Thernstrom (Ed.), *Harvard encyclopedia of American ethnic groups* (pp. 128-136). Cambridge: Harvard University Press.

Naff, A. (1985). *Becoming American: The early Arab immigrant experience*. Carbondale, IL: Southern Illinois University Press.

Naff, A. (1988). *The Arab Americans*. Chelsea House.

Newell, D. (1986, Jan.). Arab-bashing in America. *Newsweek*, p. 21.

Nigem, E. (1985). Arab Americans: migration, socioeconomic and demographic characteristics. *International Migration Review, 20(3)*, 629-649.

Noor Al-Deen, H. S. (1991, April). *Arab-Americans and the Gulf crisis*. Paper presented at the meeting of the Southern States Communication Association, Tampa, FL.

Orfalea, G. (1988). *Before the flames: A quest for the history of Arab Americans*. Austin: University of Texas Press.

Sadd, D. J., & Lendermann, G. N. (1985, Fall). Arab American grievances. *Foreign Policy, 60*, 17-30.

Samovar, L.A., Porter, R. F., & Jain, N. C. (1981). *Understanding intercultural communication*. Belmont: Wadsworth.

Shaheen, J. G. (1984). *The TV Arab*. Bowling Green: Bowling Green State University Popular Press.

Shaheen, J. G. (1990, August 19). Our cultural demon—The "Ugly Arab." *The Washington Post*, p. Cl.

Spindler, L. S. (1977). *Culture change and modernization*. Prospect Heights: Waveland.

Suleiman, M. W. (1988). *The Arabs in the mind of America*. Battleboro: Amana Books.

The Arab Stereotype. (1980). In C. Morris (Ed.), *The Arab image in western mass media*. London: Outline Books.

Wasserman, P. (Ed.). (1988). *Ethnic information sources of the United States* (2nd ed.). (Vol. 1). Detroit: Gale Research.

Zogby, J. (1984). *Taking root bearing fruit: The Arab-American experience*. American-Arab Anti-Discrimination Committee, Washington, D.C.

4

How I Came To Know 'In Self Realization There is Truth'

Sydney A. Ribeau
California Polytechnic State University

A recent reading of *Multi-Cultural Literacy: Opening the American Mind* (1988) prompted this paper. In this anthology, the editors present a number of essays which challenge readers to analyze critically their world through the writing of women and men who see a diverse America. Education, history, and culture are discussed from a critical perspective which includes groups traditionally considered "outsiders." The authors provide cultural critiques in a manner designed to expand our understanding of America, and thus strengthen the fabric of our culture. Bell hooks (1990) has referred to this approach as education for a critical consciousness. Through speaking and writing, she suggests, academics can make critical interventions which lead to altered perceptions of social reality. "A Journey into Speech" by Michelle Cliff, a selection from the reader, is particularly useful in understanding the difficulty of overcoming personal alienation and establishing an empowered ethnic identity.

Issues discussed in *Multi-Cultural Literacy* seem especially important for those interested in the study of culture and communication. In this paper, I use these issues to establish the context for a discussion of my personal search for an African American academic identity to guide my career. Michelle Cliff insightfully describes her struggle to find her literary voice after years ". . .of assimilation, indoctrination, passing into the anglo-centricism of British West Indian culture. . . ." She describes the British domination of Jamaican culture as leading to the internationalization of white supremacy which marginalized her culture and traditions. Works written in the "King's English" were literature, while indigenous stories written in patois were not. This led to a gradual alienation from her ethnic identity which culminated in the completion of her education at the Warburg Institute, University of London.

> My dissertation was produced at the Warburg Institute, University of London, and was responsible for giving me an intellectual belief in myself that I had not had before, while at the same time distancing me from who I am, almost rendering me speechless about who I am. At least I believed in the young woman who wrote the dissertation—still I wondered who she was and where she had come from. (p.57)

The inception of an academic career further immersed Cliff in the culture of dominant society. Her academic success depended on her ability to create knowledge in a form and for an audience rooted in cultural hegemony. Academically trained and intellectually prepared, she found herself personally isolated and marginalized. Psychological introspection and participation in the feminist movement enabled her to "approach herself as subject," and begin to reveal who she was in her work. As subject, she was required to rediscover her ethnocultural past.

> To write [she says] as a complete Caribbean woman, or man for that matter, demands of us retracing the African part of ourselves, reclaiming as our own, and as our subject, a history sunk under the sea, or scattered as potash in the cane fields, or gone to bush, or trapped in a class system notable for its rigidity and absolute dependence on color stratification. On a past bleached from our minds. (p.59)

The transformation from a muted, detached, alienated outsider to a centered, connected, articulate actor is not unique to Cliff. In *Breaking Ice*, Terry McMillan (1990) describes a similar realization:

I couldn't believe the rush I felt over and over once I discovered Countee Cullen, Langston Hughes, Ann Petry, Zora Neale Hurston, Ralph Ellison, Jean Toomer, Richard Wright, and rediscovered and read James Baldwin, to name just a few. . . . My world opened up. I accumulated and gained a totally new insight about, and perception of our lives as "black" people, as if I had been an outsider and was finally let in. (p. xvi)

While reading about the experiences of Cliff and McMillan, I was drawn to memories of my graduate school years. "Communication theory," "interpersonal communication," "research methodology," the list continued, but none of the courses listed considered the African American experience, nor the experience of Latinos, Asians, or Native Americans. There was, in our requirements, no intercultural communication course or mention of the ethnic experience. The "Message from the Grass Roots," a speech by Malcolm X, was brought up in one class, but other than that, rhetoric, communication theory, and all other areas of the discipline were decidedly Eurocentric. During this period, I maintained intellectual balance by taking courses in African American literature and anthropology. Like Terry McMillan, literature enabled me to experience the aesthetic life of the African American while groping for a connection between my experience and the discipline which seemed to ignore it. Was there an African American rhetorical tradition? Did interpersonal communication theory consider the unique cultural history of African Americans here and in Africa? Was there form and content which distinguished African American communication from that of the dominant group? These questions and other similar ones were felt but not stated as I struggled with Greek rhetorical tradition and social scientific theory which seemed to render me invisible. I should add that my graduate program was an excellent one. The faculty was nationally recognized; the research facilities exceptional. It was not the quality of the program that was restricting; it was the limitations placed on curricula by a Eurocentric paradigm which dominated graduate work in my disciplinary area—and in most others. I was briefly connected to another dimension of communication study by Arthur L. Smith (1969, 1972, aka M.K. Asante). His *Rhetoric of Black Revolution and Language, Communication and Rhetoric in Black America* ignited in me a desire to expand my understanding of the communication processes to include a voice, albeit muted, which recognized my presence.

Graduate school reflections were quickly replaced by the demands of my first full-time university teaching position. I felt prepared to teach courses in interpersonal and group communication, my areas of concentration, and was beginning to develop an interest in intercultural communication. My colleagues were supportive, and academic life was fine. However, as time passed I was compelled, for personal and professional reasons, to prepare a paper for submission to a scholarly journal. This decision vividly reminded me of the absence in the literature of non-mainstream voices.

African American rhetoric had surfaced momentarily, but faded with the dissipation of the Black protest movement. Papers on the subject were not being published. Intercultural communication was considered an interesting instructional area because of its focus on improving race relations (Rich, 1974), but was not represented in the scholarly journals. Surely, I thought, ethnicity and culture were variables which significantly influenced communication; my time would come. When it didn't, I forged ahead with a colleague, who shared similar interests, and conducted an empirical study on what we called "domestic ethnic cultural groups." It was submitted to a regional speech communication journal and rejected by the reviewers because African Americans did not constitute a unique culture. They were merely a "subcultural" group. My colleague and I wrote a rebuttal, citing the works of W.E.B. DuBois (1903), Melville Herskovits (1941), and Geneva Smitherman (1977), which clearly traced the evolution of African American culture from the shores of West Africa to America. The editor was not persuaded by our evidence, and the paper was not published. My anger slowly cooled and assumed the form of quiet resignation. The ethnic culture which was not included in my formal education, but gave form and definition to my life, was casually dismissed. As in graduate school, again I did not exist.

Eventually the paper was resubmitted and accepted for publication in an international journal outside of my discipline. I recount these events to make a point: the academic experience can empower or silence. It empowers through the inclusion of content which speaks to the breadth of the human experience; it silences through the exclusion of those outside the mainstream. In America we readily identify these groups. The examples discussed above consider the process by which academics of African descent come to a sense of ethnic identity which focuses their intellectual interests and creates a cultural foundation for their work. Academic training alone, in programs dominated by a Eurocentric paradigm, do not equip one to conduct research, write, or teach about issues which grow from cultural experiences. A recent issue of *Liberal Education* (June 1991) considers the limitations of traditional educational approaches which lack diversity and argues for a more pluralistic approach.

> Most commonly . . . applicant institutions report a pervasive parochialism among their students: they lack either knowledge of or interest in both the complexity of their own society and the variety of cultures, claims, and world views mingling across the boundaries of nations and societies. (p. 4)

Parochialism is not only a characteristic of the students, it grows from school curricula which ignores the experiences of outsider groups. These omissions separate the academic world from the realities students encounter in daily life and see on television or film. Many students live in a world very different from the one studied in school. Because of this, it is easy for them to become academically isolated and psychologically removed from the intellectual stimulation that schools should provide. This situation is intensified for many ethnic students whose language, family structure, and traditions move them further from the mainstream culture. Years of such educational experiences can extinguish natural intellectual curiosity, or significantly dampen it. The results, all too often, are invisibility or silence.

This does not have to be. Along with Cliff, McMillan and others, I discovered an intellectual space through an awareness of my African American ethnic identity. Ethnic identity is the ethnic culture with which one identifies. It includes traditions, "people-hood," heritage, orientation to the past, religion, languages, ancestry, values, economics, aesthetics, and social organization. The term currently used by academics to explain the intellectual framework for African American identity is "Afrocentricity." The intellectual threads of this idea date back to the early work of W.E.B. DuBois (1903) and Carter G. Woodson (1933), but the most articulate of its current advocates is Molefi K. Asante (1987). Five central measures undergird the approach:

1) People of African descent share a common experience, struggle, and origin.
2) Present in African culture is a non-material element of resistance to the assault upon traditional values caused by the intrusion of European legal procedures, medicines, political processes, and religions into African culture.
3) African culture takes the view that an Afrocentric modernization process would be based upon three traditional values: harmony with nature, humaneness, and rhythm.
4) Afrocentricity involves the development of a theory of an African way of knowing and interpreting the world.
5) Some form of communalism or socialism is an important component of the way wealth is produced, owned, and distributed. (Covin, 1990, p. 126)

While these measures are both descriptive and prescriptive, they gain their greatest potency from the ability to connect the African diaspora to its early cultural roots. Connection to a nation, philosophy, languages, and cultural values enables the Afrocentric scholar to replace noticeable curricular omissions with substantive information leading to a sense of self-awareness. This in turn redefines the role of the outsider and can help remove the mantle of invisibility.

Afrocentricity is mentioned here to illustrate a mechanism through which a people alienated by educational institutions and social practice can discover a sense of ethnic identity which leads to renewed positive self-awareness. It suggests how an outsider group can confront the paradoxes of a racially stratified America. This approach, however, is also of value for other marginalized ethnic academics, especially communication scholars. In addition to being a powerful liberating force, Afrocentricity frames significant questions regarding communication and social interaction. Asante suggests that it involves

> the systematic exploration of relationships, social codes, cultural and commercial customs, oral traditions and proverbs, and the interpretation of communicative behavior as expressed in discourse, spoken or written, and techniques found in jazz studies and urban street vernacular. (p. 16)

This focus is replete with research opportunities for the scholar interested in African American communication. It grounds the field in expressive forms and rituals central to African American culture. From it, one can begin to formulate a perspective on African American communication which begins with the fundamental cultural experiences of the people. Oral traditions, for example, are key elements in understanding African American communication and cultural continuities which connect Africa to the African American experience. Smitherman (1977) explains this important point:

> Naturally, Black Americans, having to contend with slavery and Euroamerican ways, have not been able to practice or manifest the traditional African world view in its totality. But, as we shall see in closely examining the many facets of the oral tradition, the residue of the African world view persists, and serves to unify such seemingly disparate groups as preachers and poets, bluesmen and Gospel-ettes, testifiers and toast-tellers, reverends and revolutionaries. (p. 76)

Here we see a meshing of world views which gives rise to a number of African American expressive forms. The Afrocentric perspective, through its foundational assumptions, guides the researcher to fundamental questions regarding African American communication.

Thus far my discussion has focused on the African-American experience, for through it I have established an academic ethnic identity. I am convinced that this identity has enabled me to focus professional interests in a manner consistent with the way in which mainstream scholars research and write about the reality that defines their worlds. For them, years of education identify, explain, and validate their intellectual interests because the curriculum mirrors them. The controversy surrounding multicultural education hinges on a belief that liberal education should be inclusive rather than exclusive, thus capturing the varied intellectual wealth of our nation. To accomplish this objective, ethnic scholars must be empowered to interpret the world through the eyes of those who have been forgotten. We all have much to learn, for example, from the lives of American Indian women. Paula Gunn Allen (1986) comments on the importance of the female in Indian culture:

> There are many female gods recognized and honored by the tribes and Nations. Femaleness was highly valued, both respected and feared, and all social institutions reflected this attitude. Even modern sayings, such as the Cheyenne statement that a people is not conquered until the hearts of the women are on the ground, express the Indian's understanding that without the power of women the people will not live, but with it they will endure and prosper. (p. 16)

This information can help both feminist scholars and social historians extend the debate regarding the role of patriarchy in the development of American culture. Also, this information might ignite a spark of ethnic awareness for an American Indian woman psychologically buried in Eurocentric culture and searching for a sense of self. In both instances, new information enlightens and empowers.

Certain factors of racism and discrimination are shared by people of color in America, whatever their cultural group. These factors significantly contribute to outsider status and lend themselves to similar remedies. African Americans, Native Americans, and Latinos have all been subjected to de facto and de jure segregation. History documents the evolution of these events (Zinn, 1980), while sociology describes the vestiges of this legacy found in ghettos, barrios, reservations, and other communities of the marginalized. In these areas, ethnic marginalization is usually accompanied by its economic counterpart, poverty. The combination is often a death sentence to the dreams of the young (Kozal, 1991). With limited educational opportunities, the clouds of alienation begin to settle. Those who escape this trap must still grapple with curricula which ignore them and a society largely indifferent to the plight of their people. But they are the ones who might defy the odds and make it into the academy. If they are fortunate, an opportunity for a university degree affords a range of new possibilities. But there is a price. Achievement in the academy requires a kind of acculturation which can challenge the foundation of one's cultural life. Mainstream values designed to prepare one for success in a capitalist society are usually not derived from traditional ethnic cultures. All too often the price for academic success is the loss of self, described earlier by Michelle Cliff. Fortunately, there are ways to obtain educational goals and maintain a healthy ethnic identity. This process, however, begins with an education based on the premise of inclusion. Those in the communication discipline must take a new leadership role in this process.

The study of human communication assumes as its domain the formulation, transmission, and interpretation of messages. It is bound by a cultural context which frames interactional patterns. The history of the discipline is grounded in classical rhetoric and British public address, which places it well within the Eurocentric paradigm. As mentioned previously, this paradigm does not speak to the diversity which constitutes our nation. Implicit in our field is the assumption that most communication is a social act that emerges from a context. It is a short distance from these assumptions to a culturally-sensitive communication perspective. What are the outlines of the requirements of such an approach?

Communication research must utilize a perspective on ethnic communication based on the cultural experiences of the group being studied. Just as an Afrocentric approach attempts to ground African American communication research in established cultural traditions of African Americans, research pertaining to other ethnic groups should begin with the cultural experiences of the people rather than theories developed on data from mainstream groups. The current methodological sophistication of our discipline makes this quite possible.

New initiatives must be taken to encourage ethnic students to pursue graduate work. The study of a culture differs from the experience of it. Insights gained from "living a culture" are assets in the study of cultural life. Ethnic students trained in communication theory and research methods can combine these with insider insights to explain the complexity of inter- and intracultural communication.

In the instructional area, intercultural communication must focus on the problematic aspects of intercultural encounters. Many of the problems in contemporary society are the result of cultural misunderstanding. We read of them in newspapers, see them on television, and experience them in our lives. For the most part, unfortunately, they do not find their way into the classroom to be analyzed. We must use our theory and skills to develop intercultural improvement strategies. We must connect the academy with the larger society.

The communication discipline has much to offer a truly liberal education. I have briefly discussed what I consider to be some possibilities. More importantly, I have attempted here to describe a space characterized by W.E.B. DuBois as "behind the veil." As I emerge from it, a new academic environment seems possible. One which is inclusive, empowering, and sensitive to the challenges which face our contemporary world.

I would be remiss, in closing, not to mention how the emergence of my ethnic identity has directly influenced the direction of my career. The implied impact is probably apparent to the careful reader, yet there are more pronounced manifestations. I mentioned earlier that I could not have written this essay prior to my search for a personal ethnic identity to ground both teaching and research interests. Unknown to me was a world of ideas, constructs, and feelings which would eventually direct my professional life. A result of this self-realization process was the acceptance of the chair position in the Pan African Studies Department at my university, a decision which forced me to confront alternative ways of experiencing and interpreting the communication discipline and long-range professional objectives. I interacted regularly with social scientists, literary scholars, and film critics who connected teaching, learning, and scholarship to ethnic issues and community service. In addition, my emerging personal and professional ethnic identity led to a redirection of career plans. It became apparent through discussions with a number of colleagues that the educational experience that had fostered my sense of personal alienation was not an isolated case. If this was to change, I reasoned, university policy must change. Thus, I embarked on an administrative track which has led me to serve as chair, dean, and now academic vice president. In my current position, it is possible to mobilize institutional resources to confront race, class, and gender bias while promoting an environment of inclusion which values the unique attributes of each individual.

Organizational change is a process which takes place over an extended period of time. Success in this area must begin, however, with personal self-realization. The intellectual journey described in this paper has brought me to a place where the personal and professional are fused in ways that affect my work, who I am, and what I might become.

REFERENCES

Allen, P. G. (1988). Who is your mother? Red roots of white feminism. *Multi-cultural literacy: Opening the American mind*. Saint Paul: Graywolf Press.

Asante, M. K. (1987). *The Afrocentric idea*. Philadelphia: Temple University Press.

Cliff, M. (1988). A journey into speech. *Multi-cultural literacy: Opening the American mind*. Saint Paul: Graywolf Press (originally published, 1985).

DuBois, W.E.B. (1903). *The souls of black folk*. Greenwich, Conn.: A Fawcett Book.

Herskovits, M. (1941). *The myth of the Negro past*. Boston: Beacon Press.

hooks, b. (1990). *Yearning: Race, gender, and cultural politics*. Boston: South End Press.

Kozal, J. (1991). *Savage inequalities*. New York: Crown Publishing.

McMillan, T. (1990). Introduction. *Breaking ice: An anthology of contemporary African-American fiction*. New York: Penguin Books.

Rich, A. L. (1974). *Interracial communication*. New York: Harper & Row.

Schneider, C. (1991). Engaging cultural legacies. *Liberal Education, . 77 (3) 4*.

Simonson, R., & S. Walker (1988). *Multi-cultural literacy: Opening the American mind*. Saint Paul: Graywolf Press.

Smith, A. L., aka M. K. Asante (1969). *Rhetoric of black revolution*. Boston: Allyn and Bacon.

Smith, A. L., aka M. K. Asante (1972). *Language, communication, and rhetoric in black America*. New York: Harper & Row.

Smitherman, G. (1977). *Talkin and testifyin: The language of black America*. Boston: Houghton Mifflin.

Woodson, C. B. (1933). *The Mis-education of the American Negro*. Washington, D.C.: The Associated Publishers, Inc.

Zinn, H. (1980). *Peoples' history of the United States*. New York: Harper & Row.

5

Names, Narratives, and the Evolution of Ethnic Identity

Dolores V. Tanno
California State University, San Bernardino

When being an "American" does not yield empowerment and acceptance, marginalized groups look for labels around which to proclaim identity and rally for political and communal purposes. The emergent theory of ethnic identity proposed by sociologist Felix Padilla in *Latino Ethnic Consciousness* (1985) suggests that ethnic identity is adaptive and evolving. It adjusts to the institutional and structural forces of the dominant culture. In the process, ethnic identity evolves in several ways. There is ethnic identity based on symbolic themes such as a common language, rituals, or shared world views. There is ethnic identification as historical consciousness, a sequence of events and struggles over time that reflect continuity from past to future. There is also ethnic identity as social consciousness, a seeking after communal or group acceptance. Finally, there is ethnic identity as a strategy, a way of gaining political voice. Padilla's focus is on the evolution of communal ethnic identity, but individuals also go through a similar process in understanding and coming to terms with their ethnic identity.

The individual process may be understood by examining the different terms or names persons use to identify themselves over the course of their lives.

Each "name"[1] is a rhetorical device insofar as it communicates a particular story. Walter Fisher's (1987) narrative paradigm suggests that every person has life experiences that become his/her own "story." According to Fisher, these experiences are biographical, cultural, historical, and moral, and they define the efforts of reasoning and valuing beings to conduct their lives in some semblance of order. Padilla's definition of ethnic identity and Fisher's focus on the narratives of our lives come together to help us understand the rhetorical impact of names placed on individuals and groups by themselves and by others. These names are "not merely a dilemma of self-identity, but of self-in-group-identity" (Rendon, 1971, p. 324). In this essay, I will trace the unfolding of my own ethnic identity from Spanish to Mexican American, to Latina, and to Chicana by briefly examining the story behind each name. I will also address the value of, indeed the necessity for, multiple names.

Unfolding Ethnic Identity

Over the course of my life one question has been consistently asked of me: "*What are you?*" I used to reply that I was American, but it quickly became clear this was unacceptable because what came next was, "No, really, what are you?" In my more perverse moments I responded, "I am human." I stopped when I realized people's feelings were hurt. Ironic? Yes, but the motive behind the question often justified hurt feelings. I became aware of this only after asking a question of my own: "Why do you ask?"

The answers sometimes astounded me and almost always saddened me. I was astonished by outright hostility based on the assumption that I am where I am today because of "an easy affirmative-action ride." My sadness resulted from a growing knowledge of the desperate need of students who timidly ask, "What are you?" in the hopes of finding a role model. The combined result of my responses to "What are you?" and others' responses to "Why do you ask?" has been an enlightenment. Confronting the motives of people has forced me to examine who I am. In the process I have had to critically examine my own choices, in different times and contexts, of the names by which I am "placed" in society. The names are "Spanish," "Mexican American," "Latina," and "Chicana."

"I am Spanish"

Behind this label is the story of my childhood in northern New Mexico where I was born and raised. New Mexico was the first permanent Spanish settlement in the Southwest, and New Mexicans have characterized themselves as Spanish for centuries. My parents, grandparents, and great-grandparents considered themselves Spanish; wrongly or rightly, they attributed their customs, habits, and language to their Spanish heritage, and I followed suit. In Fisher's terms, this was the biographical aspect of my life story. From Padilla's perspective, this would be considered ethnic identity based on symbolic themes such as rituals and practices. The rituals and practices included covering paths with flower petals for religious processions, speaking Spanish with some regional peculiarities, and listening to the religious ballads of the Penitentes. We never talked about whether we were *really* Spanish. Only in later years did I hear the argument that the intermarriage of Spaniards with Indians invalidated the use of the name "Spanish." Its continued use, according to Mario Garcia (1989, p. 281), communicates the idea that "racially and culturally they [New Mexicans] had to do more with Spain than with Mexico"; therefore, to be Spanish is to consider oneself "racially pure" or an "anglicized Mexican American." Garcia's argument may or may not be valid, but, in my young mind, the story of being Spanish did not include concepts of racial purity or assimilation; what it did do was allow me to begin my life with a clearly defined identity and a place in the world. For me, the story of being Spanish incorporates into its plot the innocence of youth, before the reality of discrimination became an inherent part of the knowledge of who I am.

"I am Mexican American"

When I left New Mexico, my sense of belonging did not follow me across the state border. When I responded to the question "What are you?" by saying, "I am Spanish," people corrected me: "You mean Mexican, don't you?" My initial reaction was anger; how could they know better than I who I was? But soon my reaction was one of puzzlement, and I wondered just why there was such insistence that I be Mexican. Reading and studying led me to understand that the difference between Spanish and Mexican American could be found in the legacy of colonization. Mirandé and Enriquez (1979) make a distinction between the "internal" colonization of the Southwest and the "classic" colonization of Mexico. A central consequence of internal colonization is that "natives are deposed from power and native institutions are completely destroyed" (p. 9). There is no formal or legal existence; it is as if the natives are re-invented in the conqueror's image. Therefore, behind the name "Spanish" is the story of internal colonization that does not allow for prior existence.

On the other hand, classic colonization "allows for more continuity between the pre- and post-conquest societies" because "native institutions are modified but retained," allowing formal and legal existence of the natives (p. 9). Thus, behind the name "Mexican American" is the story of classic colonization that allows for prior existence and that also communicates duality. The name itself signifies duality; we are, as Richard A. Garcia (1983, p. 88) argues, "Mexican in culture and social activity, American in philosophy and politics." As native-born Americans, we also have a dual historical consciousness—the history of America and the history before America—that we must weave into the narrative of our lives to create a collective "biography." We have dual visions: the achievement of the American Dream and the preservation of cultural identity. To be Mexican American means "'navigating' precariously between both worlds, inhabiting both in good faith, and finally. . .

forging a span between. . . original Mexican and. . . acquired American enculturations" (Saldívar, 1990, p. 168).

"I am Latina"

If the story behind the name Mexican American is grounded in duality, the story behind the name "Latina" is grounded in cultural connectedness. The Spaniards proclaimed vast territories of North and South America as their own. They intermarried in all the regions in which they settled. These marriages yielded offspring who named themselves variously as Cubans, Puerto Ricans, Colombians, Mexicans, etc., but they connect culturally with one another when they name each other Latinas.

Renato Rosaldo (1989, p. 26) argues that culture encompasses "the informal practices of everyday life." One of the most fundamental practices that unites those belonging to the Latino culture is religion, probably because Catholicism was another Spanish legacy. The Virgin Mary is appealed to in the course of daily living; the title by which she is known changes, but her importance is never questioned. For example, she is La Virgen de Guadalupe in Mexico, Nuestra Señora de la Caredad del Cobre in Cuba, La Virgen de la Macarena in Colombia, and La Conquistadora in New Mexico. She symbolizes the deep spirituality that is a definitive characteristic of the Latino culture. To use the name "Latina" is to communicate acceptance and belonging in a broad cultural community. This is ethnic identity as a type of consciousness that addresses the cultural aspect of Fisher's conception of the life story.

"I am Chicana"

This name suggests a smaller community, a special kind of Mexican American awareness that does not invoke others (Cubans, Puerto Ricans, etc.). In *Chicano Manifesto*, Armando Rendon (1971, p. 320) argues that "to be Chicano[a] means that a person has looked deeper into his [her] being." To appropriate the name for oneself signifies the most

intense ethnic identity, because, as Arnulfo Trejo (1979, p. xvii) suggests, "Chicano/a" is "the only term that was especially selected by us, for us." Padilla would define this ethnic identity as a strategy, and he would be right; the name was the primary political as well as rhetorical strategy of the Chicano movement of the 1960s. Mirandé and Enriquez (1979, p. 12) argue that a dominant characteristic of the name "Chicana" is that it admits a "sense of marginality." There is a political tone and character to "Chicana" that signifies a story of self-determination and empowerment. As such, the name denotes a kind of political becoming. At the same time, however, the name communicates the idea of being American, not in a "melting pot" sense that presupposes assimilation, but rather in a pluralistic sense that acknowledges the inalienable right of existence for different peoples (Trejo, 1979).

The Worth of Multiple Names

What, then, am I? The truth is that I am all of these. Each name reveals a different facet of identity that allows symbolic, historical, cultural, and political connectedness. These names are no different than other multiple labels we take on. For example, to be mother, wife, sister, and daughter is to admit to the complexity of being female. Each name implies a narrative of experiences gained in responding to circumstance, time, and place and motivated by a need to belong. As such they possess great rhetorical force. So it is with the names Spanish, Mexican American, Latina, and Chicana. They reveal facets of complex cultural beings. In my case, I resort to being Spanish and all it implies whenever I return to my birthplace, in much the same way that we often resort to being children again in the presence of our parents. But I am also Mexican American when I balance the two important cultures that define me; Latina, when I wish to emphasize cultural and historical connectedness with others; and Chicana, whenever opportunities arise to promote political empowerment and assert cultural pride.

It is sometimes difficult for people to understand the "both/and" mentality that results from this simultaneity of existence. In *To Split a Human*, Carmen Tafolla (1985) traces the theme of duality that gave rise to the both/and mentality. Beginning with pre-Columbian civilizations, the mythic polarities of life/death, half male/half female, and the Mother/Father god represented dual natures. In contemporary times, this duality manifests itself rhetorically as "otherness," which Alberto González (1990, p. 276) defines as "expressions of the [Mexican American] cultural identity. . . that includes simultaneous themes of separation and desire for inclusion." While some may lament this duality, Tafolla finds joy in it. Chicana women expressed to Tafolla their feelings about living in the midst of two cultures: "What is most exciting. . . is the constant thought in my mind that I am actually two"; "Being bilingual and bicultural has sensitized me. . . I can then live intensely and not merely exist"; "There are several words that we can use to describe a feeling, thing, etc. that cannot be translated into English . . . and some that cannot be translated into Spanish. We have both" (pp. 93-94).

We are indeed enriched by belonging to two cultures. We are made richer still by having at our disposal several names by which to identify ourselves. Singly, the names Spanish, Mexican American, Latina, and Chicana communicate part of a life story. Together they weave a rhetorically powerful narrative of ethnic identity that combines biographical, historical, cultural, and political experiences.

NOTE

[1]"Name" is the term I use to describe the confluence of historical, cultural, biographical, political, and symbolic themes that express membership in a particular group.

REFERENCES

Fisher, W. R. (1987). *Human communication as narration: Toward a philosophy of reason, value, and action.* Columbia: University of South Carolina Press.

Garcia, M. T. (1989). *Mexican Americans: Leadership, ideology, and identity, 1930-1960.* New Haven: Yale University Press.

Garcia, R. (1983). The Mexican American mind: A product of the 1930s. In *History, culture, and society: Chicano studies in the 1980s* (pp. 67-93). Ypsilanti, MI: Bilingual Press.

González, A. (1990). Mexican "otherness" in the rhetoric of Mexican Americans. *Southern Communication Journal, 6,* 276-291.

Mirandé, A. & Enriquez, E. (1979). *La Chicana: The Mexican American woman.* Chicago: University of Chicago Press.

Padilla, F. (1985). *Latino ethnic consciousness.* Notre Dame: University of Notre Dame Press.

Rendon, A. B. (1971). *Chicano manifesto.* New York: Collier.

Rosaldo, R. (1989). *Culture and truth.* Boston: Beacon Press.

Saldívar, R. (1990). *Chicano narrative: The dialectics of difference.* Madison: University of Wisconsin Press.

Tafolla, C. (1985). *To split a human: Mitos, machos y la mujer chicana.* San Antonio: Mexican American Cultural Center.

Trejo, A. (Ed.). (1979). A word from the editor. In *The Chicanos: As we see ourselves* (pp. xv-xviii). Tucson: University of Arizona Press.

PART II

NEGOTIATING SEXUALITY AND GENDER

6

Tejana Music and Cultural Identification

Alberto González
Bowling Green State University
Gloria Flores
Texas A&M University

In *The House on Mango Street* by Sandra Cisneros (1989), the fictional Esperanza Cordero remembers the life of her great-grandmother and namesake. Born in Mexico in the Chinese year of the horse ("Bad luck if you're born female," thinks Esperanza), the great-grandmother was "a wild horse of a woman, so wild she wouldn't marry" (pp. 10-11).

Esperanza walks through the Mexican American neighborhood of her native Chicago recounting episodes in her family history. She describes how her great-grandmother and husband met. He threw a sack over her head and carried her away like a piece of property. Her great-grandmother's spirit was forever broken. "She looked out the window her whole life . . . I wonder if she made the best with what she got or was she sorry because she couldn't be all the things she wanted to be. Esperanza. I have inherited her name, but I don't want to inherit her place by the window" (p. 11).

Though now a figure in the family history, the fate of *bisabuela* (great-grandmother) haunts Esperanza; even in Chicago, that fate could be her own. In this short passage, Cisneros reveals the symbolic connection as well a geographic and temporal distance between the Mexican woman, whose influence is acknowledged with ambivalence, and the Mexican *American* woman, whose social and political presence in the U.S. is increasingly visible.

In her book, Cisneros captures our own bicultural experience. Like Esperanza, we feel removed from our cultural origins even as we surround ourselves with artifacts of Mexican life and thought. We have black-and-white photographs that show not-too-distant relatives wrapped in blankets sitting on the desert floor near Ocampo and Monterrey, Mexico. We still imagine that *La Llorna* ("the crying woman") is hovering over our homes, searching for her lost children, eager to snatch us away if we misbehave. We remember the stories told at family gatherings about our ancestors' vivid encounters with talking, mischievous animals and battles with hideous human-beasts who hid in the mountains. How we accommodate the Mexican world of magic, music, and surprise (and sustain it for our children) with the linear world of Euro-American professionalism is the challenge of our lives.

We Mexican Americans frequently lament our "invisibility" in the mass media. Yet in the writings of Sandra Cisneros, the comedy of Culture Clash, and the music of Los Lobos and Shelly Lares, we encounter something very familiar: the sounds and experiences of living astride two cultures. Tejana music is a meeting point between them, one in which women's identity is being renegotiated.

This essay will examine the Latina experience that is being transformed through the artistic form of song. Texas Mexican American women (Tejanas) have utilized the rhetorical potential of song to overcome a cultural stereotype that stresses romantic fantasy. We will show how Tejana singers are drawing from the resources of two cultures to advance an alternative identity that stresses historical accommodation and self-determination. To answer Cisneros, we will conclude that the contemporary Tejana is "making the best with what she's got."

First, we will describe several cultural tensions that frame Latina life in Texas. Second, we will discuss the musical form as a vehicle for the symbolic transformation of the lived experience of Tejanas. Finally we will trace the musical and lyrical expression of historical accommodation and self-determination from the Mexican *rancheras* of Ana Gabriel to the Tejana pop of Shelly Lares. Our essay describes Tejana music as reflective of a particular Latina cultural awareness and encourages the reader to regard this music as both entertainment and cultural artifact.

Latina Cultural Identity

Traditional Images of the Latina

The Latina has been the subject of growing description and commentary (Sanchez and Cruz, 1977; Mirandé and Enriquez, 1979; Gonzáles, 1979; Mirandé, 1985; Tafolla, 1985). Much of this literature is a critique of previous social science research on Mexican Americans. According to Mirandé (1985), traditional social science "[has] reinforced a negative conception of Mexican Americans that sees them as (1) controlled and manipulated by traditional culture; (2) docile, passive, present-oriented, fatalistic, and lacking in achievement; (3) victimized by faulty socialization which takes place in an authoritarian family system, dominated by the cult of *machismo*; and (4) violent and prone to antisocial and criminal behavior" (p. 2). Using the Anglo family ideal as a model, motivated by the politics of assimilation, many current writers argue, traditional social science research has viewed the Mexican American family as pathological and culturally defective.

The impact of such negative conceptions of the Mexican American woman are equally clear. "This research has had dysfunctional consequences for the Chicana, because it perpetuates false and stereotypical images of the roles and function of women within the Chicano community" (Gonzáles, 1979, p. 83). These images of women are reductionistic. Originating in the Catholicism of the conquistadors, they they draw upon two mythic types: the submissive, virginal Mary, and, as Elizabeth Almquist (1989) describes, "the self-serving temptress, Eve" (p. 421).

Mirandé and Enriquez (1979) elaborate the alternative images reproduced in social science research:

> Women are divided into one of two categories. The good, one's mother, wife, and daughters, are saintly, virginal figures to be protected, idealized, revered, and held on a pedestal so that they are kept out of reach of male predators. They are virtuous creatures who do not enjoy sex. Sexual enjoyment is to be had with bad women: less respectable females that one can take as mistresses, girlfriends, or playmates. (p. 110)

Tafolla observes that neither the *Marianisma* ideal (or its variant, the Spanish noblewoman) nor the image of the "bare-shouldered cantina girl" is "comfortable *or* satisfying" (44). Almquist states, "Real people do not fit either category, but they are pressured to do so" (p. 421).

Latino/a researchers have responded to the recommendation of Amado Padilla (1971) to develop new ways of representing the bilingual-bicultural experience, not just of Mexican Americans, but of all Latinos. Books such as Carman Tafolla's *To Split a Human: Mitos, Machos, y la Mujer Chicana*, and anthologies such as *Essays on la Mujer* (1977), edited by Rosaura Sánchez and Rosa Martínez Cruz, describe a variety of Latina experiences from the barrio to the sub-division.

Who is the Latina? Tafolla observes that the Latina is

> . . . bicultural, drawing from the heritage of two nations, two cultures, two languages. Although she shares many values and cultural traditions with her Mexican sister, her own culture is a unique blend of dual experiences and a creative invention of new forms expressly her own. (p. 13)

Cisneros (1991) argues that the "unique blend of dual experiences" that defines Latinas is virtually unknown beyond *La Raza*. "Very, very few people know us intimately," she says. "They haven't cared to know who we are. Very few white women are my friends, because they haven't made the effort to know that culture" (p. 2c). What unites current Latina literature is the desire to begin with the Latina herself—her culture and her interpretations.

La Tejana in Cultural Discourse

Texas Mexican American communication is rich in symbolic resources. In his public oratory, former San Antonio mayor Henry Cisneros (1989) reminded audiences that "the very name of the place, 'Texas' is the Indian word for friend." And while many Mexican American students appear assimilated, just below the surface we hear narratives about regal *quinceñeras* (15th birthdays) and the mysterious cures of the *curandera*.

At the same time, the discursive world of *la Tejana* easily displays features of patriarchy and class repression that limit her expression. It is this bleak discursive landscape, this destructive environment of meaning, which she seeks to influence rhetorically.

Traditional class stereotypes are occasionally directed toward Tejanas in various professions. For example, during her campaign for Texas Railroad Commissioner, Lena Guerrero's opponent referred to her as the "liberal handmaiden" of the Governor. Though Guerrero has served in the Texas State Legislature since 1985, her Anglo female opponent chose to invoke the image of the passive, dutiful, Mexican servant. The opponent did not emphasize Guerrero's public record; she emphasized her *subservience*.

Women's repression is also instigated from within the culture. As in all patriarchal cultures, language is often employed to marginalize women. The Spanish phrase "*hay que dar su puesto*" (remain in your place) reminds the woman that she must always defer to the judgment of her elders and her father. Proverbs such as "*donde hay mujeres, hay problemas*" (where there are women, there are problems) invoke the presumption of woman as divisive temptress. These proverbs seek to diminish women's participation in the roles men have defined as important.

It is not surprising, then, that Tejana artists have used their recordings not simply to entertain audiences, but to influence listeners by affirming women's consciousness. Examples of such musical rhetoric are given in the following section.

Latina Rhetoric and the Musical Form

Music and Communication

Communication scholars have observed the unique capacity of songs to reflect and reinforce cultural ideology and identity to audiences (Conrad, 1988; Doucet, 1989; González, 1991; Grossberg, 1986; Lull, 1987a; Mulvaney, 1987). In her overview of several Cajun "classics," Sharon Doucet argues that Cajun music "goes far beyond the sound of the instruments; the lyrics reach and reflect the heart of the Cajun psyche. The themes of the songs mirror certain basic preoccupations and cultural tendencies of this socio-ethnic group" (p. 93). In a previous essay, González wrote that rhetorical critics focus "upon the potential for music lyrics to influence an audience toward a shared identity, new understanding, or action" (p. 310).

As communication, the musical form can be thought of as a symbolic resource for community members to use creatively to reproduce competing and complementary values, ideas, and events that are the substance of the shared experience. Put another way, music grows out of audience experience, becomes a part of its experience, and adds to the thoughts, verbal response, and movement of audiences. As Lull (1987) states, "Music promotes experiences of the extreme for its makers and listeners, turning the perilous emotional edges, vulnerabilities, triumphs, celebrations, and antagonisms of life into hypnotic, reflective tempos that can be experienced privately or shared with others" (p. 10).

As we were growing up, in what might best be called Mexican American *enclaves*, the *baile* (dance) was a very special event. The *baile* was a time when we were happy, when weary and discouraged individuals were transformed into colorful, rhythmic, flirtatious sources of energy. At the center of this event was live music—the band.

The level of anticipation before the dance was established by how far the band had to travel to get to the hall. Local bands were good, but people knew what to expect from these groups. Bands hired from nearby big cities generated more excitement, particularly if they came from "the Valley" of south Texas. For those of us not born in Texas, the excitement was infectious and mysterious. After all, we never heard this music on the radio, we could barely understand the song lyrics, and we *never* saw anyone dance like this on TV! Still, within the confines of the rented hall, in the span of a few hours on a Saturday night, it all made sense. The magic of our past was revealed to us.

Tejana Music as Rhetoric

The majority of Tejana music draws from two distinct Mexican styles: *ranchera* and *cumbia*. The Mexican *ranchera* has been introduced to the U.S. pop audiences through the recordings of Linda Ronstadt's *Canciones de Mi Papá* (1987) and *Mas Canciones* (1991) and Los Lobos' *La Pistola y el Corazón* (1988). In a review of Ronstadt's *Mas Canciones* and Ana Gabriel's *Mi México*, Daisann McLane (1992) writes, "A theater of human emotion, written in vernacular poetry of pain, pride and sexual braggadocio, *ranchera* is dramatic, at times hyperbolic, never merely pretty" (p. 79). The sound of the Tejana *ranchera* is a mix of influences: Spanish (guitar and violins), Mexican (trumpet and emotional vocal delivery), country and western, and pop. In contrast, the *cumbia* is a dance; the lyrics of the *cumbia* are simple and repetitive, functioning to reinforce the rapid rhythm of the instrumentation. Musically, the *cumbia* often displays a German/Czech influence from East Texas (polka-like rhythm and accordion).

In several recordings, Ana Gabriel demonstrates that women's consciousness is strong and distinctive. In "*Es Demasiado Tarde*" ("It's Too Late"), Gabriel writes an angry song to her lover reminiscent of Bob Dylan's rock classic "Positively 4th Street." The song is directed toward a lover who takes for granted the singer's devotion. Not willing to be a compliant toy, the lover is made accountable for a series of choices that have hurt the singer. Gabriel reminds her lover that all she has given will

now be taken back, "because you chose to be away."

In "*Cruz y Raya*" ("That is Enough"), the singer has become impatient with a deceitful lover. "Look," she says, "I also have courage/I'm not just a doll for your decoration." She has the realization that no one is indispensable and, besides, she doesn't want to begin again in this relationship. Similarly, the singer in "*Amor Con Desamor*" ("Love with False Love") tells her lover that "your false love doesn't interest me anymore."

At the same time, Gabriel reveres the passion and mystical knowing of women. "*Ven Cariño*" is an invitation to a night of lovemaking, where "*tus manos me dan calor*" (your hands make me hot), and the heart beats without control "*se unsen en una voz*" (unite in one voice). Only the moon and the night understand "*la magia*" of love. In "*Pecado Original*" ("Original Sin"), it is "*la magia de mujer*" (the magic of woman) that cannot be avoided and that makes dreams come true. "*Hechizo*" (charm or spell) describes the singer swept away, not by her partner, but by the irresistible and benevolent powers of love.

The narrative voice that Ana Gabriel brings to her lyrics is far removed from the expectations of a compliant, deferential, and uncritical Mexican woman. Through her songs, Gabriel presents an image of women that stresses self-awareness, self-determination, and an openness to forces beyond male-defined scientific rationality.

Simultaneously, her songs honor historical Mexican culture. Her live performance of "*Es Demasiado Tarde*" at the 1991 Latino Music Awards featured a mariachi band in full costume. Her public comments—for example, her greeting to the audience on the CD "Ana Gabriel: *En Vivo*"— proclaim a pride in the music of Latin America. Rhetorically, Gabriel's songs serve to revise the image of women while affirming Mexican culture.

This strategy of revision and affirmation is not lost on Tejana artists. Lyrically, the Tejana songwriters lack the emotional depth of such Mexican lyricists as Ana Gabriel. Rather, the music of Lares and Selena is more fun and entertaining with such themes as love and loss predictably following the conventions of U.S. pop music. Still, the music of Tejana artists is an example of how the mix of various styles and influences produces a totally unique sound. Further, we can look to this music to gain some understanding of how Tejanas are interpreting and expanding their social boundaries.

Shelly Lares is among the best known Tejana performers. In 1991, Lares was selected the best female vocalist by *Latin Times* magazine and was a featured performer at the 1991 Tejano Music Awards. She performs extensively in Texas, the Southwest, and the Midwest and has appeared on Univision's *El Show de Johnny Canales*.

In the 1990 album entitled "Dynamite," Lares wrote one song and co-authored two others. "Here We Stand" is notable for two significant reasons. First, it is the only English-language song that appears in the collection. The inclusion of this song is a bold move for Lares. The myth within the Tejano music industry of unqualified loyalty to Spanish is not so easily shattered. Lares risks accusations by purists of "selling out" in order to reach the Anglo market.

"Here We Stand" is an expression of the bilingual and bicultural reality of the Tejana. Appropriately, it is a song about a Tejana who has a relationship with someone who is not Mexican American. "Why should our love be what we have to hide?" Lares sings. The lyrics describe a crossroad decision of the couple to break up. Though difficult, the decision to stay together is tempting because "only you and I know what's inside." Ultimately, "Here We Stand" is a song of hope. The singer knows that the couple can survive any crisis. If we read the song as constructing a metaphor for the competing forces of traditionalism and acculturation, we can see that, as with Ana Gabriel, the situation is left purposefully ambiguous. Both worlds are accommodated. Like Cisneros' Esperanza Cordero, the singer is intrigued by her past but prefers to avoid the fate of her namesake. So while Lares may depict herself as a reluctant participant in English, she makes it clear that the writing on the wall is intended for "dudes" as well as *vatos*.

"*Fuiste una Ilusión*" ("You Were an Illusion"), is a *ranchera* that tells of lost love. This song invokes the intuitive knowledge of women, similar to the songs of Ana Gabriel. Does the lover exist? "You were an illusion/Nothing more than a dream for me," she sings. The lover may have existed and left, or the lover may be an *anticipation* of someone the singer will meet. Because of the imaginative power of the singer, "It doesn't matter that you're not at my side," which attests to the significance of dreams. In this song, the subconscious vision of the lover is sufficient. The song is a subtle tribute to women's autonomy and sensitivity.

"*Porque Tu Eres Mi Cariño*" ("Because You Are My Love") is a simple declaration of devotion. The singer is happily in love and confident that it will last. This song temporarily allays the tension of the previous two songs. Thematically and musically, the listener is back on familiar ground.

Remarkably, the strategy of revision and affirmation seems to unfold across this musical trilogy. First, "Here We Stand" is written from that cultural middle ground, where the confluence of the Mexican and the Anglo is both thrilling and confusing. It questions the imposition of expectations based upon rigid conceptions of cultural identity. Second, "*Fuiste Una Ilusión*" is informed by "*la magia de mujer*" that is celebrated by Ana Gabriel. The singer is attracted to romantic relationships but clearly transcends them. Finally, "*Porque Tu Eres Mi Cariño*" returns the listener to, and affirms the norms of, traditional culture.

Conclusion

Ana Gabriel and Shelly Lares, in different though related ways, mediate their Latina experiences with mass audiences. Their songs, like the writing of Sandra Cisneros, are part of a cultural discourse that attempts to describe and influence listeners' understanding of the terms "Tejana," "Mexicans," and "Mexican American."

Such a cultural dialogue will not be heard unless it is engaged. Tejana music is fun and innovative. It makes for great listening. For example, Selena Quintanilla is very popular at creating what we call

"Tejana funk." It was a long way from Hank Williams to Garth Brooks, from Buddy Holly to Axl Rose, and from Little Richard to Ice-T. So, too, Tejana pop is a long way from *"La Cucaracha."*

DISCOGRAPHY

Gabriel, A. (1989). *Pecado original*. CBS Discos International: CD-80187.

Gabriel, A. (1990). *En vivo*. CBS Disco International: CD-80438.

Gabriel, A. (1991). *Mi México*. Sony Discos: CDZ-80605.

Lares, S. (1990). *Dynamite*. CBS Discos International: CDA-80399.

México voz y sentimiento. (1990). [Various artists]. CBS Discos International: CD-80437.

REFERENCES

Almquist, E. A. (1989). The experiences of minority women in the United States: Intersections of race, gender, and class. In J. Freemen (Ed.), *Women: A feminist perspective* (pp. 414-445). Mountain View, CA: Mayfield.

Italie, H. (1991). Author unmasks Mexican culture. *Bryan-College Station Eagle*, 7-18, p. 2C.

Cisneros, H. (1989). *Texas heros*. Speech delivered at the Amarillo, Texas Civic Center, February 7.

Cisneros, S. (1989). *The house on Mango street*. New York: Vintage.

Conrad, C. (1988). Work songs, hegemony, and illusions of self. *Critical Studies in Mass Communication*, 179-201.

Doucet, S. A. (1989). Cajun music: Songs and psyche. *Journal of Popular Culture*, 89-99.

Gonzáles, S. A. (1979). The Chicana perspective: A design for self-awareness. In A. D. Trejo (Ed.), *The Chicanos: As we see ourselves* (pp. 81-99). Tucson, AZ: University of Arizona Press.

González, A. (1991). Rhetoric, culture class, and Dylan's *Blood on the tracks*. In M. J. Medhurst & T. W. Benson (Eds.), *Rhetorical dimensions in media: A critical casebook* (pp. 308-321). Dubuque, IA: Kendall/Hunt.

Grossberg, L. (1986). Is there rock after punk? *Critical Studies in Mass Communication*.

Lull, J. (1987a). Thrashing in the pit: An ethnography of San Francisco punk subculture. In T. R. Lindlof (Ed.), *Natural audiences: Qualitative research of media uses and effects*. Norwood, NJ: Ablex.

Lull, J. (1987b). Popular music and communication: An introduction. In J. Lull (Ed.), *Popular music and communication* (pp. 10-35). Norwood, NJ: Ablex.

McLane, D. (1992). Recordings. *Rolling Stone*. February, 6, 77-79.

Mirandé, A. (1985). *The Chicano experience: An alternative perspective*. Notre Dame, IN: Notre Dame University Press.

Mirandé, A. & Enriquez, E. (1979). *La Chicana: The Mexican-American woman*. Chicago: University of Chicago Press.

Mulvaney, B. M. (1987). Popular art as rhetorical artifact: The case of reggae music. In S. Thomas (Ed.), *Communication and culture: Language performance, technology, and media* (pp. 177-197). Norwood, NJ: Ablex.

Padilla, A. M. (1971). Psychological research and Mexican Americans. In M. M. Mangold (Ed.), *La causa Chicana: The movement for justice* (pp. 65-77). New York: Family Service Association of America.

Sanchez, R., & Cruz, R. M. (Eds.). (1977). *Essays on la mujer*. Los Angeles: Chicano Studies Center.

Tafolla, C. (1985). *To split a human: Mitos, machos y la mujer chicana*. San Antonio, TX: Mexican American Cultural Center.

7

When Miss America Was Always White

Navita Cummings James
University of South Florida

I am a child of the American baby boom. I am a person of color, and I am a woman. All of these factors have influenced the creation of the person I am today, just as the time and place of each of our births, our genders, races, and ethnicities influence the people we are today. On some level, we all know that the configurations of these factors is intertwined with the unique life stories we each have to tell. But some stories are not as well known as others. For example, the lived experiences of everyday Black[1] women are not reflected very well in the academic knowledge base. Any student of the Black female experience in the United States, who is interested in how this female and racial identity has emerged, would be better served by studying the music written and performed by Black women, their novels, short stories, essays, and poems, or their oral and written life histories—rather than relying on traditional social scientific research.

In this essay, I will use my own life history and personal narrative to illustrate how family stories about race that I heard as a child influenced the development of my racial identity. These family stories were a powerful counterforce to the negative images of Blacks in the dominant culture, and they helped me to grow up believing that I could be a doctor, a lawyer, or whatever I wanted to be, assuming that I had the talent and that I worked hard. Nevertheless, I also knew a "colored girl" in the 1950s, no matter how smart, talented, or attractive she was, could never grow up to be President of the United States or Miss America.

Two related conceptual frameworks for studying the human experience inform my analysis of racial identity. The first framework assumes that individuals take an active role in constructing themselves within particular cultural contexts. The second framework assumes that one's personal story is a powerful way to gain insight into the way people construct their lives and social worlds. Each of these approaches is briefly addressed here.

The first framework undergirds much contemporary thinking on human behavior and is sometimes labeled social constructivism. It is based on the works of Berger and Luckman (1967), who argued that reality, culture, and personal identity are socially constructed by humans. The construction of personal identity, they suggest, is a dialectic between the self and the culture in which it evolves. Individual personal identities or selves evolve differently in given cultures, in part because those cultures provide different scripts and experiences for different people. What script one receives is based on socially significant constructs in the culture. For example, in the United States, gender, race, age, and class are socially significant. In other cultures, other social constructs might be important. Because cultures change over time, the scripts and resulting meanings of gender, race, class, and age in a given culture may also change. So the meanings of gender, race, and class are not only culturally but historically bound. Another way to phrase this is that being a "colored" middle-class girl in the 1950s was not the same as being an "African American" middle-class girl in the 1990s.

The second framework of this essay addresses the role of narrative or personal story in social inquiry. The personal story is an important research strategy that gives us new insights into how people construct their lives. Anthropologist Mary Catherine Bateson in *Composing a Life* (1990) studied the personal stories of five extraordinary women. She revealed how women of significant achievement constructed their lives in a society that did not provide role models for female success outside the family.

Stories are memorable in ways that statistical studies are not. As they are recalled and given meaning, stories are not "right" or "wrong." Facts can be challenged, but a person's story *just is*. Also, as individuals and their life experiences are products of particular socio-cultural milieus, no one story is so unique or idiosyncratic that it cannot provide us insight into the overall human experience. One of the most powerful ways to gain an understanding of "the other" (e.g., a person from a culture other than one's own) is to hear or read the story of "the other" *in his or her own words*.

Family Stories

The telling of family stories not only informs children about their past, but also passes on family values and helps prepare them to live in the world beyond the family. I was born in 1952 in Columbus, Ohio. One of the duties of my parents in the 1950s and 1960s was to help prepare my sister and me for a world that would attempt to put limitations on what we could achieve because of our race. Our family always refuted the dominant culture's message of what it meant to be "colored" or "Negro." Race was a frequent topic of discussion in our family, especially among the adults.

The most vivid race-related stories of my youth were about the treachery and violence of White men, how Whites could get away with any crime committed against Black people. These stories led me to believe that Black life was not highly valued by White people and that, in the eyes of White society, Black women had no virtue worth respecting or protecting.

The single most upsetting story I can recall, related to me by an aunt, happened to a young Black girl in Georgia in the 1920s. Two young school girls were walking down a road and met a drunken White man carrying a gun. He pulled one of the girls aside, put the gun in her mouth, and began to play a form of Russian roulette. One of the chambers was loaded, and he blew the back of

the girl's head off. I expected my aunt to say that the man was punished and sent to jail. But *nothing* happened to him. Instead, White people felt pity for the man because he was drunk and had to witness his own folly, rather than for the murdered child and her family. I remember my horror that such a man could get away with killing a little Black girl *like me*.

The story taught me that White men were violent and not to be trusted. Other stories I heard about lynchings only served to reconfirm this for me. I was horrified when I learned about the practice of castrating Black men during lynchings and placing their genitals in their mouths or in jars to be displayed in community stores as trophies or warnings.

The other family stories I vividly recall were about the Cummings family from my father's side and the Pearson family from my mother's.

The Cummings Family

According to my father, my great-grandfather "Gramps" was a slave in his youth and always carried the scars of the beatings he received as a child. One of the stories I recall was about Gramps' mother. She was the child of a slave woman and a White Virginia plantation owner. Apparently she resembled her father so much that the owner's wife became upset and had the child sold off. Because of her father's betrayal, the child hated Whites so intensely that she married the darkest man she could find.

There were several interesting stories about Gramps himself. At the age of 16 he was freed from slavery. As an adult he became a land owner in Laurens County, Georgia. He learned to read and passed his love of reading on to his children and grandchildren. He gave his daughters an education so they would not have to work in "Miss Anne's"[2] kitchen, and he gave his sons land. Gramps was one of the first people in his county to own a car. As the story goes, the Whites did not like the idea of a Black man owning a car when the vast majority of Whites could not afford them. So Gramps had to carry a shotgun with him to protect himself from jealous Whites.

The stories about Gramps and his family reinforced what I had been told about the evil of White men. I was shocked that a father would sell his own flesh and blood. As I grew up, I came to believe that being White was nothing to be proud of and that the light skin color of some Blacks (including myself) was a badge of shame. It seemed to me that Whites would resort to any means—even murder—to keep Blacks beneath them.

I later learned other families in the Black community educated their women so that daughters would not have to work in the homes of Whites. This strategy helps to explain, in part, why Black women often had more education than Black men and why this difference did not create tension in the Black community.

My father's stories about his own life also influenced me. Among the most vivid were those of his experiences during World War II. My father was a Tuskegee Airman. He was very proud to have been part of a U.S. Army experiment to test whether Black men were intelligent enough to fly airplanes. The Tuskegee Airmen units that ultimately served in Europe and North Africa had one of the most distinguished records of the war. After the war, however, Black pilots were not hired by the airlines unless, perhaps, they were interested in being janitors.

Some of the most painful memories of my childhood revolve around my father's business. Since he couldn't get a job as a civilian pilot, he fell back on skills he learned as a boy in Georgia—masonry and carpentry—and started his own contracting business. But racial discrimination followed him here as well. My father often complained that when Whites contracted with him, they would pay him less than what they paid the White contractors for the same work. Even after he finished the work, some would not pay him for weeks or months. However, I began to notice that not all Whites were alike. Jews seemed to be different. They would pay for quality regardless of whether a Black or White man did the work. At least they were more likely to hire and less likely to delay payment.

Perhaps the most important lesson I learned from my father's stories, that would later be reflected in my own life and the lives of my children, was the idea that many Whites fail to see the talents and accomplishments of Black people—even when the evidence is right before their eyes.

The Pearson Family

The stories about Whites from my mother's family were less violent and shocking. Nat Pearson, my grandfather, was also a land owner. He lived in Wheeler County, Georgia. According to my mother, Whites respected "Mr. Nat" and his children. He was a hard-working and fair man. His wife was also respected in the community. She took food to the sick and the poor, Black or White, in addition to taking care of her nine children.

The Pearson family emphasized the importance of getting a college education. My mother and her eight siblings all attended college and earned degrees. (In my generation it was just expected that all 26 of us would earn at least *one* college degree.) In my mother's generation, the older children helped the younger ones through college by providing financial support. The family stuck together, helping one another. That was very important.

My mother emphasized different things than my father did when she talked about race. For example, she stressed how my grandmother helped poor Whites. My mother did not believe in any way that Blacks were inferior to Whites. She was very proud of her family, and there was no false humility here. However, as the mother of daughters, she did give us one race-related warning: "There is only one thing a White man wants from a Black woman." She warned that Black women should be wary of White men, because, in the event of rape, the White man would probably go unpunished. We should never think of marrying a White man, because, according to her, a Black woman's virtue meant nothing to Whites.

My Pearson cousins were another source of information about race. While I was going to racially integrated schools in the North, most of them attended segregated schools in the South. I was amazed that they had all Black teachers, just as they were amazed that mine were all White.

My cousins and their friends loved to tease and tell jokes. They sometimes used profanity just out of hearing distance of the adults. During one of our visits to Georgia, I learned an interpretation of the origin of the word "motherfucker." They said it was used by the African slaves in the Old South to describe White men who raped their African slave mothers.

Beliefs and Stereotypes of My Youth

From these significant stories of my youth emerged a set of beliefs and stereotypes which provided a backdrop for my own lived experience. These beliefs and stereotypes about Blacks and Whites can be summarized as follows:

Black People

- Black people are "just as good" as White people—and in some ways (e.g., morally) better.
- Black people are just as smart and capable as White people, if not more so.
- Black people should always be prepared to fight for fair treatment from Whites.
- Black people have to be twice as good as Whites to be considered half as good.

White People

- White people are often violent and treacherous.
- White people probably have some kind of inferiority complex which drives them to continually "put down" Blacks and anyone else who is not White.
- White men often rape Black women. If they say they love a Black women, they are doing so to gain sexual favors. A White man would never marry a Black woman.
- Most White people do not want to see Blacks rewarded for their abilities and accomplishments.
- Most Whites, especially Northerners, cannot be trusted. They can hardly ever be a real friend to a Black person.
- White men are usually arrogant. White women are usually lazy.

- There are some good White people, but they are the exceptions.

These childhood beliefs and stereotypes, however, did *not* become an intellectual prison of my self-identity or beliefs about Whites. Below, I address how these beliefs and stereotypes blended with my own experiences. From this dialectical interaction, my racial identity emerged.

The Dialectic of Family Stories, Culture, and Identity

Earlier, I suggested that the construction of personal identity is a dialectic between self and culture. In some circumstances, families may reinforce the messages of the dominant culture, but as we have seen in my case, my family's messages ran counter to it. The social-cultural milieu of the integrated North in the 1950s was rife with overt and covert messages about Blacks. Whites often pretended that there was no prejudice in the North. Yet the dominant culture portrayed Black people as stupid, lazy, dirty, dishonest, ugly—and invisible. We were unwelcome in many public places, even if it was legal for us to be there. If my self-image had relied solely on the messages of the dominant culture, I might have grown up with low self-esteem and seen no value in being Black.

Instead, my family's stories gave me pride in my people and in myself. They encouraged me to reject the dominant culture's scripts and embrace those from my family and the Black community that said I was a person of value and worth. The stories became a sort of metaphorical shield that protected me from the larger, hostile culture. In high school, I learned that there were many times I did not need the shield, e.g., with some of my White schoolmates. But I also learned that, because racism is a constant feature of our culture, I would be a fool to ever throw that shield away.

Moreover, I had to revise my stereotyped ideas about Whites and Blacks—hence about myself. For example, I learned that race was not a good predictor of violence—gender was; and that race was not a good predictor of intelligence—income and opportunities were. I further came to believe that all people, regardless of color, deserve to be treated with dignity and respect. We are all equal in God's eyes and in principle in American cultural mythology. Finally, I learned that prejudice existed on both sides of the color line, but sometimes for different reasons.

Through this dialectical process, my beliefs and stereotypes changed and evolved. I made definitive choices about how I would relate to others. Unlike some Blacks who preferred to socialize only with Blacks, I chose to have friends of diverse backgrounds, including Whites.

I am now the mother of two girls. What is the role of family stories related to race in *my* family? I have already had to reassure my four-year-old that "brown" people are good and beautiful. I have stressed the importance of reading and education in our family—values which span generations. And I have passed along my parents' stories, along with my own experiences. For example, I have told my twelve-year-old how as children my sister and I used to run excitedly into the living room whenever there was someone Black on TV. In the 1950s, it was a rare occurrence to see someone Black on TV. And I told her how beauty pageants such as the Miss America Pageant celebrated only European standards of beauty, so Miss America was always White.

In the course of my daughters' childhoods, Black women have finally been crowned Miss America. But when I was a child, I secretly yearned for a Black Miss America. To me that would have been a sign that our culture was learning to value Black women—that we could be viewed as beautiful, smart, and virtuous.

As I grew up, I fantasized about what my life might have been like were race not such a socially significant construct in the United States: after World War II my father would have been hired as a commercial airline pilot and our family would have flown the world for free. I would have been able to afford the Ivy League school I could not attend for lack of funds. I would have studied in Paris, become an anthropologist/pilot, and gone to Africa. . . .

As for Miss America? I would have been too busy traveling to have cared about her.

NOTES

[1]The use of the upper case "B" in the word "Black," when Black refers to African Americans, is a convention dating back to the 1960s and is still currently utilized by some writers. In the late 1960s and early 1970s, the common usage of the word "Negro" changed to "black." However, since black referred to a people and not just a color, some writers thought the upper case "B" in Black seemed more appropriate and dignifying. (Some of these writers also adopted the equivalent use of the upper case "W" when referring to Whites.) Also, since terms used to describe other ethnic and racial groups utilized upper case first letters, for the major descriptor for Black to appear with a lower case "b" seemed an unfortunate, yet grammatically correct, way to reinforce the stereotypical view of Blacks as less important. Black writers using this convention recognized the subtle power of language and that rules of language and grammar are arbitrary and evolve over time. These writers chose to take an active role in promoting what they viewed as a useful change.

[2]"Miss Anne" is an unflattering term referring to White women.

REFERENCES

Bateson, M.C. (1990). *Composing a life*. New York: Plume.

Berger, P.L. & Luckman, C. (1967). *The social construction of reality*. Garden City, N.Y.: Anchor Books.

Leeds-Hurwitz, W. (1992). Forum introduction: Social approaches to interpersonal communication. *Communication Theory, 2*, 131-139.

8

Illusive Reflections: African American Women on Primetime Television

Bishetta D. Merritt
Howard University

Images of African American women in popular culture have run the gamut from the oversized, sexless mammy and yellow gal of nineteenth-century race literature to the boisterous comediennes and witty lawyers of contemporary situation comedies. Television, one of the most ubiquitous forms of popular culture, exposes its audiences to a refined, updated version of these images and has become for many Americans, particularly white Americans, their only window on the African American world. Through this window, television viewers have been exposed to characterizations of African American women that seldom reflect their myriad numbers or diverse roles in society. This essay will review the imagery of African American women on television and suggest a fairer, more multidimensional portrayal of this ethnic group.

The history or development of the black image on network television reflects a picture of stereotypes, tokenism, paternalism and neglect. Early television offered the promise of developing as a color-blind medium. Yet as network schedules were created, this promise became an unfulfilled dream for African Americans, particularly African American women (MacDonald 1983). Images crystallized in film and radio became the order of the day on the small screen, unless one viewed the "Ed Sullivan Show" on which blacks appeared as performers or were recognized as members of the audience. (We phoned excitedly to tell our neighbors to watch a particular show whenever an African American personality was scheduled to appear. Frequent visitors to the Sullivan program included Sarah Vaughn, Hazel Scott, and Pearl Bailey.) As D. W. Griffith's epic silent film, "Birth of a Nation," crystallized the image of African American women on the large screen, "Amos 'n Andy" performed the identical role for Blacks on television. Black images in "Birth of a Nation" ranged from the devoted slave to the vamp. African American women were either cast as mammies or mulattos. Portrayed as sexless, aggressive females devoted to their owners or employers, or as wild, untamed "party girls" whose lives generally ended tragically, African American women retained remnants of these early characterizations well into the 1980s (e.g., Nell Carter in "Gimme A Break" and Sondra in "227"). Louise Beavers, a mammy in such films as "Imitation of Life" (1934) and "The Last Gangster" (1937), moved to television and starred in the 1950s comedy "Beulah." The hardy, pervasive, and long-lasting mammy image of film became the central image of African American woman on television after the airing of "Amos 'n Andy." To her other characteristics were added the role of "nag" and "shrew" through the portrayals of Ernestine Wade as Sapphire and Amanda Randolph as Mama. The name "Sapphire" became synonymous with an African American woman who raised her voice beyond a certain accepted level and who spoke harshly to African American men. She was an extension of the mammy character created in film, only more vocal and assertive. These roles made a significant contribution to establishing the image of African American women in the consciousness of the television audience. In addition, women were featured as secretaries or romantic interests for Andy. The latter characters are seldom discussed or remembered by the viewers of the program.

As a child, I enjoyed the show. It was not until I gained some maturity and a more critical view of the world, television, and the power of images that I realized how pervasive and detrimental these portrayals were to African Americans and black women in particular. The contribution of this program to the molding of perceptions about African American women on television and, by extension, in society is significant and irreversible.

As the civil rights movement flourished in the 1960s, one of the most significant characters to develop was Julia, played by Diahann Carroll. Completely different from Sapphire in temperament and physical appearance, Julia represented an educated African American woman with a successful career, raising her son in a wholesome environment. On another level, however, the image was shallow and one-dimensional, merely a reflection of what whites thought of middle-class black women. Although set in the late 60s, Julia and her son Cory never discussed racism, the civil rights movement, what it meant to be black and male in the United States, or African American culture and history. Like the sexless mammies characterized in films, Julia's life was devoid of romance. She was husbandless because of the Vietnam war and manless because the writers on the show decided that her only contact with black men would be fleeting romances.

Julia seemed very far removed from the married, middle-class Southern women I knew, who all seemed constantly surrounded by family and friends. Yet these women were proud of her and pleased with the relationship she shared with her son. I, on the other hand, the young, so-called revolutionary woman, viewed her as an unrealistic fantasy. She didn't have an Afro hair style, wear dashikis, or discuss Malcolm, Rap, or Stokley with her son. It seemed that every African American, save Julia, was touched in some way by the exciting and turbulent period when sit-ins, marches, and rallies were everyday occurrences. Moveover, I could never understand her closeness to the white woman who lived in the apartment upstairs or to other people at her job. I also could not understand her lack of family and lack of black female friends. Julia was for my generation what we called an "Oreo"—a person who is black on the outside and white on the inside.

During a lecture I attended at Fisk University, Nikki Giovanni spoke on the authenticity of Julia. She indicated that Julia was a beginning, and the portrayal of black women would hopefully expand and develop positively from this initial image. She encouraged us to use Julia as a stepping-stone, and, as media consumers, to demand better and less stereotypical images of African American women. But our voices were never heard, and any attempts at airing relevant television images of black women disappeared as the 1970s approached and public interest shifted to the Vietnam war. African American women in this decade were reminiscent of minstrel show caricatures. Situation comedies began to flourish and the Norman Lear comedies, among others, featured women in starring or co-starring roles. From "That's My Mama" to "The Jeffersons," black women were portrayed as oversized females with boisterous voices and numerous problems.

However, Isabel Sanford's Louise Jefferson ("The Jeffersons") and Esther Rolle's Florida Evans ("Good Times") did make a significant contribution to the image of African American women on primetime television during the 70s. Through these series, the television audience was exposed to women who were no longer isolated from their families and communities like Julia, but who were people with nuclear families and female friends. Media critic William Henry (1983), in his analysis of "The Jeffersons," described Louise as the long-suffering wife of George Jefferson, the owner of a chain of dry cleaning businesses. Louise may have appeared submissive, but in reality she outmaneuvered and outfoxed George in most episodes. Assisted in her housework by the live-in maid, Florence (Marla Gibbs), Louise smoothed over the *faux pas* George committed in his quest to climb the social ladder and make more money (Henry, 1983). Through this activity, the wit and intelligence of her character was revealed.

Louise worked constantly to maintain a pleasant relationship with George's mother in addition to serving as a bridge between George and their son Lionel. Louise volunteered at a community center and adjusted to her newly acquired middle-class status with little difficulty. She became very close to her neighbor Helen Willis, the female half of an interracial marriage. The bond between the two women deepened once their children, Lionel and Jenny, married. Louise and Helen worked at the community center and enjoyed shopping excursions. Helen's appearance on the program was a positive experience for me. She was statuesque, assertive, and articulate. I ignored her marriage partner and her status as a housewife because her physical appearance broke the mold of most black women on television. She shed the mammy stereotype and presented another dimension, however shallow, of the African American female.

Florence, Louise's maid, completes the circle of women on "The Jeffersons." Her relationship with Louise was positive and supportive, yet the distance between employer and employee was maintained. Florence was not treated like and did not act like a typical maid—another milestone.

Florida Evans, mother and housewife, depicted a black woman diametrically opposed to Louise Jefferson. Her home was a tenement in Chicago and her husband, though industrious, was seldom employed. Florida controlled and attempted to overcome her environment through a positive attitude. She lived for her three children and husband, pushing them to excel. Promoting strong family values, Florida and James worked as a team in their household and attempted to make the best of their meager circumstances.

Florida and her neighbor/confidante Winona were similar to Louise and Helen, save for their class differences. Winona portrayed the stereotypical single African American female. However, her friendship with Florida proved genuine and a positive element in the series.

Louise and Florida portrayed earth mothers and, because of their physical appearance, reflected mammy characters from 50s television. Neither character behaved like Sapphire, yet their size and "presence" in their families made them appear stronger and more secure than their husbands. Though Helen, Florence, and Winona played traditional roles, they offered a glimpse of black women released from the physical restrictions usually reserved for African American women in the media. In addition, the friendships created by these women kept them from being isolated, one-dimensional characters as Julia had been in the 60s. Progress, though linear, could be detected in the development of the image of the African American woman.

Primetime dramas aired during this decade provided meaningful portrayals of African American women with the introduction of made-for-television specials like "The Autobiography of Miss Jane Pittman," "A Woman Called Moses," and "Roots." These dramas offered a break from the situation comedies that dominated the 70s; yet the main themes of these specials and the driving force of the characters focused on suffering, struggle, and the will to survive—not the will to change the system *and* survive.

African American women on primetime television in the 80s were defined by the home and family, even though they were often cast as professional women such as school teachers (Gladys Knight of "Charlie and Company"), attorneys (Phylicia Rashad of "The Cosby Show"), or university students and administrators (Cree Summer and Jasmine Guy of "A Different World"). A study by Stroman, Merritt, and Matabane (1990) indicates that portrayals of African American women have changed in their socioeconomic milieu and physical appearance since the Kerner Report (1968), but remain controlled by the dominant myths regarding female social roles.

The Nell Carter character in "Gimme a Break" paralleled the maids' roles black women have played for generations. Carter, aware of the image she depicted, parodied Butterfly McQueen's role in

"Gone with the Wind" in one episode and defended her mammy-like behavior in another. Ever the dominating mammy, Nell neglected her own personal development and career possibilities while she physically abused the white youngsters under her supervision. Nell promised the children's dead mother she would raise them as her own and, when their aunt threatened to take the children, she fell to her knees crying and beseeched the judge to let her keep "her" children. For an African American woman to perform this obsequious act on network television in the 80s was astounding (Dates, 1990).

Nell's friend Addie (played by Telma Hopkins) encouraged her to break from this family and develop her own musical talents. Nell rejected this advice and often physically abused Addie. Their friendship lacked the warmth associated with Louise and Helen or Florida and Winona. The program, its main characters, and the friendship between Nell and Addie represented a step back for African American women on television. Watching it was worse than viewing old movies starring Louise Beavers and Hattie McDaniel. Nell's character embarrassed me as an African American woman and represented every stereotype my friends and I had worked to dispel through our research and daily behavior. We all celebrated the cancellation of "Gimme a Break."

In the late 1980s, the Marla Gibbs character in "227," Phylicia Rashad of "The Cosby Show," and Anne Marie Johnson of "In the Heat of the Night" made contributions to the images of African American women in a more positive manner. Mary, the Gibbs character, though cast as a housewife, portrayed a vital, strong black woman with a reliable husband and lively teenage daughter. "227" added another dimension to the black female image: a female friendship circle.

There were three other woman living in the apartment building where Mary resided: Sondra, Rose, and Pearl. They offered the audience a picture of four different types of African American women in one series. Sondra, the vamp, represented the single black woman who used her physical appearance to attract men with financial stability. Initially, Rose portrayed a widowed mother. After the first season, however, her daughter was dropped from the series and it was eventually revealed that she owned the apartment building where they all lived. She remarried before the program ended. Pearl, the grandmother of a young teen male, was cast as an older African American woman rarely depicted in primetime television except for Mother Jefferson on the "Jeffersons" and the grandmother on "Family Matters." Pearl, true to her name, frequently shared "pearls of wisdom" with the younger women. Mary, as described above, was the housewife, mother, and chief "cheerleader" for her husband Lester, a construction company supervisor. She portrayed a middle-class, intelligent woman whose skills at organization were utilized in her home and community. Various episodes focused on serious concerns that the women addressed within the context of their mutual friendships.

Clair Huxtable, mother, wife, and attorney, also depicted a type rarely seen on primetime television: the multi-dimensional, upper-middle-class, African American professional woman with a professional husband, children, and a career. Clair not only had daughters, but female friends, a mother, and a mother-in-law who visited her New York brownstone. This generational bond was a first for a black family on television. In contrast to "227" where the generational links were represented through friendship, the Cosby women were family. From little Winnie to grandma Cosby, the women shared family remedies, memories, and keepsakes. In one episode, Clair and her friends gathered to plan a tribute for one of their college instructors. Through their discussions, the influence this woman had on their development as African American women was explored, as well as the growth and development of their friendships during the years since their graduation from Hillman.

Trashed by the critics as unrealistic, "The Cosby Show" and its characters have never been accepted as rooted in the black experience, but rather as Bill Cosby's idea of black family life—"Leave It To Beaver" in blackface. African Americans consider this evaluation further proof of the lack of knowledge whites have of the black community. There is a failure to understand the diversity of our community and to continuously group us at one end of the socioeconomic scale. African American women, however, view the diverse storylines on the Cosby series as an opportunity to see themselves, frailties and all, through the multidimensional Cosby characters. Women like Clair, her children, her mother, her mother-in-law, and her friends permeate African American households and workplaces in every major city in this country.

One of the few African American women to have a continuous role in a primetime drama is Anne Marie Johnson who has portrayed Althea, the wife of Virgil Tibbs, on "In the Heat of the Night." A teacher by profession, Althea became the mother of twins. Regarded by her husband and the chief of police as a very intelligent and intuitive woman, Althea's opinions and counsel were highly valued. Althea, however, suffered from the isolation Julia experienced, for she had few close female friends. In the 1991-92 season, Althea and the city council member portrayed by Denise Nicholas began to bond and share a friendship. Althea represents the only black female cast in a continuous dramatic role since the women of "Palmerstown, U.S.A." in 1981.

In addition to the roles of African American women discussed above, portrayals that receive little or no attention are the background characters that merely appear as *scenery* on television programs. These characters include the homeless person on the street, the hotel lobby prostitute, or the drug user making a buy from her dealer. They may not be named in the credits or have recurring roles, but their mere appearance can have an impact on the consciousness of the viewer and, as a result, an impact on the imagery of the African American woman. These nameless woman have not been accorded the respect, competence, and friendships of Clair, Mary, or Althea, yet their presence cannot be ignored.

Of course, African American women are much more than the characters portrayed on primetime television indicate. They are multidimensional people who make daily contributions to the success and failure of their homes, places of employment, extended families, and recreational sites. They are resourceful, intelligent, sensitive people who show human frailties. They are large, fat, short, tall, slender, petite, brown, tan, black, cream, and caramel. They are presidents of universities, tellers at banks, and talk-show hosts. They also teach school, dig ditches, own businesses, perform heart surgery, plan civil rights demonstrations, fight wars, paint houses and portraits, serve as judges and mayors, preach the gospel, are elected to the House of Representatives, make movies, and write and produce television programs. Yet, when one watches primetime television, these images are illusive.

In order to provide a more multi-dimensional portrayal of African American women, the television industry must recognize the diversity of these women and create programs and series that reflect their variety and resourcefulness. Accomplishing this objective is far from impossible as evidenced in the myriad roles depicted by white women in programs as diverse as "Murphy Brown," "The Golden Girls," Designing Women," "Roseanne," "Empty Nest," "L.A. Law," "Brooklyn Bridge," "Murder, She Wrote," or "The Trials of Rosie O'Neill."

The impact of the image of African American women on audiences' perceptions should not be dismissed by the television industry. The constant reinforcement of a particular image has an effect on how a person or idea is perceived. If the majority of black women the television audience is exposed to are homeless, drug-addicted, or maids, and if viewers have no contact with African American women other than through television, what choice do they have but to believe that all women of this ethnic background reflect this television image? Furthermore, what image is transmitted to African American children regarding black women, their worth, and their contributions to this society? It is, therefore, important, as the twenty-first century approaches and the population of this country includes more and more people of color, that the television industry broaden the images of African American women to include their nuances and diversity.

I would argue that even though the commercial television industry's primary interest is ratings supremacy and profits, the medium should serve as an accurate window on the world by creating programs that go beyond old stereotypes and develop fleshed-out characters for African American women to portray. Universal situations and themes must be explored and examined in dealing with black culture and the black female experience. An increase in the number of roles for African American women on television would also broaden the types of images represented. Most importantly, African American women producers, directors, writers, and technicians with a special sensitivity to the diversity of the African American female population should also be hired and given the responsibility to ensure that these characters do not rely on archaic television stereotypes.

9

Black Queer Identity, Imaginative Rationality, and the Language of Home

Charles I. Nero
Bates College

Home and the human relationships within it are recurring referents in the artistic, critical, and theoretical discourse of late twentieth-century black queers in the United States. Home performs a dual task. On the one hand, it grounds our identities within African American culture. This grounding is necessary, as Ron Simmons (1991) asserts, in order to further "the development of a progressive view of homosexuality in the African American community" (p. 211). Too often African Americans view homosexuality as alien to our communities or as a pathological response to white racism (Nero, 1991).

Afrocentric and black feminist scholars have emphasized the importance of perspective in theoretical discussions of meaning and epistemology. In *The Afrocentric Idea*, Molefi Kete Asante (1987) asserts that the "critic's chief problem is finding a place to stand . . . in relation to Western standards, imposed as interpretive measures on other cultures" (p. 11). Patricia Hill Collins (1990) in *Black Feminist Thought* contends that "experience as a criterion of meaning with practical images as its symbolic vehicles is a fundamental epistemological tenet in African-American thought systems"

(p. 209). Collins (1990) emphasizes the importance of the experiential in the production of meaning and knowledge in order to challenge the dominance in the social sciences of positivist approaches which "aim to create scientific descriptions of reality by producing objective generalizations" by removing "all human characteristics except rationality" from the research process (p. 205). For Collins (1990), an experiential approach leads to understanding a black woman's standpoint, a stance that functions "to create a new angle of vision on the process of suppression" (pp. 11-12).

In this essay, home provides a perspective from which to theorize about black queer identity. The first part of this essay is a brief overview of some of the meanings and uses of home in black queer discourse. The second part is an autobiographical exploration of home as a site of contradiction and contention in the formation of my own identity.

Part I: Home in Black Queer Discourse

In the preface to the path-breaking *Homegirls: A Black Feminist Anthology*, Barbara Smith (1983) declared, "There is nothing more important to me than home" (p. xix). Smith, a black lesbian feminist, chose the radical maneuver of identifying home as the origin of her intellectual and political consciousness. Her maneuver was radical in the sense that it located her queerness within a black communal setting. Kitchen Table: Women of Color Press, the publishing company that Smith founded, also alludes to home imagery. Writer and critic Jewelle Gomez confirms the importance of home in black lesbian fiction. Gomez (1983) has identified a longing for home as "the driving force behind most strong writing by black Lesbians" (p. 120).

Home is also a metaphor for black community. Audre Lorde (1984) referred to familial relations and her status within the home in the title of her collection of essays and speeches *Sister Outsider*. Poet Donald Woods (1986) in "Sister Lesbos" used the home imagery of the family in referring to the possibility of any connection between male and female black queers:

What we've shared
is the strength
to be apart
what we seek
is the strength
to be together.
Liberation to love ourselves
fiercely, in the family way.

(p. 105)

In "Brother to Brother: Words from the Heart," the late essayist and anthologizer Joseph Beam (1986) defined home as "not only the familial constellation from which I grew, but the entire black community: the black press, the black church, black academicians, the black literati, and the black left" (p. 231). Beam's "brotherhood is community" metaphor has influenced the work of Essex Hemphill (1991) in the acclaimed *Brother to Brother: New Writings by Black Gay Men* and of Marlon Riggs (1989) in the controversial and award-winning film "Tongues Untied." Actors chanted and recited portions of Beam's "Brother to Brother" essay in Riggs' film. Hemphill (1991) extended Beam's concept of home to invoke a powerful call to black gay men:

Our mothers and fathers are waiting for us. Our sisters and brothers are waiting. Our communities are waiting for us to come home. They need our love, our talents and skills, and we need theirs. They may not understand everything about us, but they will remain ignorant, misinformed, and lonely for us, and we for them, for as long as we stay away hiding in communities that have never really welcomed us or the gifts we bring. (p. xx)

Home thus suggests a perspective from which black queers can articulate their reality and negotiate meaning.

Part II: 'When I Think of Home . . .'

For me, home is a site both of contradiction and contention. As a site of contradiction, home is experienced as a mediated event. As a site of contention within the home, my childhood was a mixed environment of liberation and domination.

Home as a Mediated Event

Home has been mediated by imagery from popular culture. The title of this section, "When I Think of Home," is from the black gay anthology *Brother to Brother*, which is a song from the Broadway musical and subsequent film "The Wiz." As I write this section of the essay, I imagine Rodgers and Hammerstein's "My Favorite Things." Although I am familiar with versions of the song by Mary Martin in the Broadway cast recording of *The Sound of Music* and the straight-no-chaser jazz version by Betty Carter, it is the cloying Julie Andrews version that I am humming now. Andrews sang "My Favorite Things" in the movie version of "The Sound of Music." Although I did not see that movie until I was in graduate school, "My Favorite Things" mediates my understanding of home. Often imagining my home to be like the one in "The Sound of Music," with a fun-loving ex-nun for a governess and mother figure. All day and night I could have sung "Raindrops on roses and whiskers on kittens / Bright copper kettles and warm woolen mittens / Brown paper packages tied up with strings / These are a few of my favorite things" (Rodgers and Hammerstein II, 1960, p. 29). My home, however, was never like this.

Nevertheless, I reject the scenario popularized by many intellectuals that a powerful media creates unrealistic images that necessarily lead to personal frustration. Such a notion would rob me of my own power. I was not a passive victim consuming media images. Let me use two examples to illustrate my point.

It was through television that I first imagined the possibility of being gay and living as a member of the African American post-Civil Rights professional middle class—the group I was being educated to enter. I vividly remember watching Hal Holbrook, Hope Lange, and Scott Jacobi in the 1973 television movie "That Certain Summer," in which a white man divorced his wife for a male lover. I was a junior in high school and I remember being emotionally moved by poignant scenes such as the one in which Lange, the wife, tells Holbrook, her husband, that she doesn't know how to compete with a man and the anger of young Scott Jacobi, the sensitive son with whom I identified, when he discovered that his father was gay.

Did this film create unrealistic expectations for me? Did they lead to personal frustration because I could not attain the image of home as presented in the media? No, because I also remember several disquieting moments in the movie. Holbrook and his lover, played by Martin Sheen, never displayed affection toward each other. (I had recently viewed Marlowe's "Edward II" on PBS, and it seemed to me that for the entire program the King and Gaveston did nothing but kiss.) It also occurred to me that Holbrook and Sheen, for all intents and purposes, were not the least bit effeminate like me. Yet "That Certain Summer" allowed me to imagine the possibility of being in love with another man. It also reinforced the idea that personal happiness was a worthy goal, and, on later reflection, that one's quest for personal happiness might be a cause for the unhappiness of others. In other words, I realized that announcing I was gay would require me to weigh my happiness against that of my parents. For me that became an intellectual task beyond homophobia—a critique of heterosexuality itself. This critique was aided by the music of Stephen Sondheim. In Sondheim's music, hetero-sexuality and marriage were often sources of profound unhappiness. For example, in his 1970 musical *Company*, one character who has been married "three or four times" sings, "The concerts you enjoy together/Neighbors you annoy together/Children you destroy together/That keep marriage intact" (Sondheim, p. 529). At the end of *Company*, Robert, the bachelor protagonist, appears to have accepted the idea of marriage as desirable. His final song, however, is not about marriage, but about love within a relationship. Moreover, the gender of the lovers in Robert's final song is never specified. Instead, the love interest in Robert's final song, "Being Alive," is signified by the genderless pronouns "someone" and "somebody." These genderless pronouns recur over twenty times in the song. "Being Alive" contained phrases such as "But alone is alone, not alive" and "Somebody

need me too much/Somebody know me too well/Somebody pull me up short/And put me through hell and give me support/For being alive" (Sondheim, p. 570). The deliberate absence of gendered third person pronouns affirmed the possi-bility of love and commitment outside marriage and heterosexuality. Sondheim's music enhanced my defenses against the forces of compulsory hetero-sexuality. Marriage would not guarantee me happi-ness. Rather, it might be more desirable to resist compulsory heterosexuality and to imagine, as it seems Sondheim's Bobby did, the possibility of that "someone" being a man.

Home as Lived Event

My behavior was a site of contention in my home. I was an effeminate boy, a so-called sissy. My parents did not want me to be effeminate. Fre-quently, I was chastised, told that I held cups too much like a girl, that I should try to act tougher, play football and basketball, talk in a deeper voice. I acquiesced to some of these demands. I actually practiced how to hold a cup in a more masculine manner and how to shake hands with a firm grip. But my parent's verbal and physical abuse drained my confidence. Although I know that they loved me, I began to realize that their efforts threatened the loss of my own sense of self. At a very early age, I learned not to trust my parents. Even to this day, I rarely tell them about the ordinary, everyday events in my life. This lack of trust hurts me; yet, I believe that it is necessary for my survival. Domination hurts, even when it is done to protect.

What my parents feared, of course, was that I might be gay. Social scientists, however, have shown that male childhood effeminacy is an inaccu-rate predictor of homosexual tendencies (Bell, Weinberg, and Hammersmith, 1981). My parents number among the millions of people and institu-tions who do not see the existence of gay people, as Eve Sedgwick (1991) has stated, "as a precious desideratum, a needed condition of life" (p. 23). In other words, the battle waged over my effeminate traits reflected a larger wish endemic in our culture: "the wish that gay people *not exist*" (Sedgwick, p. 23)

I would like to show how this wish manifested itself in my relationship to sports and my decision to become a scholar.

At my request, my parents bought me a basketball, and I learned how to play the game. But when the ball was stolen, I lost interest and stopped playing. I really did not have an aversion to athletics; I was just not overly enthusiastic about football, baseball, basketball, or track and field. But as a teenager, I discovered sports that I liked. I learned how to play tennis which eventually led to volleyball, the sport that I most enjoy and continue to play. However, neither tennis nor volleyball were masculine sports in African American communities, so there were few occasions to engage in these sports within my neighborhood. Moreover, even at white high schools, there was little enthusiasm from either parents or physical education instructors for boys to play volleyball.

The idea that some sports are more masculine than others harmed me, as I am certain it has harmed many other boys. I missed the opportunity of experiencing the benefits of physical activity, such as hand-eye coordination and cardiovascular maintenance, that accrue from early participation in sports.

I also experienced a great deal of resistance to my interest in a career in scholarship. The African American feminist bell hooks (1991) has written movingly about the resistance she experienced:

Many black females, myself included, described childhood experiences where the longing to read, contemplate, and talk about a broad range of ideas was discouraged, seen as frivolous activity, or as activity that indulged in too intensely would lead us to be selfish, cold, cut off from feelings and estranged from community. In childhood, if I did not place household chores above the pleasures of reading and thinking, grown-ups threatened to punish me by burning my books, by forbidding me to read. Although this never happened, it impressed on my consciousness the sense that it was somehow not only "wrong" to prefer being alone reading, thinking, writing, but was somehow dangerous to my well-being and a gesture insensitive to the welfare of others. (p. 155)

Unlike hooks, who grew up poor, my parents were school teachers with graduate degrees. Yet they opposed my desire to become an intellectual. They gave me the best education they could afford with the hope that I would become a professional, preferably a medical doctor. They were delighted by my childhood announcement that I wanted to become a pediatrician. When I later decided instead to apply for teaching and research assistantships to attend graduate school, however, their disappointment was palpable. My mother lamented, "I'm not giving you any money; who is going to pay you to go to school?" My father was more resigned. When I got my first tenure track job in academia, he said, "Well, I guess you are just going to be a teacher." Two or three years ago, he criticized my desire to write and do research by informing me that Alex Haley's *Roots* was the last book by a black person that he had seen on the shelves at his neighborhood drugstore.

Hooks (1991) suggests that being an intellectual in African American communities "meant that one risked being seen as weird, strange, and possibly even mad" (p. 149). Moreover, hooks (1991) ponders the fate of "gifted black children raised in homes where their brilliance of mind was not valued but made them 'freaks' who were persecuted and punished" (p. 149). Certainly, as a young, effeminate black male, I risked falling into the category of freak, a term often used in my community to describe gay men and lesbians. My desire for isolation in order to read and indulge in contemplation, as well as my absence from organized sports, raised the level of my parents' anxiety about me.

The desire for isolation, I have recently discovered, are historically connected in science and popular lore with pathology and criminology. The 1949 *Encyclopedia of Criminology* includes activities that require isolation in its description of the narcissistic homosexual. The people in this category included "eccentrics of all kinds, misers, collectors, *book-worms* [emphasis added], also exaggerating lovers and protectors of animals who prefer pets to men, because animals are no danger to them"

(Wittels, p. 193). In the insightful ethnography *Ways with Words*, Shirley Brice Heath (1983) gives the following account of a small town black community in North Carolina and its reaction to a young man who enjoyed reading in isolation:

> Aunt Berta had a son who as a child used to slip away from the cotton field and read under a tree. He is now a grown man with children, and he has obtained a college degree, but the community still tells tales about his peculiar boyhood habits of wanting to go off and read alone. In general, reading alone, unless one is very old and religious, marks an individual as someone who cannot make it socially. (p. 191)

It should also be remembered that the hermit who lives in isolation is a popular stereotype for men who deviate from heterosexual intercourse. In her brilliant debut novel *The Bluest Eye* (1974), Toni Morrison chillingly manipulated this stereotype of the hermit as a homosexual and child molester to create the character Soaphead Church.

'Alone Is Alone, Not Alive'

My description of home seems reminiscent of Esther Phillip's recording of Gil Scott Heron's "Home Is Where the Hatred Is." It certainly has not been my intention to say that home was an absolutely terrible place. It wasn't. Yet home was a place I associate with domination and resistance. My parents did not want me to be gay, and they tried to force me to alter such behaviors that they attributed to gayness. Because of their social class standing and their desire to educate me, they supported my attendance of the opera, ballet, and theatre. I could purchase books and music and, as long as I didn't remain cloistered in my room for unreasonable periods of time, I could consume them with abandon. My parents did not, however, realize that the activities and events they sanctioned and associated with class mobility also enabled me to oppose their wishes for my future.

The home I have created today does not resemble the one in which I was raised. For the past nine years, I have shared a home with a man whom I love deeply. The desire to be free from domination by loved ones is a constant issue in our home, and we have struggled with the issue of monogamy when our careers have forced us to live apart. Neither of us believes that we have the right to police each other's body. Belief and praxis, however, are not the same. So we struggle to avoid domination. We just want to be happy.

My parents and I have cordial relations. I speak with my mother on a weekly basis, but sometimes weeks pass before I speak to my father. Seldom do we speak of my relationship with my partner.

REFERENCES

Asante, M. K. (1987). *The Afrocentric idea*. Philadelphia: Temple University Press.

Beam, J. (1986). Brother to brother: Words from the heart. In J. Beam (pp. 230-242).

Beam, J. (1986). *In the life: A black gay anthology*. Boston: Alyson Publications.

Bell, A. P., Weinberg, W. S., & Hammersmith, S. K. (1981). *Sexual preference: Its development in men and women*. Bloomington: Indiana University Press.

Collins, P. H. (1990). *Black feminist thought: Knowledge, consciousness, and the politics of empowerment*. Boston: Unwin Hyman.

Gomez, J. L. (1983). A cultural legacy denied and discovered: Black lesbians in fiction by women. In B. Smith (pp. 110-123).

Heath, S. B. (1983). *Ways with words: Language, life, and work in communities and classrooms*. New York: Cambridge University Press.

Hemphill, E. (Ed.). (1991). *Brother to brother: New writings by black gay men*. Boston: Alyson.

hooks, b. (1991). Black women intellectuals. In b. hooks & C. West, *Breaking bread: Insurgent black intellectual life*. Boston: South End Press.

Lakoff, G., & Johnson, M. (1980). *Metaphors we live by*. Chicago: The University of Chicago Press.

Lorde, A. (1984). *Sister outsider*. Freedom, CA: The Crossing Press.

Nero, C. I. (1991). Towards a black gay aesthetic: Signifying in contemporary black gay literature. In E. Hemphill (pp. 229-252).

Rich, A. (1980). Compulsory heterosexuality and lesbian existence. *Signs*, 5, 631-60.

Riggs, M. T. (Producer & Director). (1989). *Tongues untied* [Film]. San Francisco: Frameline.

Rodgers, R., & Hammerstein, O. (1960). *The sound of music*. New York: Williamson.

Sedgwick, E. K. (1991). How to bring your kids up gay. *Social Text, 29*, 18-27.

Simmons, R. Some thoughts on the challenges facing black gay intellectuals. In E. Hemphill (pp. 211-228).

Smith, B. (Ed.). (1983). *Home girls: A black feminist anthology.* New York: Kitchen Table: Women of Color Press.

Sondheim, S. (Music and Lyrics), & Furth, G. (Book). (1973). *Company.* In S. Richards (Ed.), *Ten great musicals of the American theater.* Radnor, PA: Chilton Book Company.

Johnson, L. (Director). (1973). *That certain summer* [Television Film].

Wittels, F. (1949). Homosexuality. In V. C. Branham & S. B. Kutash (Eds.), *Encyclopedia of criminality* (pp. 189-194). New York: Philosophical Library.

Woods, D. W. Sister lesbos. In J. Beam (pp. 104-105).

10

Jewish and/or Woman: Identity and Communicative Style

Sheryl Perlmutter Bowen
Villanova University

More than ten years ago, my graduate school mentor revealed to me that only when I stopped complaining would she begin to worry about me. Over time, she had come to expect my continual complaints of work load, crises that got in the way of completing tasks, gripes about my family, and other such minutiae of life. She had learned that, as long as I "bitched," I was really doing fine. That meant that, despite all my verbiage, I was still functioning normally.

Recently, in separate incidents, two young men in leadership positions in a student organization that I advise asked me why I was "mocking them." I thought I was just having good-natured conversation with them, harmlessly teasing, trying to create identification with them. I might ask how the weekend went or perhaps retort, "Oh, you just like to have a good time." On another day I might ask how their classes were going and respond in a way that wouldn't paint me as "the professor," saying something such as, "You can't take this academic stuff too seriously." When one of these young men brought this so-called mocking to my attention, I attributed it to not knowing him very well and assumed that perhaps he was more sensitive than I had imagined. When the second man made the same comment, I recalled the earlier episode and became pensive. I tried to identify what they had found so troublesome.

Most of us do not spend considerable amounts of time ruminating about our own styles of communication. Usually it is only when our communication becomes problematic, when we fail to achieve a communicative goal or are called out for something we said or how we said it, that we really begin to notice how we communicate with others. This self-awareness is quite different from the relative ease with which we can characterize someone else's interactive style.

I have begun to understand that the complaining aspect of my interaction with my mentor (and countless others since) is in part a result of my cultural identity. I will often list the impediments to the work I *should* be getting done. My frequent teasing of students is also a part of my cultural identity, as I try to connect with students on a personal level without prying into their lives. Symbolic interactionist theorists tell us what most of us already know: all of us play a variety of roles in our daily lives and often alter our communicative styles based on the roles we perceive for ourselves. What has not been well discussed, however, is how variations in that communicative style can be highly influenced by one's cultural or ethnic heritage. Often the influences are not conscious, and surely they are also affected by individual differences among people.

In this essay, I will explore two conditions that may account for the complaining and teasing aspects of my communicative style. Specifically, they are being Jewish and being female in late twentieth-century America. Each of these aspects of my identity has shaped my being, my goals and aspirations, my lifestyle choices, interpretations of my experiences, and my communication with others.

The problematic episodes related above have come to symbolize for me the tension that exists between certain aspects of identity. What I hope to show in the pages that follow is that being Jewish accounts for some aspects of style and being a woman accounts for others. Now, there are surely other influences on my communication, such as my education and socio-economic background, but cultural influences are dominant in the complaining and teasing episodes mentioned above. Consistent with the style of this book, I will not bother to detail the scholarly literature on these topics, but rather analyze the two episodes in light of my understanding of my own cultural experiences. Perhaps readers can use this essay to learn a bit about how it feels to be Jewish and female, or to reflect on the ways in which their own cultural identities may influence aspects of their communication with others.

Jewish Identity

I am, besides being Jewish and female, a non-traditional Jew and a feminist. I was raised in a traditional Jewish home, heavily influenced by two aunts who are Orthodox Jews. I went to religious school at least once a week from age six to fifteen, and spent one year in a Jewish parochial school where the day was divided between secular and religious studies. I learned to read Hebrew with fluency and to understand a portion of what I read. The Jewish calendar was very important in marking the passage of time in my home. As my immediate family was affected by the death of a parent, remarriage to a non-religious Jew, and a move to the suburbs, my experiences in Jewish institutions were with Conservative and Reform synagogues. By the time I was in high school, my Jewish identity was primarily expressed through my active involvement with a statewide Reform youth organization. Here I celebrated Jewish rituals and culture with other adolescents in a social setting. I even flirted with the idea of becoming a rabbi.

Although I have a fairly traditional Jewish background and upbringing, as an adult I choose to affiliate with a "spiritual activist synagogue" which places emphasis on joining Jewish life and Jewish renewal with modern secular work. This synagogue is part of the Reconstructionist movement, the fourth branch of Judaism. Reconstructionism is heavily influenced by the thinking of Mordecai Kaplan and retains elements of traditional Jewish ritual and observance with understandings relevant for living in the modern multi-cultural world. I have found the Reconstructionist movement to be highly compatible with my understanding about life from my academic training, and I am able to connect my secular and religious life.

Culturally, I am a Jew. This means that I am influenced by the historical experiences of Jews in this country, in my family's Eastern European origins and, indeed, in today's Middle East. I am a product of the ways that I have received Jewish training, participated in Jewish ritual, and interacted with others, Jews and non-Jews.

I have felt a closeness to the feminist ideals espoused in academic and activist presses. I am not content to perpetuate traditional sex roles, as I am not content to perpetuate traditional Jewish roles. My personal choices have involved discovering methods to reconstruct and reaffirm aspects of both female culture and Jewish culture in ways that disturb the male-female inequities that have characterized our society. My group affiliations and political perspectives force me to continually question and evaluate situations in which I find myself.

In addition to taking a Jewish perspective, I must also consider the fact that my experiences are influenced by my gender. As many Jewish women have been describing over the last fifteen years or so, being a Jewish woman is different from being a Jewish man in this country. Differing access to religious and cultural experiences has meant that Jewish women and men traditionally have lived in different worlds. To provide an oversimplified sketch, men were responsible for public prayers, traditionally said three times per day, and for working outside of the home; while women were responsible for the domestic aspects of family life, including raising the children and keeping the household according to Jewish law to preserve traditions (for example, following *kashrut*, the Jewish dietary laws). Aside from the particulars that differentiate Jewish life, the traditional sex roles parallel those dominant in the larger culture.

Consistent with feminist moves in a variety of other areas, Jewish feminists have recently begun to appropriate some of the symbols and rituals that previously were open only to men. For example, in traditional Orthodox Jewish circles, only men were able to be counted in the prayer group, or *minyan* (which must consist of at least ten men to allow saying all of the prescribed prayers in a given service). Orthodox women in many cities across the country are gathering to pray among themselves, and some have protested their invisibility in a male prayer service, since in Orthodox synagogues, women and men sit in separate areas divided by a screen or curtain. Some groups of women have reclaimed *Rosh Hodesh*, the celebration at the new moon each month, as a women's holiday. Women's groups have developed rituals of their own to commemorate and celebrate their experiences as Jews and as women (e.g., celebrating life cycle events). Women are ordained as rabbis in most of the major Jewish dominations and can fully lead and participate in religious services and conduct rituals that were previously performed only by men. In short, over the years, many changes have been made.

Vivian Gornick (1989) has written about being "twice an outsider," expressing many of the dilemmas faced by women who struggle for cultural identity within the patriarchal confines of Judaism. Gornick notes that in American culture, being Jewish and female involves two stigmas, although ostracism for being Jewish is less prevalent than in previous decades. Put-downs for being a woman, however, have not yet been rejected in many circles. Letty Cottin Pogrebin (1991) details many of the feelings I myself have had as I confront being female and Jewish in American society. She particularly attacks the Women's Movement for its anti-Semitic undertones. In my view, these phenomena surely have an impact on individuals' behaviors.

In the communication discipline, we learn that one's communicative style is shaped and influenced by the historical and cultural events surrounding one's life, and my case shows no exception. Further, my speech may be characterized by at least some of the elements of what Deborah Tannen early on described as New York Jewish conversational style (Tannen, 1981; curiously, by 1984, she refers to this simply as New York style). Although I am not from New York, I am from a mid-Atlantic state and share recent Eastern-European Jewish immigrant history as a member of my family's second generation of Americans.

Tannen (1981; 1984) describes this conversational style as "high-involvement," which comprises a number of elements that seem to be consistent with the two "problematic" examples described in this essay. My own speech, for that matter, is often marked by a preference for personal topics, abrupt topic shifts, storytelling (in which the preferred point is the teller's emotional experience), a fast rate of speech, avoidance of inter-turn pauses, quick turn-taking, expressive phonology, pitch and amplitude shifts, marked voice quality, and strategic within-turn pauses (Tannen, 1981, p. 137). Given these characteristics, my complaining and teasing should both be seen as normal interaction strategies. Since the others in this episode did not share the same style, my conversational style became an issue. Such ill-perceived attempts to communicate might be best understood as simply strategies using humor to "keep the conversation going."

Jewish Humor

The examination of humor as one aspect of communicative style offers a perspective for understanding some of the influences on Jewish women's style. Humor provides an avenue of communication, for it includes not only jokes and stories but witticisms and sometimes sarcastic statements that punctuate everyday interaction. Humor is also somewhat ambiguous, in that one can intend to be funny and not succeed, or that something one says can be taken as humor when it was not intended as such. As feminist and Jewish styles of humor interact in today's changing world, there are often few markers that indicate "this is humor" in routine interaction.

For many years, people have tried to isolate what constituted Jewish humor and determine why it was characteristically different from other types of humor. One explanation derives from the historical experiences of Jews. Novak & Waldoks (1981) describe some of the misconceptions about Jewish humor. They contextualize Jewish humor in the nineteenth- and twentieth-century Jewish experience with such momentous influences as pogroms, anti-Semitism, the Holocaust, immigration, and assimilation. Nineteenth-century Jewish humor arose partially out of persecution, poverty, and uprootedness. On the other hand, however:

> For every joke about anti-Semitism, poverty, or dislocation, there are several others dealing with less melancholy topics: the intricacies of the Jewish mind, its scholars, students, and schlemiels; the eternal comedy of food, health, and manners; the world of businessmen, rabbis, and schnorrers (beggars); the concerns of matchmaking, marriage, and family. (Novak & Waldoks, p. xiv)

While the humor carries into the twentieth century, these authors see anxiety and skepticism as twin currents underlying much of Jewish humor of that century. As Jews increasingly moved into the American experience of the twentieth century, jokes about anti-Semitism became less central and were replaced by jokes about assimilation, name-changing, conversion, and fund-raising. Many of these jokes arose as a way to cope with surrounding hostility and rapid changes to ways of living which had been transplanted from Europe. Novak and Waldoks, in their attempt to summarize Jewish humor, have come up with five descriptors: (1) it is usually substantive, and the topics often illustrate a fascination with mind and logic; (2) as social or religious commentary, it can be sarcastic, complaining, resigned, or descriptive; (3) it is anti-authoritarian; (4) it has a critical and often political edge; and (5) it mocks everyone, including God, while simultaneously affirming religious traditions (pp. xx-xxi).

As I read through the jokes and stories included in Novak and Waldok's anthology, I felt a deep connection and familiarity with much of the contents. The witticisms sounded like comments I might interject into some of my own interactions. It is no accident in my mind that the sarcastic, ocking, and complaining notions included in thecharacteristics of Jewish humor fit the pattern of how others view my own interactions. Could I be witnessing my own Jewish roots playing themselves out in this way? I believe so.

A complaining style, despite continued productivity (as in the case with my graduate school mentor), could function in several ways. It might diffuse the tension felt between doing work and not wanting to brag about it. In the Jewish context, I was taught as a child not to be too boastful, not to call too much attention to myself, especially as a female. The complaints could also be a way of drawing attention, commiseration, or support. A stereotypical "Oy vey," a Yiddish response cry (Tannen, 1981) uttered with a sigh, would be an appropriate response from another Jew.

Complaining, therefore, would not necessarily seem to be depressing to the listener nor even a sign of depression in the speaker. Rather, it could function in a social context to maintain the connection between speaker and listener. In other circumstances, complaints from one could generate complaints from another in a "Can you top this?" fashion. But in the setting described between student and mentor, this seems unlikely. The mentor in my case accepted the complaints of the student without interjecting her own complaints. Perhaps because she did not share the same cultural identity with the student, she did not enter into the language game of comparing complaints but rather simply accepted the complaints as clues to what was happening in the student's life.

Feminist Humor

What of the episode of the two male students? Is there a way to account for it within the Jewish context? It does not seem so, unless one compares the in-group/out-group phenomena of Jew and non-Jew to women and men. Jewish humor traditionally has not included many celebratory notions of women. Gornick's connection between being an outsider because of Jewish identity and being female may invoke similar in-group/out-group aspects of humor. The demarcation of the in- and out-groups are one of the types of humor found by Cindy White (1988).

In an essay about feminist humor, White lists characteristics of the humor that in some ways parallel Novak and Waldok's characterization of Jewish humor. She notes that feminist humor "exposes sources of imbalance and attempts to eradicate them" (p. 78). It comes out of a desire for equity, an attempt to bond people together, and a need to obliterate the myths and stereotypes that have plagued women since time immemorial. White collected instances of feminist humor from feminist comics and feminist social actors in their everyday interaction. These humorous incidents often poke fun at mainstream expectations, just as they take jabs at feminist expectations. The uncertainties reflected in the changing notions of women's roles and behaviors are mirrored in this type of humor. At the same time, feminist humor is used to connect people, to point up shared experiences, and to affirm the positive strengths of women. At times, the humor can also be anti-male.

From a feminist perspective, an interpretation of my teasing behavior with the two male students suggests several things. I may have been attempting to close the gap between us. I am older, female, and perceived as an authority figure in my role as advisor. They are younger, male, and subordinate in the hierarchy of the university. In my desire to close the distance between us—since feminists often see equality as a prerequisite for satisfactory interaction or negotiation—my teasing may have functioned to show them that I could "play" with them, indeed that we could have playful interactions. Our relationship did not have to fall into the usual superior-subordinate norm. On the other hand, simply because they were men and assumed greater knowledge of everyday operations within their student organization, my attempt at non-threatening communication could have served as a safe feminist ploy to equalize roles of women and men, despite the other differences between us. Had these two leaders been women, I doubt that I would have used the same teasing behaviors with them. More likely, I would have used a strategy that would have appealed to our common womanhood, perhaps juxtaposed against the predominantly male membership of the organization. When I recall my feelings and level of awareness in these interactions, I was more conscious of being a woman than of being Jewish, even though the young male students were not Jewish.

Conclusion

The somber side to analyzing each of these episodes resides in the potential for conflict as the styles of being Jewish and being female collide, especially in interactions with Jewish men or with women who are very male-centered. Pogrebin (1991) recalls her 1982 article in which she labelled one problem faced by Jewish women as "invisibility, insult and internalized oppression." She was speaking particularly of the problems of Jewish women within the broader women's movement, but the same descriptors could be used for other situations. Jewish women are often rendered invisible because of either their Jewishness or their femaleness. The analysis offered for each of my two experiences perpetuates the invisibility of one or another dimension of my being. Jewish women are often seen by outsiders as loud, pushy, or motivated by material wealth in stereotypically negative ways. Due to a number of factors, Jewish women often face personal feelings of self-hatred and denial, thus internalizing the oppression that has been waged from outside.

In attempting to overcome the negative forces that can lower Jewish women's self-esteem and contributions to society, I would argue that micro-level communication should be examined for the strategies in which Jewish women can continuously face their challenges. As most Jewish women today interact with others who are not Jewish, as well as with men, flexibility in communicative strategies seems to be warranted. Humor provides one arena of options for overcoming obstacles to satisfactory interaction.

REFERENCES

Gornick, V. (1989). Twice an outsider: On being Jewish and a woman. *Tikkun*, *4* (2), 29-31, 123-125.

Novak, W., & Waldoks, M. (Eds.). (1981). *The big book of Jewish humor*. New York: Harper Collins.

Pogrebin, L. C. (1991). *Deborah, Golda and me: Being female and Jewish in America*. New York: Crown.

Tannen, D. (1981). New York Jewish conversational style. *International Journal of the Sociology of Language, 30*, 133-149.

Tannen, D. (1984). *Conversational style: Analyzing talk among friends*. Norwood, NJ: Ablex.

White, C. (1988). Liberating laughter: An inquiry into the nature, content, and functions of feminist humor. In B. Bates & A. Taylor (Eds.), *Women communicating: Studies of women's talk* (pp. 75-90). Norwood, NJ: Ablex.

PART III

REPRESENTING CULTURAL KNOWLEDGE IN INTERPERSONAL AND MASS MEDIA CONTEXTS

11

The Rhetoric of *La Familia* among Mexican Americans

Margarita Gangotena
Texas A&M University

"You are going out so soon? At what time will you be back, *hijo*?" the mother asks as she approaches her son and fixes the collar of his shirt. She touches his cheek with the palm of her hand while looking at him with love and pride. Manuel, a six-foot-tall, 25-year-old man, checks the rest of his attire then embraces his mother and kisses her farewell on the cheek.

"I will be back soon, no later than eleven," he replies. "Jenny and I are going to the movies. And, yes, *Mami*, I left the money for the rent on your night table, where Cristina left the money for the food."

As he departs, his sister Cristina enters the apartment. "Have fun, Manuel," she says and turns around to kiss her mother on the cheek. "*Hola, Mami*. What are we having for supper? Is Dad still at work? Where is Uncle Beto? Is Grandma asleep?" She sits on a couch.

"Cristina," the mother says without answering any of her questions, "when are you going to get married to Joe? He is four years older than you; you are 22, and you will be graduating from college this year. We will help you get started and help you along. Joe is a good, hard-working young man."

"I don't know, sounds all right, but. . ." Cristina sighs. "We have only known each other for a couple of months, and, you know how it is, he wants to have everything clear and organized before we even talk about marriage. He will have to move out of his parents' house, and there are still younger kids in the family, they need support. . . ."

If this same episode had transpired in an Anglo family, the dialogue would most likely have been different.

"See you, Mom," Tom says as he opens the door to leave. Noticing that his sister Cary has arrived, he adds, "I better leave, she's back!" Cary glares at him as he goes by. As she walks in, she says, "I have a lot of work to do, Mom." She marches off to her bedroom and closes the door. Throughout this exchange, the mother does not take her eyes off what she is doing, nor does she respond to her children's statements.

Two typical households, one Mexican American and the other Euro-American, reflect two very different underlying values and assumptions of what a family is and what it provides for its members. The communication of the Mexican American family in the above episode points to the continued interdependence of its members across generations. It also makes explicit that sharing time in conversation is a valued form of family interaction. Touch, affection, and greeting rituals are means of affirmation. In contrast, the communication in the Anglo family points to some basic assumptions about the value of individualism and the need to maintain it through more restricted communication and contact. In the Mexican American family, the formality given to greeting rituals is intended to keep both familiarity and distance. In the Euro-American family, cultural valuations seem to limit interdependence and affiliation to the family, so as to make the children leave the "nest" and form other independent, nuclear families. In my opinion, the Euro-American family rarely uses touch in its casual interactions and even less so with grown children. The cultural perception of touch for Euro-Americans seems to work as (1) a means of control and preventing any tendency towards individualism and (2) a communicative device reserved mainly for sexual encounters. The need for independence and individualism apparently fosters an emotional distance between the generations that severely impairs significant bonding among family members.

The Mexican American family is the source of many of the cultural values, attitudes, and assumptions that Mexican Americans carry with them into their interactions with mainstream society. This composite of cultural elements that influence the Mexican American character is what Mexican Americans call *la familia* (the family). Consequently, the analysis of the rhetoric that frames Mexican American family values and activities will facilitate Euro-Americans' understanding of Mexican Americans. Moreover, awareness of the Mexican American valuation of the family provides a model for society of such productive attributes as community, solidarity, respect, and discipline.[1]

The purpose of this essay is to describe the rhetorical devices that comprise and sustain *la familia* (the Mexican American family) in the United States. The essay begins with a critique of traditional social science research that has advanced a negative image of *la familia*. Then it discusses the contributions rhetorical analysis can offer toward clarifying the Mexican American valuation of the family. Finally, it introduces a new theoretical approach not yet present in the literature on Mexican Americans, nor in the Euro-American interpretation of Mexican American culture. Theoretically, this essay is significant, because it provides (1) a process for analyzing Mexican American culture and (2) a more accurate interpretation than would be the case from a Euro-American perspective.

This essay describes five rhetorical devices that emerge in family discourse among Mexican Americans: harmony/silence; rationality/emotionalism; the concept of personhood; respect for hierarchy, age, and gender; and solidarity and a sense of community. One qualification must preface this analysis: the devices described herein occur in various ways among Mexican Americans. The rhetorical vision of *la familia* is often manifested in the discourse

and behavior of most of its adherents. However, one's perception of this rhetorical vision may differ if one is neither of Mexican American background nor is an actual participant of *la familia*. Nevertheless, the vision of *la familia* holds a strong allegiance among most Mexican Americans. Any participant of *la familia*, upon hearing this discourse, should immediately feel a sense of familiarity and comfort, become emotionally moved, and consciously recognize the layers of meaning embedded herein.

La Familia and Traditional Social Science Research

Traditional social science research has studied the Mexican American family for several decades. While it has brought *la familia* to the focus of scholarly work, it has not always been able to understand it clearly. Because of this, social science studies tends to blame *la familia* for most of the problems of Mexican American acculturation.[2] Hence, *la familia* has become a scapegoat for the lack of both understanding and intercultural sensitivity.

Social science discourse on *la familia* has been biased by Euro-American conceptions of the family. Some of the elements that characterize the Euro-American vision of the family include: nuclear structure; non-generational, individualistic, non-extended, detached, permissive child-rearing practices; and flexible gender roles, all of which tend to grant respect on the basis of individualism.

Another factor may be involved in the social sciences' assessment of *la familia*: conclusions are often based on assumptions derived from incomplete information on the psycho-social background of Mexican Americans. It has been postulated that the changes *la familia* undergoes are due to Mexican Americans moving from rural to urban life. Mexican Americans have high mobility within the United States. Needless to say, as they relocate, they have to undergo some changes. However, these changes are not pronounced, because their movement is from one urban center to another. We know this is the case because a large proportion of

Mexican Americans have lived mainly in urban centers. A large percentage of those who migrate to this country are already city dwellers—many of them skilled and semi-skilled industrial laborers (Schick & Schick, 1991). The unfounded conclusions by U.S. social scientists that the Mexican American family is neither "developed," "Western," nor like middle-class America and, therefore, of a lesser, peasant-like quality, derive from generalizations based on studies of the rural enclaves of Mexican Americans. Because of such conclusions, the Mexican American population at large has been stereotyped. For example, stereotypes portray the Mexican American husband as a dictator in the family and the wife as weak and spineless. When these stereotypes are not corroborated by the urban data, researchers attribute the differences to the influence of urbanization and modernization on a peasant population. I would argue that previous studies of the characteristics of the Mexican American family may have reflected the reality of the locale and/or the people researched, but they were not really representative of Mexican American people as a whole.

Social scientists have relegated the slow progress of Mexican Americans toward assimilation on their strong attachment to *la familia*—or "familialism"— not to mention their dependence on the extended families. But they do not take into account that the reaction of Euro-Americans to Mexican Americans contributes to segregating the latter from social interactions, job opportunities, and overall advancement. I personally experienced this Euro-American perception when I was traveling by bus to a high-level seminar at the University of Portland. During most of the trip, I talked with a senior citizen, while across the aisle sat a friendly couple. The husband would occasionally eavesdrop on our conversation. Later, he queried about my destination. When I told him I was going to the University of Portland, he asked with apparent sincerity, "Are you going there to learn to serve tables better?" He had automatically pegholed me into a specific socio-economic structure.

Researchers on the Mexican American family have not brought to bear certain historic facts about *la familia*. Influenced by the slow but persistent erosion of the importance of the Euro-American family, their data has distorted the relevance of *la familia* for Mexican Americans and for the nation. Both the Meso-American and the Spanish ancestors of the contemporary Mexican American were highly urbanized, and the religious beliefs of both cultural groups valued the basic family structure. The Meso-American ancestry is obvious in Mexican American food, Mexican American discourse, and much of its folklore. The Spanish imprint on Mexican Americans today is manifested, for example, in their preference for language usage, music, family structure, and religion. Undoubtedly, one of the symbols that has strengthened the Mexican American valuation of the family is the Christian image of the Holy Family (Joseph, Mary, and Baby Jesus). This rhetorical type is continuously reinforced through the discourse of the Catholic Church. It also coincides with basic rhetorical themes commonly valued by Western culture, i.e., love, a need to belong, mature interpersonal relations, and deliverance from guilt. Thus, the force of the vision of *la familia* has its source in discourse that supports (1) life, (2) self-identity based on family belonging, and (3) human communication. The dialogue at the beginning of this essay illustrates some of the elements that sustain the rhetoric of *la familia* for Mexican Americans. For example, through Manuel, Cristina, and *Mami*, we see the importance of touch, caring, and nurturing in *la familia*. Some of social science's misunderstanding of Mexican American culture can be overcome by a proper analysis of rhetorical visions through symbolic convergence theory. Applying this theory, commonly known as fantasy theme analysis, is not only innovative but practical, because the methodology allows the culture to speak for itself without the influence of the system of analysis or the researcher's bias.

Contribution of Communication to Understanding *La Familia*

La familia is a concept embedded with meanings developed by Mexican Americans through five centuries. As we gain an understanding of these meanings, we will be better able to view *la familia* from the perspective of its participants. Thus, we can develop a deeper appreciation of the inner richness of *la familia*.

To help us comprehend the meanings associated with *la familia*, communication theory and methodology allow us to focus on the discourse of Mexican Americans. As dialogues, narratives, and symbolic references to *la familia* are analyzed, the rhetorical critic will be able to understand the development of meaning as a manifestation of the deeper layers of values and value attributions. The dialogues and narrative data found among Mexican Americans are quite rich.[3] Because of the culture's valuation of narratives as a means to transfer tradition and to interact, one of the best methods to understand *la familia* is through symbolic convergence theory.

Ernest Bormann developed symbolic convergence theory at the University of Minnesota, where he analyzed data on leaderless groups. He found that these groups seemed to create narratives on themes outside of the topic of discussion which involved their members emotionally (Bormann, 1972). When the discourse of a group's narratives was analyzed, it was found to contain such dramatic elements as heroes, heroines, and villains, and performed "action sequences somewhere other than in the 'here and now'" (Smith, 1988, p. 271). Furthermore, the drama, plot, characters, and discourse of the group were found to be symbolic of what was happening in the dynamics of the group's interaction. For example, when a group studied the benefits of the social security system, one of its members offered only minimal participation. Digressing from the topic at hand, the others told jokes and stories about the importance of working together and making contributions, which revealed the group's disapproval of the more reticent member's lack of involvement.

Bormann and his associates researched message stories in interpersonal, small groups and organizational settings, both in writing and over the electronic media. They found dramatizations of ficti-tious and non-fictitious events with a specific message, which Bormann labeled as "fantasy themes" (Bormann, 1972). The recurrence of these fantasy themes, or "stock scenarios repeated in various forms within a body of discourse," were deemed fantasy types. Bormann defined rhetorical views as "the more global symbolic realities consisting of fantasy themes and fantasy types, often including metaphors and analogies" (Gangotena, 1980, p. 24). Groups of people sharing in the same rhetorical vision comprised what was called a rhetorical community. In using the term "fantasy," Bormann did not mean that the narratives were negative or reflected negatively on the people researched, nor did he interpret them as imaginary or unreal. Rather, the term "fantasy" was used to indicate that the themes and types made reference to events not in the "here and now" of a group's task.

> When a communicator dramatizes some event, the listeners may share the drama in an appropriate way or they may ignore it, ridicule it, or reject it in some other way. Only the communication associated with the sharing of fantasy serves to build a common social reality for the participants. When people constituting a community have shared a large number of similar fantasy themes, they may allude to the basic scenarios in general terms in the form of a fantasy type. (Gangotena, 1980, p. 24)

Thus, if several Mexican Americans dramatize incidents in which a person has not displayed behaviors that in Mexican American culture demonstrate respect, and/or they praise those who have displayed those behaviors, we can safely assume that a fantasy type of respect has been introduced into the group's discourse. Once the fantasy type is present, the entire meaning for a class of fantasy types can be brought about through such expressions as *malcriado* or *sin crianza* (both terms meaning "poorly trained at home by the parents").

By utilizing this kind of rhetorical criticism, the researcher needs to look at the dramatic elements of the discourse (the plot, heroes, heroines, villains, and scenarios) to uncover the basic themes, types, and rhetorical visions involved. Subsequently, the critic focuses on the artistic manifestation and value of the discourse, the consequences of that discourse for the rhetorical community, and the consequences of that vision for the enhancement of humanity. "Did the rhetorical vision emancipate and enrich human experience, did it enslave and degrade the people affected by it?" (Smith, 1988, p. 273).

When using symbolic convergence theory, the objective is to unravel the themes, i.e., the fantasy themes, that predominate in a group or in a cultural community. These themes, each time they are repeated, create fantasy types that are shared by groups of people. The rhetorical community which shares in these themes creates a unique rhetorical vision, or paradigm, of the world. The convergence of these themes captures the imagination and emotion of people by way of a shared symbolic reality. (For further discussion on this topic, see Bormann, 1972.)

Fantasy theme analysis of discourse is one way of describing the cultural meanings expressed by members of a rhetorical community. As we uncover the basic framework of discourse through symbolic convergence, we are able to see a culture from its own perspective rather than from that of the "biased outsider." Bormann has used fantasy theme analysis to interpret the aspects of Euro-American rhetoric that has helped shape this nation in his book, *The Force of Fantasy: The Making of the American Dream* (1985).

Reports of Mexican American discourse on *la familia*, gathered by the author from participant observation, point to the existence of various fantasy types that support the rhetoric of *la familia* among Mexican Americans. It is through these themes that the Mexican American community comes to share in a common symbolic reality. The fantasy types that emerge regarding *la familia* are: harmony/silence; rationality/emotionalism; the concept of personhood; respect for hierarchy, age, and gender; solidarity and the sense of community.

Harmony/Silence

One of the main fantasy types that supports the rhetoric of *la familia* among Mexican Americans is that of maintaining harmonious relationships. The

basic fantasy type is that of a person who values relationships, gets along well with others, fulfills all family obligations, does not place others in compromising situations, and does not bring shame to the family. In this fantasy type, Mexican Americans resist creating external conflicts such as those that would draw them out of their shell, have them lose face, or cause insecurity. Not only are relationships valued, but, when faced with choices that go against harmony, their preference would be to avoid conflict through compromise. Mexican Americans generally dislike conflict, considering it to be of no social value in maintaining relationships. Only when discourse has failed to prevent conflict will they choose antagonistic exchanges. For example, if faced with a situation where the choice is between assertiveness and harmony, Mexican Americans will compromise. This is not to say, however, that they will not fight abuse and oppression from external sources. They will come out against injustice once other channels have failed. The fantasy type that will justify assertiveness and aggressiveness is the fantasy theme of "the intrinsic honor of the person" and "the honor of the family."

Much like in other Latin cultures, Mexican Americans have a cultural need to protect themselves from external influences, thus maintaining some control over their own lives and circumstances. They usually accomplish this with silence and compromise. To attain harmony, silence is often necessary. Mexican Americans may choose to grow silent and introverted rather than become a source of disharmonious relationships. This fantasy type of harmony/silence is supported by what González (1990, p. 281) has called "defense against intrusion."

The importance Mexican Americans give to maintaining relationships offsets a natural human inclination towards selfishness and the Mexican American tendency to self-absorption described by González (1992). It also tempers the cultural trait of undeterred individualism passed on by the Spanish. The characteristics that conform to the Spanish individualistic fantasy type of the 16th and 17th centuries are a preference for private property, the freedom to be one's own agents, the freedom to speak their minds, the freedom to have a divergent point of view from another, self-trust and mistrust of others until proven reliable, freedom of mobility and decision making, and freedom of enterprise. In the rhetorical vision of *la familia*, these characteristics are incorporated as qualities of the Mexican American family. Thus, trust is placed on *la familia* and not on the self alone. This *familia* is one that includes relatives on both the mother's and father's sides, both generationally (e.g., great-grandparents, grandparents, children, and grandchildren) and laterally (e.g., uncles by blood and marriage, first, second, and third cousins, brothers- and sisters-in-law, sons- and daughters-in-law, nephews and nieces by brothers, sisters, and first and second cousins).

This fantasy type of harmony and silence never includes the trust of strangers, only the trust of family members. When Mexican Americans want to trust a friend or a business partner, the fantasy type allows for two types of fictive kinship: (1) the granting of a family title (and the respect that goes with it) to the family and/or person with whom a closer association is desired; and (2) the integration of an individual into the *compadrazgo* system, which refers to "co-parents." The *compadrazgo* system is established between the parents and the baptismal godfather and godmother of a child. Originally established by the Catholic Church to oversee the Christian upbringing of the child, the relationship carries with it obligations of education and upbringing of the godchild, especially in the event of the parents' death. Among Mexican Americans, the bond between the adult members of this fictive system replaces the possible lack of blood relationship and is cultivated by both parents and godparents. A couple with three children could have six co-parents. For the sake of the child, the relationship is made "like family" and the godparents are included in *la familia's* networking structure.

The titles that express this fantasy theme of family-like closeness are *hermano, hermana,* (brother, sister), *tio, tia* (uncle, aunt), and *compadre.* Other expressions that will indicate this fictive kinship are *como hermana, como hermano* (as a

sister, as a brother). With the family role title, each new member receives the treatment of that role within the family and with the trust of that family's members.

Another theme in the fantasy type is the care for others, for *la familia*, and for relationships. In this scenario, care should not be sacrificed for the sake of self, since one's sense of self comes through caring and being cared for in the context of relationships.

One of the advantages of this discourse on care is that it provides Mexican Americans with a system for avoiding conflicts that can destroy relationships. The second advantage is that the circle of people Mexican Americans trust and depend on for support is larger than what an individual would usually have in the mainstream culture. The existence of a support system serves two basic purposes. First, it is relational. Mexican Americans need not be alone in the fight against the "rat race"; they have a greater choice of support networks on which to depend. Thus, when needed, the rebuilding of self-esteem after interacting with the outside world can be done within the "safe" *familia* network. Within *la familia*, many not only rest their minds by speaking Spanish but are also cared for through the sharing of familiar stories and through expressions of love and understanding. Expressions such as *"Mijita/mijito, mi amor, cómo le fue?"* (My child, my love, how did it go?) are used to establish a scenario of care and nurturing for both children and adults. Second, this support is not only psychological but also pragmatic. *La familia* provides help with food, clothing, child care, contacts for jobs, referral to community and government services, education, citizenship instructions, and legal procedures.

Because the structure of services in this country is organized and oriented within an individualistic frame of mind, community and government institutions and services not only do not know about *la familia*, they do not have the flexibility to attend to it. In most hospitals, for example, beds are not provided for family members to stay with an adult family member who is ill. When Mexican Americans are interviewed by government agencies in most states, their request that a family member be present is often met with disapproval. The same is true when Mexican Americans visit a physician: the examination room is often blocked, and only the patient is allowed inside. The difficulties Mexican Americans encounter are often misconstrued by agencies as the problems of individuals without support systems. In leaving out the family and its influence, a great measure of support is discounted. The use of public services, therefore, may prove ineffective. If Euro-American institutions and services would pay more attention to the particular discourse of *la familia*, the social and economic advancement of Mexican Americans would be greatly enhanced.

Rationality/Emotionalism

Mexican Americans are brought up in *la familia* with a fantasy type that encourages the expression of emotion and rationality. This contrasts with the Euro-American background that usually emphasizes, in my opinion, the use of reason over emotion—à la Sherlock Holmes. One popular Euro-American vision subscribes to a scenario in which the hero displays aggressiveness, sexuality, and forcefulness with cool reasoning—à la Rambo.

For males, the themes that tend to prevail in the Mexican American fantasy type of rationality/emotionalism are those of courage, self-defense, honor, the defense of *la familia*, and the defense of women's honor. Other themes include the control of certain expressions of emotions (e.g., crying and fear) when these expressions may be seen as weakness by an opponent or interactant; and their display, for example, when celebrating with friends of the family. The social display of emotions such as romantic love, caring, and enthusiasm, however is more encouraged in the fantasy type of rationalism and emotionalism. Hence, Mexican American men may have no problem in defending their honor physically, yet see no contradiction in reciting poetry, giving serenades to their fiancées, writing ballads or short stories, raising their voice with emotion in social circumstances, and crying when among the family or among friends. In this scenar-

io, a typical villain is unemotional, detached, calculating, manipulating, two-faced, and a bit of a coward. In contrast, the hero is "*todo un hombre*" (a total man; i.e., expressive, intelligent, caring, tender, physically and psychologically strong, masculine, emotive, assertive, understanding, honest, forward, chivalrous romantic, pragmatic, respectful, and caring towards women and children).

The Mexican American rhetorical vision excludes any conflict between the simultaneous expression of emotion and the use of reason and logic. This apparent contradiction is resolved in a scenario of caring within which the heroes and heroines of *la familia* develop actions and discourse. (In fact, one way to distinguish a villain in Mexican American discourse is by his or her cool-headed, dispassionate yet sensual attitude, and by lack of love, caring, relating, or self-sacrificing behavior. When a person in this vision stops caring, reason and logic predominate; therefore, all sense of relationship ends. In this fantasy type, interactions acquire meaning through nonverbal expressions of emotion, e.g., gestures, maintaining an appropriate space in interactions, taking the time to relate, and paralanguage. Caring is one of those meanings expressed nonverbally. Consequently, when the nonverbal communication of this fantasy type is not allowed expression, emotion is subdued and turns to introversion. Under this circumstance, the only option left for the participant is to play the role of the villain. Logic without caring means severing relationships, negating people's inner worth and thus fostering individualism and human expediency.

Some of the puzzling behavior of Mexican American gangs could be better understood if these concepts were brought to bear on the analysis of their behavior. Particular attention should be given to the gangs' strong need for affiliation to a *la familia*-like network, as well as to the alienation they feel toward society, since Euro-American society does not understand that their idiosyncrasies stem from cultural differences.

The consciously enacted script that encourages the use of nonverbal communication enables Mexican Americans to be more perceptive, receptive, and understanding of the discourse of other rhetorical visions. But in turn, this same asset can leave them frustrated, disappointed, and mistrustful when their depth of insight is not appreciated or reciprocated by those visions.

The fantasy type of rationality/emotionalism can be better understood through an explanation of the facial gestures that a Mexican American is likely to use when talking and listening. At times the Euro-American culture emphasizes the use of permanent facial expressions for some discursive situations. Usually the upper lip is fixed, while the lower lip moves to produce sound, while the eyes remain detached. In the case of the Mexican American, especially for a close descendant of a first-generation immigrant, emotion can also be conveyed through the smile and through the eyes. The seriousness of a topic is usually expressed verbally, while relationship is often expressed through the seriousness of the face ("I do not care for you") or through a smile while talking ("you are okay"), or through the expression in the eyes. If the receiver of the communication is not conversant with the cultural discourse, he or she may choose not to pay attention, since the smile for some Euro-American groups is likely to mean that he or she is not serious and does not really mean what is being said. When the topic is serious and the nonverbal expression of a Mexican American is excited and friendly (e.g., a smiling mouth and/or eyes, a rapid rate of speech, a higher pitch of the voice, and a louder volume), the listener will react attentively. They will be neither bothered, bored, nor otherwise react adversely to the message and the speaker, if they are knowledgeable about the social discourse. The reverse will be true if the listener is not familiar with Mexican American rhetoric.

The Concept of Personhood

The fantasy type of personhood is summarized by the words *la persona* (the person). Understanding the meanings and elements that conform this structure allows us to gain deeper insights into the rhetoric of *la familia* for Mexican Americans. The themes that predominate in this fantasy type are that *la persona*, has a soul, or spirit, and is superior to lower animals and endowed with qualities an animal cannot possess. In addition, a person has life, dignity, and a heart which is considered sacred. Therefore, no one has a right to use other persons, play with them, or mistreat them. A person has the right to keep his or her thoughts private, to be one's own self; in the face of conflict, he or she has the right to neither show emotions nor expose the inner self in public—though amongst the family it would be acceptable to do so. In this fantasy type, "People's definitions of persons . . . did not . . . depend on being a biologically defined human being or on other physical characteristics, but on some other way of being in the image of God, such as having an inner nature of a certain kind" (Sewell, 1989, p. 91). Hence, people, or *personas*, must be treated with dignity, courtesy, and deference.

The importance given to the person does not mean that the holders of this vision are naive and easily deceived. Mexican Americans are very aware of the evil nature in human beings: people are "difficult to understand, egoistic, tricky, often covertly hostile, prone to offensive gossip, and competitive. . ." (Sewell, 1989, p. 92). Yet, because humans are persons, they deserve respect and humane treatment.

One of the themes that holds this fantasy type together is that of good upbringing or *educación*. In turn, this theme manifests itself through two other fantasy themes: courtesy and good manners. Examples of courtesy would be greeting people cordially or offering a chair to a guest. Good manners are expressed when conversation is deferred to those who are older, or when one takes time to talk with people. If people are to be treated with respect, rules on behavior are necessary. Hence, good manners or the rules of *educación* are in order. If *personas* have undesirable qualities, rules have to be developed to test these people and to keep them at arm's length until proven reliable. These approved behaviors minimize the opportunities for people to feel offended and disregarded. Once the person proves to be reliable, basic, culturally approved rules for good manners are maintained. But many of the restrictions on psychological closeness can be relaxed. An example would be the writing of thank you cards. Mexican American culture usually does not see the necessity for thank you cards among *la familia* or with friends (except where this custom has been adopted from Euro-American culture), but it deems them necessary with formal acquaintances.

Needless to say, this fantasy type clashes with contrasting types when Mexican Americans come in contact with cultures that do not share fantasy themes that support the discourse of personhood. For example, Mexican Americans may feel deeply offended by someone raising their voice to them in public or not greeting them. Many individuals of a Euro-American background do not have this rhetorical element in their discourse and hence are not always sensitive to what the Mexican American experiences. Clashes of rhetorical visions like the one just described only serve to increase the suspicions that Mexican Americans have toward Euro-Americans, because the Euro-Americans' behaviors closely resemble those of a villain. In this rhetorical vision, the villain is one who has no regard for the personhood fantasy type.

One of the main reasons why Mexican Americans may never fully integrate with Euro-American culture is because they do not see in the latter the elements of personhood. Above all, they do not find in the Euro-American rhetorical vision the more evolved valuation of human dignity inherent in the term *persona*. Hence, they prefer to remain apart because they do not believe that Euro-American culture has these superior values to offer them.

Respect for Hierarchy, Age, and Gender

Besides the need by people to be respected because they are *personas*, a fantasy type in the rhetoric of *la familia* dictates that they should be treated with deference because they have status in the family due to their age and their gender. Of these three themes, age is the most significant characteristic that supports the theme of status in the rhetoric of *la familia*. Hence, the grandparents and great-grandparents are given more deference because of their age and birth order. In the same way, parents throughout their lives should be respected and treated with special care by sons and daughters. Uncles and aunts are given respect according to their birth order, the oldest having the most authority and deference. For example, younger individuals never look directly into the eyes of those of higher status, particularly parents and grandparents, when being addressed, nor when they are being disciplined verbally. To do so would be challenging authority.

Contrary to the usual stereotype of Mexican American women, in the rhetorical vision of *la familia*, women are never considered weak, passive, or of lesser stature than any other family member. Although age is a more important criterion for respect than gender, women are important *because they are women*. They hold the family together by transmitting the values, assumptions, and beliefs of *la familia*, which enables it to remain a viable institution. Furthermore, women are vital to the sustenance of relationships and social networks, particularly when they have to establish one-parent households. This is not the case with the men. Once a Mexican American male marries, it is the new wife who takes charge of recreating the vision of *la familia*. One popular proverb verifies this essential truth: "*la mujer es el centro del hogar*" (a woman is the center player in the home).

To understand the Mexican American rhetorical vision of women, consider the following response of one such male when asked his view on women: "From the time we were kids, we were taught to respect girls and women, not to hit them, but to protect them from harm. We were taught to take care of them." The he added that taking care of women did not mean that they were inferior, but that they were special "and had to be respected and especially cared for." While Euro-American women may perceive this attitude as patronizing and chauvinistic, Mexican American women are better aware of two basic facets of their culture: (1) the rhetoric of Mexican American culture does not hold that women are inferior, and (2) the attitude of Mexican American men lies within the context of the fantasy type of respect and honor towards women.

The importance of women does not exclude the importance of men. In this rhetorical vision, *la familia* contains two sources of power, but only one leader—the father. In his absence, the head of household is the mother with the support of the male family members. The oldest son, especially if he is already in late adolescence or early adulthood, is delegated more responsibility. Every male role in this rhetorical vision must represent and act as a spokesperson for *la familia* in the society at large. Hence, any humiliation or disregard of the Mexican American male by Euro-Americans can be detrimental to the culture's participation in the mainstream. Both males and females would rather communicate with those who would encourage and understand them and their vision of *la familia*.

The Mexican American male has yet another role in *la familia*: preserving order and discipline, and giving direction to the family. Studies show that both Mexican American men and women share in the disciplining of the children. The men consult with the family regarding decisions and encourage their wives to do the same. The responsibility of the decision, however, is carried by the male.

In a rhetorical vision where the conception of personhood is vital to relationships, women cannot exist as non-persons. It follows, then, that daughters are highly regarded. The Mexican American vision equalizes the sexes, because it does not deny the nature and contribution that these two important *personas*, man and woman, provide to *la familia*.

Solidarity and the Sense of Community

While *la familia* is an almost self-sufficient unit in regards to relationships, it still has to interact with other institutions and groups of *familias*. Their rhetorical vision of *la familia* also carries over into the *barrio*, which includes the group of households around the home. The limits of the *barrio* may be decided by the individual in relation to one's home, or by the community. In the Hispanic tradition, *barrios* were usually limited to the Catholic parishes. This limitation no longer applies to the Mexican American experience in this country. Each *barrio* is a communal unit composed of groups of *familias*, which allows each *persona* in this vision to overcome their "resistance to intru-

sion" in order to fulfill social and practical goals. They can engage in discourse with those outside the *barrio* because (1) relationships are important and (2) knowing their neighbors enables them to keep some control over strangers' intrusions. The *barrio* is also a place where one can live by *la familia's* principle of solidarity, thus making urban survival that much easier. In contrast, mobility only tends to fragment the network of the *barrio*, as every new neighbor may not share the same rhetorical vision or may even reject it.

In the rhetorical vision of *la familia*, solidarity is one fantasy type that contributes greatly to family unity. A basic theme in this context is that of sacrifice. While love and caring are part and parcel of relationships, a member of *la familia* must also give up rights, interests, and desires for the family's welfare. If child members of *la familia* have been orphaned or their mothers can no longer support them, for example, relatives of *la familia* will take the children in and raise them in spite of the sacrifice involved. This kind of sacrifice means staying together through thick and thin and giving loyal support to the family member undergoing difficulties. This would explain the lower rate of divorce and family breakdown among Mexican American families (Schick, 1991, p. 38). The social sciences, influenced by the rhetorical vision of "the deficiency theory of minorities," does not consider the influence of solidarity and sense of community when examining the stability of the Mexican American family.

Conclusion

This essay has covered some salient points of the Mexican American rhetoric of *la familia* in order to better understand the discourse associated with the rhetorical visions of Mexican Americans. It has provided a theoretical framework by which to analyze Mexican American culture in a new light and offer an alternative to the typical misrepresentation made by Euro-American studies of Mexican American culture. The communication methodology of symbolic convergence was used to identify five main fantasy types: harmony/silence; rationality/emotionalism; the concept of personhood; respect for hierarchy, age, and gender differences; and solidarity and the sense of community. Some basic fantasy themes under each of the above categories were described so as to better explain the rhetorical vision.

When two rhetorical visions come into contact, the two visions either blend together or not. Corroboration is the term used in symbolic convergence theory to refer to the ability of one rhetorical vision to incorporate another (Gangotena, 1988). Visions that are empirical in nature tend to be sensitive to corroboration; that is, if a vision embraces "facts" or "observations" as the ultimate basis for argument or proof, it will tend to be more flexible and more easily altered by other themes and visions. Those visions which are insensitive to corroboration tend to be more rigid and more idealistic (Gangotena, 1980, pp. 217-218). While we could expect the Euro-American vision to be more sensitive to corroboration, as it is more pragmatic and logical in nature, and the Mexican American vision to be less sensitive because of its more idealistic view, in practice this is not the case. Euro-American culture is less sensitive to corroboration when influenced by the Mexican American rhetoric of *la familia*.

In the search for themes in the Euro-American rhetoric that render it less flexible, we find one possible fantasy type with two supporting themes. This fantasy type is based on the principle of homogeneity by which Euro-Americans will accept those who are "like them" and will disregard those who are Spanish and Catholic. This harks back to the so-called "Black Legend," when the leaders of Great Britain in the 1600s and 1700s (and the United States in the 1800s) found it convenient to spread legends about the evil nature of the Spanish and their descendants, and of the Catholic Church and its supporters, in their attempt to prevent Spain and other European powers from controlling the Americas. Although the rhetorical vision of *la familia* is alive and well in America, Euro-Americans do not identify it as a valuable source of support for Mexican Americans. The rhetorical vision of Euro-American society is not flexible enough to include either contrasting rhetorical visions or alternate themes and fantasy types. In contrast, Mexican Americans can incorporate elements of the Euro-American vision into their own rhetoric, because their rhetorical vision is more flexible and lends itself to corroboration.

The Mexican American rhetorical vision of *la familia* has long been under siege by Euro-American culture. When the vision of *la familia* comes in contact with Euro-American culture, it loses adherents from its own ranks. This disenfranchisement is caused by a clash of visions in which the adherents to the Mexican American rhetorical vision encounter others who have succumbed to the Euro-American script of a hero and his uncaring conception of relationships. Every time one of the fantasy types and themes of the rhetorical vision of *la familia* are lost, Mexican Americans are left without the integral system of discourse that helps them survive in an alien culture. Hence, they are easy prey to the most negative elements of the Euro-American vision. Gangs, violence, child abuse, substance abuse, and crime, as portrayed through the communication channels of the Euro-American vision (i.e., public schools, radio, television, and cinema), supplant the more beneficial fantasy types and themes of *la familia*.

As the Euro-American community becomes more aware of the rhetorical vision of *la familia* and comes to respect it, Mexican Americans will be granted a more distinguished place in American life. Regardless, the vision of *la familia* continues to be a form of discourse that provides Mexican Americans with identity, support, and comfort in an often hostile environment.

ENDNOTES

[1] This "call for the family" was verified by *U.S. News and World Report* of December 9, 1991. The report indicates that 93 percent of Americans interviewed by the Gallup Poll say that the family is very important. This contrasts with an 82 percent in 1981. The increase in 1991 was stronger among the 18-29 age group. The report also indicates that two thirds of voters believe the family to be the basic core unit of the society.

²An extensive discussion on this topic is provided in the following books: Buriel, R. (1984). "Integration with traditional Mexican American culture and socio-cultural adjustment." J. L. Martinéz and R. H. Mendoza (Eds.), *Chicano Psychology*. Orlando: Academic Press, Inc., 95-129. Mirandé, A. (1982). "The Chicano family: A reanalysis of conflicting views." Duran, L. I. and Bernard, H. R. (Eds.). *Introduction to chicano studies*. New York: Macmillan Publishing Co., Inc., 430-444; Mirandé, A. (1985). *The Chicano experience: An alternative perspective*. Notre Dame, IN: University of Notre Dame Press.

³I found the Mexican American narratives to be longer, more detailed, and more vivid than those of Euro-Americans. The discourse of Mexican Americans has more interplay of characters, plot, script, and drama.

REFERENCES

Bormann, E. G. (1972). "Fantasy and rhetorical vision: The criticism of social reality." *Quarterly Journal of Speech*, *58*, (4), 396-407.

Bormann, E. G. (1985). *The force of fantasy: Restoring the American dream*. Carbondale: Southern Illinois University Press.

Gangotena, M. (1989). "Curanderas and physicians: Con--trasting rhetorics of healing." Intercultural Communication Association Mid-Year Health Communication Conference. Monterey, CA.

Gangotena-González, M. (1980). Rhetorical visions of medicine compared and contrasted: Curanderismo and allopathic family practice as held by Mexican American and Anglo patients and practitioners. (Doctoral dissertation, University of Minnesota, 1980). *Dissertation Abstracts International*, *41*, 5A.

González, A. (1989). "Participation at WMEX-FM: Interventional rhetoric of Ohio Mexican Americans." *Western Journal of Speech Communications*, *53* (Fall 1989), 398-410.

González, A. (1990). "Mexican 'otherness' in the rhetoric of Mexican Americans." *The Southern Communication Journal*, *55*, 276-291.

Schick, F. L., & Schick, R. (1991). *Statistical handbook on U.S. hispanics*. Phoenix, AZ: The Oryx Press.

Sewell, D. (1989). *Knowing people: A Mexican-American community's concept of a person*. New York: AMS Press.

Smith, M. J. (1988). *Contemporary communication research methods*. Belmont, CA: Wadsworth Publishing Company.

Walsh, K. (1991, December 9). The retro campaign. *U.S. News and World Report*, *111*, (24), 32-34.

12

Oral Rhetorical Practice in African American Culture

Thurmon Garner
University of Georgia

In an effort to characterize black modes of communication, scholars generally have accepted the notion that African Americans have molded their language behavior in an oral mode. For example, Geneva Smitherman (1977, p. 77) observes that blacks, having come from an African, orally-oriented culture, have allowed a spoken mode to shape their language behavior. Kochman (1974, p. 96) explains that a black oral cultural style is characterized by "feeling, heat, and loudness, and the establishment of a mode of confrontation" which he calls "dynamic opposition." The focus of much of the resulting research literature on black communication revolves around identifying and exploring expressive uses of language. As a result, scholars have provided a better understanding of the uses and functions of black speech acts such as "boastin'," "braggin'," "playin' the dozens or soundin'," "signifyin'," "shuckin' and jivin'," and "rappin'."

In African American culture, as in other oral cultures, communication is direct and immediate. It is free of a medium. One has to act and react spontaneously, because there is instantaneous feedback. The oral person is emotionally involved in the acts of communication and "makes decisions, acts upon them, and communicates the results through an intuitive approach to a phenomenon"

(Sidran, p. 4). There is no distinction made between the "speaker" and the "audience." The communication that transpires between them is the "creation and sharing of one's personhood," so that one retains a personal humanism.

A culture's humanism is shared in the way that it presents and performs its forms of communication. This essay explores communication in African American culture in an attempt to describe the discourse skills which allow members of the culture to act respectfully toward each other. The emphasis here is not with those forms of language in oral cultures that are concerned with the "high rhetoric"—rituals, myths, or toasts that require a great degree of memorization—but with rhetorical patterns or modes that allow members of the African American community to act out their daily personal interactions. This essay seeks to provide a better understanding of African American communication as part of a broader oral communication tradition and system of understanding rather than as isolated speech acts.

What do people value in communication? What is appropriate communication? Is there a cultural logic that leads participants to interact effortlessly with each other? What must one know to become competent in a culture? What does one's inner voice, that cultural logic, tell one to do as different communicative situations arise? What are some of the hidden assumptions underlying communication interaction in African American culture?

In an attempt to provide insight into these questions, I begin this essay by exploring concepts that help one to prepare rhetorically in African American culture. Next, I explore traditional recognized speech acts in the African American community. Finally, I examine the relationship between rhetorical assumptions and speech acts.

Rhetorical Assumptions

Black cultural communication has been influenced by a rich oral tradition with ties to American slavery and African culture. The impact of both influences has been explored in other writings

(Abrahams, 1970; Kochman, 1981; Levine, 1972; Gee, 1985; Smitherman, 1977; Asante, 1988, 1990). We see that "Nommo, the magic power of the Word" is as strongly felt in African culture (Smitherman, Asanti) as is respect and value for the "man of words" in African American communities throughout the United States (Abrahams, Hannerz, 1969; and Kochman). The oral tradition continues to be part of the African American tradition because of the homogeneous nature of the black community and "because the structural underpinnings of the oral tradition remain basically intact even as each new generation makes verbal adaptations within the tradition. Indeed, the core strength of this tradition lies in its capacity to accommodate new situations and changing realities" (Smitherman, p. 73). In this section, three rhetorical assumptions—indirection, improvisation, and playfully toned behavior—are examined.

Indirection

To illustrate indirection, we begin by providing an example of the oral tradition. In the following example, the parent is not positive about exactly at what age his daughter started this speech act. She is now over 20 years old and still uses this particular communicative approach when she wants to make an important point, to explain an unusual behavior, or to extricate herself from a potential conflict. His daughter never, or at least almost never, gets to the point by going from A to B in a straight line. She meanders around the point through a series of asides or stories and comes to the point an eternity later. So when she wants something important to her, he is often subjected to expanded historical narratives which carry the message that she has not borrowed the car lately. For good measure, she throws in other explanations, analogies, metaphors, or extended illustrations to help make her point. Finally she gets to the point: she wants to borrow the car.

Let me get to the point. Indirection is essential to understanding African American oral discourse. Indirection is characterized by a speaker's use of innuendos, insinuations, inferences, implications,

and suggestions to make the point. The speaker can use circumlocution, avoiding the major point and only coming to it in a circular manner.

African Americans have retained, it appears, an essential circular quality of African discourse. Sidran (1971, p. 6) notes that, "In language the African tradition aims at circumlocution rather than at exact definition. The direct statement is considered crude and unimaginative; the veiling of all content in ever-changing paraphrases is considered the criterion of intelligence and personality." Researchers have noted the same phenomenon in African American culture. According to Kochman (p. 99), "blacks regard direct questions as confrontational, intrusive, and presumptuous."

For the African American community, the philosophy behind indirection suggests that everyday discourse should not be used to put one on the spot. Indirect message preparation has a latent advantage. Mitchell-Kernan (1973, p. 318) observes that, "Such messages because of their form—they contain explicit and implicit content—structure interpretation in such a way that the parties have the option of avoiding a real confrontation." Consequently, indirection is not a speech event in African American communities, but a strategy or tactic employed during the daily ritual of communicating. As a strategy, it is a rhetorical method and philosophy for attacking and handling communication behaviors. Therefore, as a concept, indirection implies something about how African Americans understand what is appropriate cultural conduct. When used in conjunction with speech acts such as rapping and signifying, the indirect message might not be a result of what is actually said, but of the meaning assigned to it by the hearer.

Normally, indirection has been treated as a function of the speech acts and not as a rhetorical strategy in oral discourse. Boasting, bragging, loud talking, rapping, signifying, and, to a degree, playing the dozens have elements of indirection. Mitchell-Kernan observes the following about indirection:

Meaning conveyed is not apparent meaning. Apparent meaning serves as a key which directs hearers to some shared knowledge, attitudes, and values or signals that reference must be produced metaphorically. The words spoken may actually refer to this shared knowledge by contradicting it or by giving what is known to be an impossible explanation of some obvious fact. The indirection, then, depends for its decoding upon shared knowledge of the participants. (p. 325)

Strategically, indirection is used to entertain and reduce conflict. The value of indirection lies in the ability of the speaker to be creative.

Improvisation and Inventiveness

It goes without saying that spontaneous daily communication interactions are unrehearsed. Orality and rhetorical preparedness require that speaker and audience devise, originate, compose, or invent without preparation when engaged in dialogue. The spontaneous non-analytic nature of an oral tradition demands such action. African American culture places a high value on inventiveness, spontaneity, and improvisation. Although writing about music, Sidran (1971) makes an important point about oral improvisation when he states, "The complexity of this rhythmic approach is in large part due to the value placed on spontaneity and the inherently communal nature of oral improvisation" (p. 7). "The oral man's inner world is a tangle of complex emotions and feelings that the Western practical man has long ago eroded and suppressed within himself in the interest of efficiency and practicality" (McLuhan, p. 59). Each moment is a unique experience, and "the celebration of the feeling of any given moment as a unique experience, rather than as a part of some elaborate syntactical structure, has made the black man flexible and helped him to improvise" (Sidran, p.18).

It is reasonable to assume that improvisation and inventiveness is a result of historical black and white struggles, particularly slavery and its aftermath. But subsequent language innovation became important as a means of influencing white behavior, either keeping certain messages away from whites or assigning meanings to words that were opposites, such as "hold tight" which in certain situations can mean "let go," "do not proceed," or "stop." "Improvisation is based on the ability to 'hear' with internal ears the sound of an internal voice. This reliance on 'internal hearing' is part of the more general approach of the oral orientation" (Sidran, p. 62). Invention is creating new ways of saying the same thing, while improvisation is taking a message and manipulating it in new directions.

Holt (1975) provides a suitable explanation of verbal inventiveness when she notes that, "Rote verbalizations are usually abandoned as 'juvenile' by practitioners who have progressed to the creation of metaphorical language when needed to control a situation" (p. 91). She goes on to say that, "Valuation of creation/invention invites involvement of the 'personhood' of all participants in a communication event. Performed reality is viewed as an entity of the speaker/listener which the performer manipulates. The communication created equals the person" (p. 91). She finds that, "The expert 'creator of personhood' is one who creates endlessly ethnotropic language, who uses his skills in novel, inventive ways. The more novel the creation, the more the listener/participant is skillfully challenged to accurate interpretation, to discover hidden meaning which calls forth his personhood" (p. 91). Finally she notes that, "Satisfaction of the cultural pressure for invention, implementation, and creativity accounts for the frequent use of forms which are semantically different and which serve the purpose of implementation even though phonetic form of constant, e.g., 'bad' to mean 'good', etc." (p. 93). Such inventive powers are a result of mastering the "metaphor," which has a high level of abstraction, its meaning never fixed.

Black communication through inventiveness and improvisation maintains the integrity of the individual's "personal" voice in the context of group activity. Black metaphoric language is a vehicle for individual expression, perfectly suited to improvisation and spontaneous composition. It stimulates and increases the importance of innovation or, at least, of individuation within a normally group-oriented society. This integration of the individual into the society at such a basic level of experience is the root of black group actionality. One effect of the oral mode of perception is that individuality, rather than be stifled by group activity or equated with specialization, actually flourishes in a group context. Thus, members of the oral culture are not differentiated by their specialist skills but by their unique emotional mixes. African American communication, then, is "an act to be performed on a stage of life; the creation and sharing of one's personhood with others of similar acculturation" (Holt, p. 90).

Playfully Toned Behavior

Ong (1982) notes that oral cultures are "antagonistic in their verbal performance and indeed in their lifestyle" (p. 44). He also observes that orality situates knowledge in a context of struggle. Riddles, proverbs, and stories are used to store knowledge as well as "to engage others in verbal and intellectual combat" (p. 44). At the same time, he claims that "violence in oral art forms is also connected with the structure of orality itself" (p. 44). Verbal communication by nature, direct word of mouth, dynamic give-and-take, and high interpersonal relation add to the antagonisms of daily life.

If Ong is correct, the antagonistic nature of orality is found in any culture which uses verbal behavior as its primary means of communicating in interpersonal relationships. Certainly African Americans engage in these daily verbal struggles, influenced by orality, in a more noticeable manner than white Americans. A distinctive difference between cultures might be in how each handles, practices, and controls the antagonistic nature of verbal communication. Abrahams (1976) appears correct when he concluded that "perhaps the clearest indication of the distinctiveness of the black speech community lies in the use of speech in the pursuit of public playing" (p. 37). Play, in African American communities, is a non-serious, sometimes non-threatening, verbal exchange. It is a symbolic exchange of selves, an entertainment of each by the other (Hannerz, 1969).

Abraham's discussion of play provides some insights about the way antagonistic practices might be understood in African American culture. Beginning with the idea that play is difficult to describe in any culture, he considers that play as practiced in African American cultures relies on distinguishing between it and the "real" or the "serious." For play as entertainment to operate successfully, he finds that "there must be a sense of threat arising from the 'real' and 'serious' world of behavior" (Abrahams, 1976, p. 40). That threat must be constant, and the constant message must be ambivalent. The message is carried out by the use of curses, boasts, and devices of vilification used in real arguments. These explanations provide critical commentary concerning the inability of other participants to determine if one is cursing in a playful or serious tone.

If we take football as an example, the importance of the role of play in African American society and the cultural position play assumes as real and serious can be better explained. For the sake of clarity, playing football will be divided into sandlots (spontaneous gatherings to play) and competitive football (organized play where prestige is on the line). Given that the rules and organization for both are the same, what distinguishes sandlot football from competitive football is the reason why both are played. Sandlot football is played for the entertainment of each team by the other. In this context, creativity and spontaneity are essential. It is football played, for the most part, out of joy for the game and to perform for an audience. It is performance-oriented, but at times, participants can act seriously about the game. Competitive football is organized, and the group's long-term respect is on the line. Each game is played seriously, and the group's action is focused on winning. It is not performance-oriented, nor is it considered entertainment for one by the other for the sake of individual pleasure; however, at times, players entertain each other with end-zone dances. Verbal play in the African American community is both performance- and entertainment-oriented like sandlot football. But it can, on occasion, be as serious play as is competitive football.

African American culture has found through verbal play a mechanism to reduce and restrict daily hostilities brought on by the antagonism and struggle inherent in oral communication. It is not enough to know that play exists as an important phenomenon in African American culture. Cultural understanding demands that you know when to use it. Understanding the importance of play as a strategy in public discourse allows a speaker to interact. Play in the African American community operates as a norm in the public environment. By public environment I mean what has commonly been called the street or secular world: street corners, barber shops, pool halls, garages, and such places other than church and home where people congregate to enjoy themselves. Play in African American communities functions in a recreational and performance sense. Verbal play is found in much of the good-natured banter in which African Americans engage. But when the unexpected happens and confrontation takes place, the use of playfulness can often quell emotionally charged conflicts that may bring the contestants to blows (Folb, p. 92).

The notion of verbal play or entertainment suggests that in African American culture the same speech acts or language behavior function expressively and instrumentally. An expressive or stylistic function is one in which communication is used to influence an audience by drawing attention to the character of the speaker. An instrumental or rhetorical function is one in which communication is used in the traditional sense of influencing or manipulating others. The decision as to which function to use is often a matter of personal assessment by the speaker of the relationship between play and seriousness. If a situation is considered serious or the potential for hostility is great, the speaker uses the instrumental function. In contrast, if the shared cultural knowledge is that participants are in play, then the expressive function is used.

Rhetorical Speech Acts

African Americans do speak differently from whites, thus establishing a separate speech community. As a community, blacks use different varieties of speech, share different rules for conduct and interpretation of speech, and assign special in-group names to manners of speaking. It is these shared names that "constitute one important dimension of their [African American] system of speaking" (Abrahams, 1976, p. 16). The following section explores the form and function of four of the many speech acts that are part of the African American community: playing the dozens, rapping, boasting, and signifying.

Playing the Dozens

While the name of this particular speech event might be called joaning, talking about your mama, capping, or playing the dozens, there is considerable agreement about the characteristics of the game. It is an aggressive verbal contest which makes use of obscene language. One talks about females in another's family, usually the mother, but the speech acts are not restricted to her. Males are less of a target for biting and caustic insults. There is a clean dozens and a dirty dozens. The clean dozens is often devoid of obscenity or sexual references, and the language is humorous rather than caustic. "Your mama is so short that she can crawl under a penny" is an example of the clean dozens. The dirty dozens makes use of derogatory and obscene language: "Your mama is so short that she can crawl under a penny and give Lincoln a blow job." The dozens can consist of one-liners or a long poetic discourse. Males between the ages of 7 and 20 play the game more than females. Fighting is considered taboo and the initiator of a fight is labeled a loser.

One function of the dozens is to act as "a valve for aggression in a depressed group" (Dollard, p. 20). Rather than African Americans directing their hostility toward whites who have neglected or oppressed them, blacks use the dozens as a mechanism of aggression toward themselves. The dozens also functions as "an exorcism which liberated black males from the dominant influence of strong mothers" (Abrahams, 1970, pp. 38-54). Young black males come to realize that they have identified with the mother rather than the father, and the dozens, through vilification of the mother, helps young boys become men. The game is also "a pedagogic device that instructs citizens in communication strategies for the resolution of conflict in routine daily interactions" (Garner, 1983, p. 48). Participants in the game learn self-control and how to measure the attitude of others. Unlike rapping, this game is an artificial and playful form of conflict and conflict resolution.

Rapping

Rapping, like signifying, is often laced with ambiguity. As a rhetorical form it is a personally stylized, lively, and fluent way of talking. It can be used as a means by which someone engages in ordinary conversation, as a romantic way of talking to a woman, or a means of devastating an opponent. Smitherman (1977) and Folb (1980) report on meaningful ways by which rapping can be used in ordinary conversation, where one provides information but not in a preachy manner. While the current use of the term is associated with the act of conversation, its most common uses in African American communities refer to interactions that are often more private. "That is," according to Abrahams (1976, p. 66), "rapping in its more pointed uses is something generally carried on in person-to-person exchanges, ones in which the participants don't know each other well." Smitherman (p. 69) notes that "in the white mainstream, rap is used to mean talk, usually serious, but in its indigenous black meaning, rap refers to romantic talk from a black man to a black woman for purposes of winning her emotional and sexual affection."

Rap's more traditional role in male-female interactions, is provided by Smitherman who writes, "The existence of love rappin' in the oral tradition allows a strange black man to approach a strange black woman without fear of strong reprisal. Black women are accustomed to—and many even expect—this kind of verbal aggressiveness from black men. Black culture thus provides a socially approved verbal mechanism with which the man can initiate conversation aimed at deepening the acquaintance" (p. 85).

Consequently, rapping can be a private or semiprivate activity. It is not performed in the presence of large audiences. The following is an example of a romantic rap, as Mitchell-Kernan (1973, p. 319) explains:

> The following interchange took place in a public park. Three young men in their early twenties sat down with the researcher, one of whom initiated a conversation in this way:
>
> I: Mama, you sho is fine.
> R: That ain no way to talk to your mother.
>   (laughter)
> I: You married?
> R: Um hm.
> I: Is your husband married?
>   (laughter)
> R: Very.
>
> (The conversation continues with the same young man doing most of the talking. He questions me about what I am doing and I tell him about my research project. After a couple of minutes of discussing "rapping," I returns to his original style.)
>
> I: Baby, you a real scholar. I can tell you want to learn. Now if you'll just cooperate a li'l bit, I'll show you what a good teacher I am. But first we got to get into my area of expertise.
> R: I may be wrong but seems to me we already in your area of expertise.
>   (laughter)
> I: You ain' so bad yourself, girl. I ain't heard you stutter yet. You a li'l fixated on your subject though. I want to help a sweet thang like you all I can. I figure all that book learning you got must mean you been neglecting other areas of your education.
> I: Talk that talk!
> R: Why don't you let me point out where I can best use your help.
> I: Are you sure you in the best position to know?
>   (laughter)
> I: I'mo leave you alone, girl. Ask me what you want to know. Tempus fugit, baby.
>   (laughter)

"Rapping, then, is used by the speaker at the beginning of a relationship to create a favorable impression and be persuasive at the same time" (Kochman, 1972, p. 243). The rapper expects to teach, educate, impress, get on one's case, or just play around (Folb, p. 91). Raps have a built-in safety device, because they are worded so that a male is able to say he was only kidding and can escape conflict or reprisal for an unintended insult.

Rapping as a speech event is usually associated with male behavior, although women have been known to be good rappers when they want to get on someone's case.

Boasting

Blacks and whites generally agree that boasting and bragging refer to "vocal self-praise or claims to superiority over others" (Kochman, 1981, p. 63). Boasting is characterized by intensive talk about oneself, a source of humor with obvious exaggerations about one's strengths or shortcomings, and is not intended to be taken seriously. Although one praises himself or claims superiority over others, the boaster does not have to emphasize positive traits. And one does not have to prove what was claimed. "Boasters can exercise the full range of their comic inventiveness" (Kochman, p. 64-65).

The themes in a boast can cover a variety of topics, such as physical strength, personal appearance, personal accomplishments, and economic well-being. "For the most part, a boaster builds his rhetorical image through the sheer power of words" (Garner, 1985, p. 232). A boaster normally associates himself with desirable status symbols found in clothing, cars, women he knows, sexual conquests, and demonstrations of knowledge. The following boasts were reported by Kochman (1981, p. 66). Black players (ladies' men) will say, "I got more women that Van Camp has pork and beans." Muhammad Ali boasts, "I can hit you before God gets the news." He notes that women also boast. A black female boasts, "I can look through muddy water and spy dry land. I can look through any bush and spy my man." The normal use of boast then is to build status for the speaker. One can build a reputation as having a way with words. Boasts are another form of play and entertainment in African American culture.

Boasts are sometimes used in tense situations to send messages so that conflict can be avoided. When situations turn tense and participants in interactions find themselves in potential conflict, the art of boasting is used instrumentally where a participant is intent on influencing the attitude of the listener. The structure of the boast might remain the same, but changing intonation, word emphasis, or facial expression can signal a change of attitude.

Signifying

Signifying is one of those terms where confusion exists over its use in the African American community. It is a form of language behavior, a method of provocation, goading, and taunting. Signification "refers to the verbal art of insult in which a speaker humorously puts down, talks about, needles—that is, signifies on—the listener" (Smitherman, 1977, p. 118). This act tends to be more subtle and circumlocutory that the other verbal activities. Signifying, according to Abrahams, is language behavior used to, "imply, goad, beg, boast by indirect verbal or gestural means" (1970, p. 267). It is at best a way of talking that carries an alternative message or, as Mitchell-Kernan (1972, p. 311) notes, "a way of encoding messages or meaning which involves, in most cases, an element of indirection." But Mitchell-Kernan also reports:

> Labeling a particular utterance 'signifying' involves the recognition and attribution of some implicit content or function. The obscurity may lie in the relative difficulty it poses for interpreting (1) the meaning or message the speaker is adjudged as intending to convey; (2) the addressee—the person or persons to whom the message is directed; (3) the goal orientation or intent of the speaker. A precondition for the application of the term signifying to some speech act is the assumption that the meaning decoded was consciously and purposely formulated at the encoding stage. (p. 314)

The significance or meaning of the words must be derived from known symbolic values. Signifying is characterized by the exploitation of unexpected and quick verbal surprises.

Signifying functions instrumentally to make a point. At times, it is used expressively for fun. When used expressively as entertainment, the participants who are being signified on are not supposed to get upset. It is ritualistic play that is accepted at face value. As a cultural mechanism, it can be used to talk about someone indirectly.

Because humor is used, "it makes the put-down easier to swallow and gives the recipient a socially acceptable way out" (Smitherman, 1977, p. 119). As a form of play, signifying can function instrumentally "to put somebody in check, that is, make them think about and, one hopes, correct their behavior." It can make a point or deliver a message without preaching or lecturing (pp. 120-21). The following example is provided by Mitchell-Kernan:

> The relevant background information lacking in this interchange is that the husband is a member of the class of individuals who do not wear suits to work.
>
> Wife: Where are you going?
> Husband: I'm going to work.
> Wife: (You're wearing) a suit, tie and white shirt? You didn't tell me you got a promotion. (1973, p. 317)

The wife is testing the truth of her husband's statement. She is signifying that he is lying, but she has done it indirectly. He is wearing a suit that he does not normally wear, received a promotion she knew nothing about, or he is telling the truth. The burden of proof is on him.

According to Smitherman (p. 121), signifying has the following characteristics: "indirection, circumlocution; metaphorical-imagistic (but images rooted in the everyday, real world); humorous, ironic; rhythmic fluency and sound; teachy but not preachy; directed at the person or persons usually present in the situational context (siggers do not talk behind yo back); punning, play on words; introduction of the semantically or logically unexpected." Confusion about signifying abounds, because some of these characteristics are found in other rhetorical speech acts such as playing the dozens, rapping, and boasting. Yet, to signify means to engage in rhetorical games.

Signifying can exhibit all or a combination of the characteristics above. As an example, Smitherman (1977) cites a passage from the novel *Hot Day, Hot Night* By Chester Himes, which later became the movie *Cotton Come to Harlem*. The main characters, Coffin Ed and Grave Digger, have been assigned by their white superior the task of finding out who started a riot in Harlem. The result:

"I take it you've discovered who started the riot," Anderson said.

"We knew who he was all along," Grave Digger said.

"It's just nothing we can do to him," Coffin Ed echoed.

"Why not, for God's sake?"

"He's dead," Coffin Ed said.

"Who?"

"Lincoln," Grave Digger said.

"He hadn't ought to have freed us if he didn't want to make provisions to feed us," Coffin Ed said. "Anyone could have told him that."

"All right, all right, lots of us have wondered what he might have thought of the consequences," Anderson admitted. "But it's too late to charge him now."

"Couldn't have convicted him anyway," Grave Digger said.

"All he'd have to do would be to plead good intentions," Coffin Ed elaborated. "Never was a white man convicted as long as he plead good intentions."

"All right, all right, who's the culprit this night, here, in Harlem? Who's inciting these people to this senseless anarchy?"

"Skin," Grave Digger said. (pp. 122-123)

Not only are Coffin and Digger signifying because they used the characteristics associated with the act, but they have described a situation and individuals in a telling manner.

As a term, the standard use of signifying signals a meaning it conveys or is intended to convey. In this sense of the word, to signify is to give the apparent or denotative meaning to a term or act. When African Americans signify, they are concerned with the playful puns on words, what is suspended or left out of words, and what language they might connote through shared knowledge. That is why Mitchell-Kernan noted that

> The black concept of signifying incorporates essentially a folk notion that dictionary entries for words are not always sufficient for interpreting meanings or messages, or that meaning goes beyond such interpretations. Complimentary remarks may be delivered in a left-handed fashion. A particular utterance may be an insult in one context and not another. What pretends to be informative

may intent to be persuasive. The hearer is thus constrained to attend to all potential meaning carrying symbolic systems in speech events—the total universe of discourse.

Signifying is a clever way of conveying a message, because it implies a meaning but never makes the message explicit. Signifying relies for its rhetorical impact on verbal indirection. The surface meaning carries the hidden or implied meaning. Consequently, signifying is an intended or deliberate attempt to say one thing and mean something else. It is a complex rhetorical activity in the adult speech act.

Rhetorical Practice

In African American culture, an understanding of the role of indirection, improvisation, and playfully toned verbal behavior is essential for communication interaction. In addition to this fact, one must know that different routines (speech acts) may employ the same front (rhetorical strategy). That is, playing the dozens, rapping, boasting, and signifying make use of indirection, improvisation, and verbal play. Knowing what to use at what moment depends on one's cultural knowledge of the significance of an act or behavior. There are no hard and fast rules. The purpose of this section is to explore the relationship between speech acts and the cultural knowledge that guides them. This is not an exhaustive examination, but one that demonstrates how cultural knowledge shapes interactions.

Indirection is a cultural assumption that has as its function the reduction of conflict. This assumption is based on the idea that it is important to address issues in a circuitous fashion rather than straightforward or head-on. While each speech event involves indirection at some level, the decision as to how much indirection is necessary is a result of a participant's understanding of a situation as play or serious. If the context is one of play, then speech acts are used expressively. Likewise if the context is serious, a speech event is used instrumentally. The major function of playing the dozens and boasting is an expressive one. While some ambiguity or hidden message exists, the audience is not asked to use its powers of interpretation. Each

event is done to entertain the group. The entertainment value of playing the dozens comes from dramatic attempts of participants to demonstrate their wittiness and verbal dexterity. Boasting entertains because it relies on humorous invectives and exaggerated claims to please the crowd. Both events rely more on indirection when used to function instrumentally. Boasts, for example, are used to send warnings when situations become tense. When used in this manner, the speaker either voices a situationally appropriate boast or changes the tone of the boast to send an intended message. The listener now has to interpret the message and the meaning behind it. The dozens makes use of indirection in a more subtle way. The game is an artificial form of interpersonal conflict, indirectly establishing itself as real conflict. It indirectly suggests ways to handle conflict by retaining one's emotional control and personal poise while under attack.

Rapping and signifying are speech acts that serve to deliberately influence ideas and behavior. The major function each serves is instrumental; the expressive function, although important, is secondary. Rapping entertains because of the lively way by which the message is delivered. One's personality and style are important attention-getters. Signifying is expressive because the speaker draws attention to himself or herself by framing the message in an ambiguous but stylized manner. As a source of entertainment, signifying can be used to present humorous messages about someone else. It is used to entertain, to display one's wit, and often to vilify. Yet signifying is an artistic, clever way of conveying messages and controlling the situation. Because it is a complex speech event, a speaker must be a skilled critical thinker.

Instrumentally rapping and signifying function to reduce tension in situations that are potentially confrontational. In situations where rapping is used by an African American male to meet a woman, the rapper implies or suggests a romantic involvement. The approach is indirect. The speaker's language is ambiguous and the listener must make an effort to interpret the message. The message is deliberately constructed to present multiple levels of meaning. Signifying is an indirect means of avoiding conflict in long-standing interpersonal relationships. It is a means of seeking information without placing the listener on the spot. In the example cited earlier, the wife did not directly ask her husband where he was going, but implied, suggested, and hinted that his wearing a suit to work was not his normal behavior. Therefore, he was lying. There was an implicit message in the wife's comment, but the real message was not made explicit. Signifying, because it is indirect, forces the listener to take additional steps. The husband had to interpret the wife's intent: was it an accusation of lying or genuine interest? But the wife, because of the ambiguity of her remarks, does not have to accept his interpretation that he was wrongly accused. She simply denies it (Mitchell-Kernan, 1973, p. 319), thus controlling or avoiding possible conflict.

Rapping, playing the dozens, boasting, and signifying are events that rely for their effectiveness on invention, creativity, and improvisation. Because community members constantly interact with each other, a speaker must voice ideas in a way the listener has not experienced. Playing the dozens must be done in a fresh way. New ways of saying the same thing must be accomplished. One has to "top" his opponent by improvising on a previous remark or by creating or inventing new put-downs. In boasting, a speaker, because he or she interacts with known others, must find new ways of exaggerating strengths and weaknesses. In rapping, a speaker does not want to be accused of "using the same old lines as everyone else." Inventiveness in approach and improvising, by building from previous statements, receive favorable responses. In signifying, the message is constructed with multiple meanings. Therefore, the nature of constructing remarks that signify compels one to be clever and inventive. An important aspect of signifying is that it is spontaneously constructed. Each event calls for constant invention and improvisation which involve participants by challenging them to make an accurate interpretation and to discover meanings which call forth their personhood.

Conclusion

Rhetorical understanding in any culture may mean that one understands some of the basic assumptions individuals have about the nature of orality. Oral discourse is the mechanism by which interactants work out their daily routines. At the same time, cultural preparation implies a recognition of the rhetorical tactics in daily use and the names of speech acts that signal a particular rhetorical strategy. In African American culture, learning to act rhetorically is a life-long process. How such practice develops, that is, how a culture goes about instructing members in rhetorical assumptions and rhetorical acts that lead to rhetorical understanding, will require continued exploration.

REFERENCES

Abrahams, R. D. (1970). *Deep down in the jungle: Negro narrative folklore from the streets of Philadelphia.* New York: Columbia University Press.

Abrahams, R. D. (1972). Joking: The training of the man of words. In T. Kochman (Ed.), *Rappin' and stylin' out: Communication in urban black America* (pp. 215-240). Urbana: University of Illinois Press.

Abrahams, R. D. (1976). *Talking black.* Rowely, Massachusetts: Newbury House.

Asante, M. K. (1988). *Afrocentricity.* Trenton, NJ: Africa World Press.

Asante, M. K. (1990). *Kemet, Afrocentricity, and knowledge.* Trenton, NJ: Africa World Press.

Dollard, J. (1939). The dozens: Dialectic of insult. *American Imago, 1,* 3-25.

Folb, E. A. (1980). *Runnin' down some lines: The language and culture of black teenagers.* Cambridge, MA: Harvard University Press.

Garner, T. (1983). Playing the dozens: Folklore as strategies for living. *The Quarterly Journal of Speech 69,* 47-57.

Garner, T. (1985). Instrumental interactions: Speech acts in daily life. *Central States Speech Journal, 36,* 227-238.

Gee, J. P. (1985). The narrativization of experience in the oral style. *Journal of Education, 167,* 9-35.

Hannerz, U. (1969). *Soulside: Inquires into ghetto culture and community.* New York: Columbia University Press.

Holt, G. (1975). Metaphor, black discourse style, and cultural reality. In R. L. Williams (Ed.), *Ebonics: The true language of black folks* (p. 89). St. Louis, MO: Robert L. Williams and Associates, Inc.

Kochman, T. (1974). Orality and literacy as factors of "black" and "white" communicative behavior. *International Journal of the Sociology of Language* 3.

Kochman, T. (1981). *Black and white styles in conflict*. Chicago: The University of Chicago Press.

Levine, L. W. (1977). *Black culture and black consciousness: Afro-American folk thought from slavery to freedom*. New York: Oxford University Press.

McLuhan, M. (1964). *Understanding Media*. New York: A. S. Barnes.

Mitchell-Kernan, C. (1973). Signifying as a form of verbal art. In A. Dundes (Ed.), *Mother with from the laughing barrel: Readings in the interpretation of Afro-American folklore* (pp. 310-328). Englewood Cliffs: Prentice-Hall.

Ong, W. J. (1982). *Orality and literacy: The technologizing of the word*. London: Methuen.

Sidran, B. (1971). *Black talk*. New York: Holt, Rinehart and Winston.

Smitherman, G. (1977). *Talkin and testifyin: The language of black America*. Boston: Houghton Mifflin.

13

When Mississippi Chinese Talk

Gwendolyn Gong
Texas A&M University

As an undergraduate at the University of Mississippi during the early 1970s, I can recall thinking about how I spoke and how I sounded to others. I remember boasting proudly to a classmate of mine from Illinois that a native Mississippian with a true Southern drawl could enter an elevator on the ground floor, push 5, say "Delta, Delta, Delta," and—lickety split—the doors would open on the fifth floor, long before even the second "D-el-l-ta" had been uttered.

While this anecdote makes an amusing conversation piece, it is not really true that most Mississippians with Southern accents speak slowly. In fact, when I consider my own siblings, all native Mississippians with genuine Southern twangs, I know that, if anything, Southern talk can be lightning fast and full of the colorful expressions and melodic rhythms of dialogue from a Faulkner novel. Given that my siblings—in truth, my entire immediate family—served as classic, prolific producers of Southern speech, I find it peculiar that, when I went to graduate school in Indiana, my Hoosier peers and professors saw me as some sort of enigma—an oddity. They would joke, "The picture's fine but adjust the sound." This same type of remark followed me to Texas, where indeed another version of English is spoken. "Adjust the sound." What did that mean? Hadn't these folks ever encountered a Mississippian before? The truth was that

they had. But I was different. I was a Mississippi Chinese.

Though my family heritage traces back to an ancestral village in Canton, China, I am a Chinese American, born and reared in the Mississippi Delta:

> In the northwest corner of the state of Mississippi lies a vast alluvial plain, formed from the rich black flood deposits of the Mississippi and Yazoo Rivers. Almost perfectly flat, rimmed by low bluffs to the east and south, the basin is called the Yazoo-Mississippi Delta. The Delta stretches over nearly the entire 185-mile distance from Memphis to Vicksburg, though it includes neither of those cities, and at its widest point extends sixty miles east of the Mississippi River. (Loewen, 1988, p. 1)

Since the late 1800s, this lush farming area has served as a homeland for approximately 1200 Cantonese Chinese from Southern China who have gradually assimilated into being Southerners of another ilk: Mississippi Chinese (MC). As a consequence, the MC represent a melding of primarily Confucian and Southern Genteel cultures, distinct yet powerfully complementary in terms of thought and action. For example, despite the apparent geographic and physical European-versus-Asian or Western-versus-Eastern contrasts, both cultures valorize the past, family, elders, traditions, secular rituals, land, business, hospitality, and propriety. And it is this mutuality of values, along with an unyielding emphasis on education, that has allowed the MC to adapt successfully in the Mississippi Delta, not only surviving but flourishing in a place lost in time, a place time has lost.

My family operated a general store in Boyle, a small, dusty town located on Main Street. This location—like most everything in the Delta—represented for us a strange and wonderful cross-cultural intersection. Our store sat in close proximity to the Post Office, City Hall, and the defunct Fire Station and Depot—landmarks that suggested the Caucasian milieu of the plantation South. Our business was also tightly sandwiched between two dirt and gravel alleys where most of the African Americans in town lived. Thus, my family and I were situated in the middle of a populace whose convictions, behaviors, and social and linguistic conventions epitomized Southern Genteelism. It is from this perspective that I now write about the communicative interactions of the MC with others and among themselves.

In my experience, one of the most interesting ways by which I have observed how Southern Genteelism and Confucianism reveal themselves is in the talk of the MC. A major rhetorical feature that typifies MC speech is deference, the courteous yielding to others, which may manifest itself in two forms: accommodation (i.e., making the non-MC speaker feel comfortable and welcome) and topic shifting (i.e., changing the subject of the conversation). Ironically, accommodation that may provide comfort for the non-MC listener may, on occasion, result in discomfort for the MC speaker; conversely, topic shifting oftentimes provides relief and control for the MC speaker but frustration for the non-MC listener. As an MC, I know that the discomfort and frustration which non-MC listeners may experience is very recognizable by MC listeners. As an in-group participant in this communicative act, I find myself keenly aware of the MC speaker's conversational shifts, which are designed to manage the conversation and my level of involvement in it, no matter how deftly and graciously these rhetorical strategies are executed. My recognition of the linguistic turns enables me to interact felicitously and reciprocate with my own conversational deference: accommodation. For non-MC speakers and listeners, understanding how deference operates among the MC helps to provide a more effective, informed exchange between these two groups.

Deference and Accommodation

Deference refers to the submission or acquiescence to the opinion, wishes, or judgment of another speaker. The courteous yielding of the floor results in an MC accommodating the topic designated by a speaker, whether or not it may be interesting, logical, tasteful, or pertinent. Part of the motivation of this act may be to seek approval, to demonstrate respect, to allow others to perceive that they are respected or even "superior" to the speaker, or simply to cooperate and not "make waves."

Most of the time, accommodating others' topics in conversations can be quite easy, mutually satisfying, and pleasant. I recall customers like Mr. Schaefer (the town sheriff, who insisted we call him "Uncle Charlie") and Preacher (an African American Southern Baptist lay minister), who would stop in the store at supper time to pick up groceries and chat with my father about the weather and fishing.

"How hot was it today, anyhow?" Uncle Charlie would ask Daddy, chomping on his King Edward cigar. "Summers are gittin' hotter every year, don't ya think?"

Daddy would reply, "It was a scorcher, all right. But I didn't see no monkeys dancin'. Now that's when I know it's really hot."

"Monkeys dancin'. Yep, that'd be mighty hot, hell yeah," the sheriff would agree.

Then Preacher would break in, "Good thing we wasn't on the lake in this heat, though. The water's probably so hot the fish ain't bitin'—they just put out a sign sayin' 'Out to lunch' or some such."

They would all laugh and lean on the counter top, while my mother or I totaled their bill, took their money, and sacked their groceries. The chit-chat would end at this point, everyone feeling as if an enjoyable conversation had taken place and that something significant had been said.

As I reconsider this snippet of talk, I realize now it was more than mindless chatter and mere politeness. These three men, all of different races, professions, ages, and socio-economic backgrounds, were interacting socially and linguistically. The Caucasian sheriff initiated the talk and the subject, and my MC father accommodated him, as did the African American minister. This exchange illustrates deference and accommodation in its purest form as both a Confucian and Southern Genteel phenomenon. The MC speaker, as well as the Southern non-MC preacher, courteously participated and played the linguistic game, partly out of respect for the sheriff, partly out of a code of social etiquette—convention or propriety—and partly out of their own genuine interest in the topic and their ability to communicate as equals in this informal rhetorical situation.

While this example of deference is one in which all participants—MC and non-MC alike—accommodated one another and felt "at home" with the conversation, this is not always the case. For MC, certain topics or types of discussion are simply inappropriate, in both an MC to MC as well as non-MC to MC context. Topics such as death (especially a violent one), terminal illness, and sex are seen as particularly personal and private. MC subscribe to the notion that living things, good fortune, and happiness should never be intermixed with the dead, bad luck, or inauspiciousness in either their conversations or their activities. Consequently, in my parents' home, my mother would never place a photograph of my deceased older brother, Dwight Arnold, among other family pictures of the living. In fact, until I was six years old, I never knew I even had another brother, for Arnold was never talked about.

My first memory of Arnold was when I noticed his name on a headstone at the cemetery the day our family went to "bow three times in silence" to pay honor and respect to our ancestors. Though his bronzed baby shoes and faded snapshots were treated with reverence, I later learned, these reminders of him were segregated from all other items that families typically display—reunion and wedding pictures, annual school photos, trophies, awards, baby books, and so on. Even in my siblings' and my own home, no picture of Arnold is displayed. I keep my photographs of him in a filing cabinet drawer, along with the portraits of my father's deceased parents. Moreover, I have never queried my parents about the brother I never knew. To accommodate myself about this topic would have caused them great pain and discomfort. Even writing about this now is troubling for me and would be unsettling for my family, were they to read these words. As this clearly illustrates, the MC valorize the family, the past, and secular rituals in very specific, often nonverbal ways.

That example shows how I, an MC speaker, could have engendered discomfort for other MC listeners, such as my parents, in order to satisfy my own need to know. Instead, I understood the delicate nature of death and the need to respect my elders, as well as family, ritual, and MC's tendency to accommodate others; thus, I refused to invoke the tragic subject of Arnold. There are other people and events I long to know more about: my father's involvement in World War II and the Korean War; the KKK's burning of our original family store in Merigold, Mississippi; and Principal Akins, who had a fist-fight with a prominent school board member in his attempts to ensure Chinese Americans would be allowed to attend the Boyle public school. Out of my sense of deference and accommodation, however, I have never asked my parents to explain these parts of our family past that surely must have shaped their lives over the years. For propriety's sake, I have refrained from mentioning anything from the past, especially if it was traumatic. Most MC hold that the "unlucky" past lies behind us, yet the past also represents auspicious events and times such as weddings, births, and family traditions. Consequently, most MC can learn from the auspicious past how to proceed with the present and the future.

Unfortunately, however, this sensitivity in regards to accommodating others may not always be contemplated or realized in conversations between MC and non-MC speakers. A number of years ago at the institution where I was teaching, I developed a friendship with a colleague. This woman was a master teacher who spoke with authority and often openly revealed to me her earnest but prejudicial concerns about me as a person. Occasionally, we would see each other in passing and chat:

"Hi, Gong. I went to a Thai restaurant on Sunday. I asked for some soy sauce, and the waiter looked at me like I was crazy. What was wrong with askin' for some soy sauce? The food was so bad—like bad Chinese food—that I covered it with everything. Why was the guy so mad at me?"

"Asking for soy sauce isn't a crime. I don't know why your waiter was upset," I replied sheepishly. I was not certain why she was broaching me on the topic of Thai food; I'm no expert on it, though I do enjoy that particular cuisine.

"We ought to have lunch. What's your schedule?" my colleague inquired.

delicate nature of death and the need to respect my elders, as well as family, ritual, and MC's tendency to accommodate others; thus, I refused to invoke the tragic subject of Arnold. There are other people and events I long to know more about: my father's involvement in World War II and the Korean War; the KKK's burning of our original family store in Merigold, Mississippi; and Principal Akins, who had a fist-fight with a prominent school board member in his attempts to ensure Chinese Americans would be allowed to attend the Boyle public school. Out of my sense of deference and accommodation, however, I have never asked my parents to explain these parts of our family past that surely must have shaped their lives over the years. For propriety's sake, I have refrained from mentioning anything from the past, especially if it was traumatic. Most MC hold that the "unlucky" past lies behind us, yet the past also represents auspicious events and times such as weddings, births, and family traditions. Consequently, most MC can learn from the auspicious past how to proceed with the present and the future.

Unfortunately, however, this sensitivity in regards to accommodating others may not always be contemplated or realized in conversations between MC and non-MC speakers. A number of years ago at the institution where I was teaching, I developed a friendship with a colleague. This woman was a master teacher who spoke with authority and often openly revealed to me her earnest but prejudicial concerns about me as a person. Occasionally, we would see each other in passing and chat:

"Hi, Gong. I went to a Thai restaurant on Sunday. I asked for some soy sauce, and the waiter looked at me like I was crazy. What was wrong with askin' for some soy sauce? The food was so bad—like bad Chinese food—that I covered it with everything. Why was the guy so mad at me?"

"Asking for soy sauce isn't a crime. I don't know why your waiter was upset," I replied sheepishly. I was not certain why she was broaching me on the topic of Thai food; I'm no expert on it, though I do enjoy that particular cuisine.

"We ought to have lunch. What's your schedule?" my colleague inquired.

"I've already eaten. Plus, I've got so much work to finish in my office today. Sorry that I can't join you while you eat." I was uncomfortable, yet truthful.

"What'd ya eat? Betcha had egg rolls, eh? Gong, you're always eatin' egg rolls—at least you used to. Remember when you first came here years ago? I couldn't believe it—a Chinese, teaching English—with a Southern accent, too. I used to share an office with a fellow named Joe, who'd eat tacos and avocados all the time, and then I'd see you across the hall, eatin' egg rolls. Right, Gong? Don't ya remember?"

"Well, no, I really don't remember, but I suppose it's true," I replied, trying to go along with my colleague. "I do recall Joe and I ate take-out food sometimes. It was a quick way to have lunch," I added, my voice trailing off, diminishing with every syllable. I wished I was anywhere else but here, "talking" with this person. It was embarrassing enough that she made these kinds of remarks to me at all, much less within earshot of other faculty and students. Where could I hide? I thought to myself: "Hang in there; it'll be over soon."

This is only one conversation among many that this professor and I have shared. Out of my deep belief that she did care about me and out of my respect for her professional accomplishments, I always accommodated this individual's topic selection and conversational moves. I self-consciously defended her, rationalizing that she was just "tone-deaf" and didn't understand her audience very well. She admitted that she never knew an American-born Asian like me before. As a result, I reasoned to myself that I should give her a break, help her avoid "losing face," and prevent her from feeling awkward. Despite my desperate efforts to excuse her inappropriate comments, I always experienced regret that I voluntarily subjected myself to being bullied, demeaned, and belittled by someone espousing true friendship. Yet I can still hear her explanation regarding her response to me as a colleague: "I've never known a 'foreigner' who wasn't a foreigner, like you are." She offered this remark with great bravado.

In these types of conversations, the non-MC speaker initiates talk and the MC allows it to subjects beyond "self"; that is, when her attacks are personal, I try to ignore or avoid interacting with her. But when they are directed toward others or issues, I am compelled to respond. This is certainly true when she once asserted, for example, that there is no difference between the KKK and the NAACP. If we in society can see the NAACP as respectable, she adamantly asserted, then we should do likewise for the KKK. After all, "they're both merely special interest groups." I wondered, how can she broach such matters with me? Should I be honored that she looks at me, hears my Southern drawl, and then "accepts" me as just a salt-of-the-earth country woman? Or should I be absolutely offended that she fails to realize that I am a person of color whose family has experienced firsthand the ways that groups like the KKK mete out their own particular brand of "special interest?" At times like this, I cannot be silent and passive. Deference and accommodation serve no purpose in these instances. As I illustrated earlier, I believe that I can hear this person's verbal jabs directed at me, and I can weather and survive them by staying above the fray. This is an opportune time to present another conversational strategy that enables MC speakers to participate conversationally with greater ease and comfort: deference and topic shifting.

Deference and Topic Shifting

Ironically, accommodations that may at times provide a sense of deferential comfort for the non-MC speaker may instead result in estrangement and embarrassment for the MC speaker. Accordingly, MC often use a second strategy: topic shifting. This is a linguistic strategy which turns the tables, oftentimes providing relief and empowerment for the MC speaker and confusion and frustration for the non-MC listener. To understand this type of conversational move requires that we explore when and why topic shifting may occur, as well as consider which topics MC speakers may commonly switch to.

Topic shifting happens most frequently when an MC speaker is the subject of discussion, whether being complimented or spoken of in any positive way, but does not want to respond to the issue. For example, this scenario:

"Good morning, Annie," says Mrs. Alexander warmly, dressed in a floral-patterned knit dress.

"Hello," replies my mother, Annie Gong, busy hauling two massive platters of food into Fellowship Hall. Annie and Mrs. Alexander are both in their early 60s, attending a Sunday potluck lunch at the Boyle Baptist Church.

"I made deviled eggs, my specialty. They go like hot cakes ever' time I make 'em. You make sure you sample one." Scooting over a crystal bowl containing a mustard potato salad, Mrs. Alexander positions her egg plate smack dab in the center of the long table dedicated to salads. "Whatcha got there? I surely do hope it's Chinese food. You make the best Chinese food, Annie."

"I love deviled eggs," my mother says to shift the topic, as she concentrates on removing tin foil from her cashew chicken and sweet and sour pork. She continues to talk, never looking up. "How do you make your filling so tasty?" Garnishing her dish, she persists in her egg-talk: "Some folks just put Miracle Whip or mayonnaise in their filling; some like Underwood deviled ham mixed in with their mashed yolks. What do you think, Mrs. Alexander? I trust what you do."

Mrs. Alexander, however, prefers to talk about Annie's food. "How do you do it? How did you learn to cook like this, Annie? Now, that's sweet and sour, isn't it? And what's that other dish with the nuts? Can it be chicken almond ding? No, well. Last year, you brought fried rice, too. There wasn't a grain left inside of ten minutes when the line started moving. Wish you'd give lessons on Chinese cookin'. Everybody at the church would be your student in nothin' flat. Mark my words."

But Annie just coyly smiles and begins her egg talk once more. "Your eggs, do you boil them all at once? Put sweet or dill pickles or relish in them? And what about white or black pepper, because that's something I've never understood about makin' that." Annie stuffs her tin foil back into her bag and looks Mrs. Alexander in the eye.

"I'm fixin' to go back to the car to get the chow mein. Before I do, though, you tell me about your recipe, okay?"

At this juncture, Mrs. Alexander commences telling Annie her deviled egg recipe. "Well, you know, I always go out and buy the freshest dozen of eggs I can find. I put all my eggs in one pot at room temperature. Never try to boil an egg straight out of the ice box."

Relieved by this egg talk, Annie listens intently, nodding her head as each ingredient and instruction is described. "I never had anybody teach me about cookin' in the formal way," she then says. "I just learn from good cooks like yourself and by doin'—makin' mistakes." With that, the small MC woman saunters out of Fellowship Hall to fetch her noodles, breathing a sigh of relief that she avoided having to talk about herself or her cooking without being perceived as rude by not accommodating Mrs. Alexander.

As is evident, Annie diverts attention and conversation away from "self," a subject that she is uncomfortable with, despite the fact that Mrs. Alexander's topic selection would allow this MC speaker a chance to showcase her personal accomplishments as a cook. Annie can't take a compliment, a common phenomenon among most MC. Rather than demonstrate her deference to Mrs. Alexander by accommodating her topic selection, Annie is deferential—polite and respectful—through her topic shifting to highlight the culinary skill of the other speaker. To cap it off, she is even a bit self-effacing at the end of the exchange, thus countering the compliment. This topic shifting, consequently, is a move to accomplish modesty. That is, by persistently re-introducing her egg-talk, she eventually leads Mrs. Alexander to talk about *her*self and *her* dishes, two topics in which most any Southern Genteel woman excels. Hardly any other region of the U.S. compares to authentic Southern cooking and the talk that goes with it.

While Annie didn't choose to talk about the entree that she prepared, she does engage in talking about food. This is a topic to which most MC shift routinely, especially with in-group speakers or non-MC they regard as close friends. To share food talk with an MC is, by and large, a sign of trust and acceptance. In my own MC family, food-talk epitomizes being Chinese. Be it good or bad fortune, the event can be ritualized with sumptuous, bountiful amounts of food. The more impressive or auspicious the occasion, the longer the menu. Rituals require ceremony, and ceremony always entails food. For example, weddings call for nine-course dinners; births—"red egg and ginger" banquets and a vat of *gai djil gahng*, a chicken-whiskey soup often referred to as "mother's brew"; birthdays—chicken, noodles, and a cake with some shade of Chinese red in or on it. (Chocolate cakes and frostings are perceived by many superstitious MC as inappropriate for happy celebrations.) Red is a good-luck color and a standard for every celebration; in fact, brides often don bright red, silk *cheung sahms* (a type of Chinese dress) to their wedding receptions and banquets.

While food-talk is not the focus of this essay, it is such an unquestionably important subject to all Chinese that it deserves further mention here. After all, one conventional way to greet someone in Chinese is "Nay heck fan?" (Have you eaten your rice?) The MC maintain this traditional valorization of food and the Confucian notion of dining rather than eating. As I was once admonished by my sister, "When planning any MC event, always remember that, if everything else is a disaster but there are lots of good, exotic dishes, then you're okay. Everyone will leave bragging about what a great time they had because all they'll remember and tell others about is the food."

Here is another example of topic shifting: Every week I phone my parents in Mississippi. Inevitably, I always spend the majority of the call reviewing the MC current affairs with my mom. She and I cover the general topics—health, work, and family—rather swiftly. Then, without any linguistic cue at all, Mama commences with the food talk:

"Grilled chicken, that's what we ordered. Daddy and I went to our exercise class at the Mall this morning and ate at the Food Court. I like that. It was grilled, yes, not pan-fried with no liquid smoke," Mama speculates. She carried on this dramatic monologue of sorts: "Daddy didn't like it 'cause of the mayonnaise; he likes his sandwiches dry." Reminded of my sister-in-law's poultry, Mama then reminisces: "On Monday, Josie barbecued chicken. It was real good—she left the skin on."

I hear my daddy's voice in the background. "The girls didn't have tennis or basketball—they're all playing sports now, you know—so we all went over there and watched football," he says, alluding to my brother Stephen's big-screen TV and the Monday night NFL game.

Without skipping a beat, my mother returns to revealing the supper guests and their contributions to the buffet. "And Annette made homemade rolls and a broccoli-rice casserole—too rich, but Daddy likes it. Ginger and Eddie ate there, too; think Ginger had a tin of brownies, still warm from the oven. And that Lynette. She made a batch of cookies, and I sampled one—everybody fussed at me, said 'Mama, better watch your diabetes.' Juanita just phoned and told Josie she and her family had already eaten, but she'd come on over later, if she had time. She had laundry and house cleaning to do. Just like a family reunion."

Throughout this part of the phone call, I never get a word in edgewise—nothing but an intermittent "a-huh," barely audible amidst Mama's recollection of the communal meal (i.e., an important interpersonal function that unites everyone, strengthens family ties, and provides a sense of "village" life from Canton) at sister-in-law Josie's. From her food-talk, I intuit that everyone there is fine. My siblings and their spouses are well; the grandchildren are doing well in school; Daddy's blood pressure and cholesterol are reasonably low, but Mama's sugar is high. Among MC speakers who know each other well, food-talk can be as natural, effortless, and meaningful for MC speakers as alternating between English and Cantonese in a single conversation. One MC's divulgence of the context, people, and events, along with a cataloguing of the edibles, can provide information for another MC—data that could only be otherwise fathomed by folks who were present at the family gather. This food-talk demonstrates our common bond as individuals in family and culture; it serves as a vehicle to express our love and respect for one another as members of a single, cohesive community whose "separateness" is merely geographic. A seasoned food-talker myself, I usually sense there is more to the story than the abbreviated menu suggests. I ruminate on my suspicion, wondering what Mama isn't telling me in what she is saying.

There is a pregnant pause on the other end of the line, and I chime in, "What was the reason you all decided to eat at Stephen and Josie's, Mama? Didn't you all do turkey and dressing for Stephen's birthday the day before? Goodness, what'd y'all do with all the leftovers, anyway?"

"Oh, C.W. had a stroke, and Audrey drove him to town to see a specialist." C.W. is Mama's nephew, Audrey his wife. "They were supposed to stop by Stephen's to see all of us and have a bite before the drive back, but all they did was call. They have a daughter in town here now, see." There's another lull in the conversation. "We warmed 'em up. Flavor's the best the next day when the turkey and dressin' have set awhile," Mama then says. "We don't waste leftovers here."

I understand now, having discovered the missing link: Mama had arranged the family's Monday night communal potluck at my brother's house because relatives were in town; they had expected C.W. and Audrey to drop by and visit. But the couple never showed up. Never mind that their expectations were never fulfilled. They still enjoyed their own informal reunion, an interpretation that my mother construed. And even more important was this ultimate reality: They had lots of delectable home cooking. Given a satisfying meal, a body can strive to overlook the out-of-town guests who never came to dinner—and C.W. was, after all, sick. The graciousness with which Mama handles this situation is both very Confucian and Southern. But one should never be deceived by the surface politeness: C.W. and Audrey's minor transgression will not be soon forgotten. And you can bet your last shiny penny that I'll hear about this matter next week, when Mama shifts into food-talk. Her message will be loud and clear.

Food-talk is but one topic that MC speakers are predisposed to shift toward. It is a rather clever, witty, and powerful topic, though, for it enables speakers to shift to or intermingle with additional topics. These topics tend to be in narrative form, stories of self-disclosure about the MC's family, cultural, or historical past and traditions. Some of the narratives are "stock" or "ritualized" tales, repeated in public again and again; others are akin to "sacred texts," seldom uttered under any circumstances. The more "ritualized" the narrative, the less trustworthy or familiar the MC speaker may feel toward the other speech participants. Conversely, the more "sacred" the text, the more the MC speaker may identify with and have regard for the other speakers in the communicative act. To break out of the safe, ritualized narratives in topic shifting means risking greater self-disclosure and thus greater vulnerability. Perhaps my best example of the trust and deference involved in topic shifting is apparent when examining the narratives that I have chosen for use in this essay. I really don't know you, my readers. Yet, I am convinced that you will be as interested in MC talk as I am, as I have topic shifted to some very "sacred" subjects: my family, its cultural and historical past, and its rituals. The conversations reconstructed here are the embodiment of one of the most precious revelations of all: the way we MC talk to ourselves and to others.

Lotuses in the Land of the Magnolias

When I was in high school, I remember Mama, brother Stephen, and myself driving an old aunt from Canton to visit my cousins in Duncan, a neighboring town some 35 miles north of Boyle. It was fall, the weather was cold and wet, and the expanse of rice and cotton fields were flooded, reflecting an eerie mirror image of the full moon on the black water. The ribbon of road we drove along was surrounded on either side by encroaching rain water. We were all concentrating on the road, silent; my brother drove fast, nonetheless. Then the silence was broken by our elder's deep voice, difficult to decipher because she really spoke no English. She muttered softly. Mama translated: "This looks like Canton." The old aunt scanned the landscape, waving her hand toward the window as if to bless the land itself. We heard her utter more sounds. "No wonder you live here; it's just like home," relayed Mama, fixing her own eyes on the blackness. My mother broke the silence once more: "Home." With this, she peered out her fogged window and reached over to grasp the old woman's hand. Three generations of our family drove the narrow Delta road that night—Chinese with cultural and linguistic roots in two Southern regions: Canton and the Mississippi Delta.

*   *   *

To explain and exemplify deference as it manifests itself in accommodation and topic shifting during MC talk, I have offered here a very small sample of the linguistic interaction of Chinese Americans from the Mississippi Delta as I know it; the milieu that I depict is from my own perspective, as seen through my own eyes. Furthermore, the conversational strategies that I have selected represent linguistic phenomena drawn from my own experiences as an MC speaker.

As mentioned in the introduction, I have always been sensitive to voices—mine and others'. I have always been conscious of how I and other MC were distinct yet complementary in the way we sounded and expressed ideas. My hope is that understanding deference and the ways by which it can be expressed through specific rhetorical strategies will provide keys to greater appreciation for the culturally distinct communicative acts of the Mississippi Chinese lotuses living in the land of the magnolias.

REFERENCES

Loewen, J. W. (1988). *The Mississippi Chinese: Between black and white* (2nd ed.). Prospect Heights, IL: Waveland Press.

14

Understanding Traditional African American Preaching

Janice D. Hamlet
Shippensburg University

Growing up in the South, I fondly remember Sunday morning worship services. The service would begin when the pastor stood and read the scripture, "This is the day which the Lord hath made; we will rejoice and be glad in it" (Psalms 118: 24). Then he would say, "Let us stand to receive the choir." And the choir would come down the aisle, swaying from side to side, in step with the music from the organ. Sometimes there would be drums and tambourines. The voices were melodious and filled with excitement and praise. Some members of the congregation would clap their hands in time with the music while others would wave their hands over their heads. Once the choir reached the choir stand, the singing would drop to a whisper while the pastor prayed. Afterwards, the choir and congregation would sing the morning hymn. Sunday morning worship was now in progress.

When finally the last song had been sung, announcements read, testimonies given, tithes and offerings taken up, the pastor would approach the pulpit where his great Bible awaited him and a spirit-filled aura was about him as if there was no doubt in his mind that God had placed him there. A hush would fall over the congregation as the preacher "took" his text. What followed was a strong sermon, which was never less than an hour, punctuated by a great deal of animation and "talk-back" from worshippers.

Even as I visited other Holiness and Baptist churches, I came to accept without question that African American worship services existed to worship and glorify God by achieving a mass catharsis which offered an escape from the harshness of reality and left worshippers drained in spiritual ecstasy. It was an experience I took for granted. It was not until I became an adult and began to visit churches outside of my culture that I began to realize that there is something distinct about African American worship, especially in its preaching. The purpose of this essay is to explain this distinction.

Roots of the Traditional African American Preaching Style

In her work on black language, Geneva Smitherman (p. 90) notes that to speak of the traditional black church is to speak of the holy-rolling, bench-walking, spirit-getting, tongue-speaking, vision-receiving, intuition-directing, Amen-saying, sing-song preaching, holy-dancing, and God-sending church. This church may be defined as one in which the cognitive content has been borrowed from Western Judeo-Christian tradition, but the communication of that content has remained essentially African, deriving from the traditional African world view. This view assumes a fundamental unity between spiritual and material aspects of existence. Though both are necessary, the spiritual domain assumes priority (Smitherman, p. 90).

There are no irreligious people in traditional African society, for to be without religion amounts to a self-excommunication from society. The heart of traditional African religions is the emotional experience of being filled with the power of the spiritual. In the traditional African American church and culture, this aspect of the traditional African religion continues to exist (Smitherman, p. 91). African Americans believe that soul, feeling, emotions, and spirit serve as guidelines to understanding life and others. All people are moved by spirit forces, and there is no attempt to deny or intellectualize this fact (Smitherman, p. 92). This convergence of Judeo-Christian content and African delivery is found in Protestant denominations, such as Baptist, Methodist, and Holiness where the worship patterns are characterized by a spontaneous preacher-congregation relationship, intense emotional singing, spirit possession, and extemporaneous testimonials to the power of the Holy Spirit (Smitherman, p. 90).

The African American Preaching Style

It is often difficult for an outsider to understand what is going on in a traditional African American worship service. However, one cannot approach this experience as an outsider intending to simply take notes on how African Americans behave in church. One must come as a participant, willing to be transformed by the presence of "the spirit." African American congregations have claimed the promise that "where two or three are gathered together in (God's) name, there (is God) in the midst of them" (Matthew 18:20). It is this belief that creates the distinctive style of the traditional African American worship service.

Because African Americans believe that no worship service can exist without the presence of "the spirit," the preacher is seen primarily as a prophet who speaks "God's message" to them. For this reason, African American preachers are known to take their time. While they are preaching, there is nothing more important than the sermon they are delivering at that moment. As a result, the length of church services is unpredictable. On one Sunday the service may last an hour; on another Sunday, as long as three hours. This unpredictability may be irritating to an outsider, but African Americans believe that "you can't hurry God"; therefore, it is an acceptable characteristic of the traditional African American worship experience.

It is important also to note that African American preachers typically preach extemporaneously from an outline, while their white colleagues often prepare complete manuscripts delivered in lecture style. African Americans believe that an extemporaneous sermon is more spiritual.

Finally, it should be noted that African American preachers are diverse in their preaching styles. For example, some African American preachers are fluent in African-based black English dialect, delivered with force and oratorical rhythm. Some are more bourgeois in their language style yet equally skilled in voice techniques. Others are skilled in forceful, animated delivery. They work themselves into an emotional frenzy and stir their audiences profoundly.

Despite this diversity, the African American preaching style includes the following commonalities: black idiom, storytelling, poetic diction and rhythm, and call-response. Each of these components will be discussed from a cultural perspective.

Black Idiom

Effective African American preaching requires the use of black idiom or language. Black idiom or language is simply the rich rendition of English spoken in the black community (Mitchell, 1970, p. 149-178). The oratory of Dr. Martin Luther King, Jr. provides an excellent example of the effective use of black idiom. It is a powerful medium used to influence, inspire and often mobilize the masses. It is important for the preacher to use because it serves to assure the congregation that there is no social distance between members. It establishes rapport and achieves the desired effect. The congregation is not usually conscious that the preacher has deliberately chosen this language to manipulate for the common good.

In his work on African American preachers, Charles Hamilton (p. 28) wrote that during the 1960s, civil rights activists had been arguing about segregation and integration long before Martin Luther King arrived on the scene. They would go into Mississippi and Alabama and tell people that they needed to get organized. But their messages didn't stick. However, when King talked about "leaving the slavery of Egypt and wandering in the wilderness of separate and equal and moving into the Promised Land," somehow that made sense to people. It was that vernacular that mobilized people to act. African American preachers use the scriptures for the interpretation of their audience's experiences. In so doing, the sermons are constructed with language from the people's culture.

Storytelling

Although African Americans believe that academic degrees in theology, philosophy, and so forth are commendable credentials for their preachers, the dominant criterion in accepting a pastor in the African American church has been "Can he or she preach?" This simply means "can he or she tell the story?" Hermeneutics is an essential tool for telling the story. As it relates to religion, hermeneutics may be defined as the process through which the bible is read, examined, interpreted, understood, translated, and proclaimed (Stewart, p. 30).

In the following excerpt from the sermon "Recipe for Racial Greatness," African American preacher Dr. Manuel Scott paraphrases the story told in Joshua 17:14-15. Through application of the hermeneutical process, the story of the children of Israel is told. The preacher argues that African Americans should use the Israelites' lifestyle as a role model.

> They (Israelites) would not permit four hundred years of bondage, biological distinctiveness, material meagerness, educational retardation, and exaggerations by their enemies to strip them of a sense of worth and dignity. Without apology or ambiguity, they affirmed to Joshua: "We are a great people." This was another way of saying that they liked themselves without being ashamed. They were not inclined to mimic, mindlessly, other people. They had a sense of being somebody. They comprehended in themselves usefulness and a capacity to meet meaningful needs. They included in their self-image the idea of equality with the rest of mankind. They were not cringing and crawling and bowing and blushing before anyone. (Scott, p. 93)

In another sermon, dramatizing the biblical story of Jesus feeding 5,000 with the limited resources of a child's lunch, one African American preacher interrupted the story with a personal testimony. He said that he was a school dropout. God called him to preach, and he said, "Lord I haven't completed my education and I am not properly trained, but God told me:

> Give me your lunch!
> Give me your life!
> Give me your heart!
> Give me your all.
> And you sit down and wait.
> And whatever you need,
> I will give it to you.
> You just give me what you have.
> (Moyd, p. 59)

The preacher took the bare facts of God's story and wove them into the structure of the audience's own lives.

Poetic Diction and Rhythm

African American preachers have always understood that poetry is the language of emotion and imagination, and their sermons have appealed to both of these as well as to reason. Poetic diction uses symbolic and presentative words and sets up a musical structure of alliterative expression. In utilizing poetic diction, sentences are short, crisp, and clear. Verbs are filled with energy. Sentences build to a climax.

An equally significant feature of this preaching style is rhythm. The voice is considered the preacher's trumpet for proclaiming the gospel. It can challenge, convince, comfort, and charm. An example of the use of poetic diction and rhythm is illustrated by the following excerpt from a sermon preached by the Reverend Adam Clayton Powell, Jr., who, during his ministry, preached to the largest Protestant congregation in the world.

> It's not the color of your skin, brother, it's what you have in your heart and in your mind that makes you a man or a woman. Remember that. And if you will stand together there's nobody in this world than can stop a united mass of people moving as one. . .
>
> Standing together
> Working together
> Picketing together

Loving together
Worshipping together
You'll win together
Walk together children, don't you get weary.
There's a great camp meeting in the Promised
Land. (Powell, 1990)

An important component in implementing poetic
diction and rhythm is the use of repetition. The
text and other significant statements are restated for
emphasis, memory, impact, and effect. Through
repetition, the preacher ensures that the gist of what
he or she is saying is not lost in the emotionalism
of the audience. An example of the use of repetition can be noted in the following excerpt from the
Reverend Jesse Jackson's celebrated "I am Somebody" message:

I am somebody.
I may be poor,
But I am somebody.
Respect me.
Protect me.
Never neglect me.
I am somebody.

(Jackson, 1987)

Call and Response

Finally, it is not uncommon for African American
preachers to receive responses from their congregations during their sermonizing. Some preachers call
out for a specific response, such as "Can I get a
witness?" or "Somebody ought to say Amen,"
thereby soliciting responses. The response may
come voluntarily from members of the congregation
as an affirmation of the presence of "the spirit"
and/or as encouragement to the preacher. Such
responses as "Amen," "Preach!," "Tell it!," and
"Well?" are commonplace and essential in traditional African American worship services.

This interactive process, commonly referred to as
"call-response" is an African-derived process
between speaker and listener in which each of the
speaker's statements is punctuated by expressions
from the listener. Whether solicited or voluntary,
this participatory technique makes the listeners
believe that they are experiencing God's presence in
their midst, for African Americans believe that if
you don't put anything into the service, you won't
get anything out of it.

Summary

African American preaching is not simply a religious presentation. It is the careful orchestration of
the biblical scriptures interpreted in the context of
a people's culture and experiences. It is presented
with logic blended with creative modes of expression, tonal and physical behaviors from a tradition
that emphasizes emotionalism, interaction, spirituality, and the power of the spoken word.

Beginning with the enslaved Africans, Sunday
after Sunday, African American preachers have
breathed new life into a downtrodden people. They
have interpreted the Bible in view of their historical, cultural, and daily experiences. Their tones are
powerful, their gestures natural, and their words
keep audiences spellbound, touching the souls of
African Americans.

REFERENCES

Hamilton, C. V. (1972). *The black preacher in America*. New
    York: William Morrow Co.
Jackson, J. L. (1987). "It's Up to You," presented at the
    "What's Happening Teen Conference" in Atlanta, Georgia,
    June 19, 1978. In R.D. Hatch and F. E. Watkins (Eds.), *Jesse
    L. Jackson: Straight from the heart*. (p. 205). Philadelphia:
    Fortress Press.
Mitchell, H. (1970). *Black preaching*. New York: Harper &
    Row.
Moyd, O. P. (1971). Elements in Black Preaching, *The Journal
    of Religious Thought*.
Powell, Jr., A. C. (Speaker). (1990). *Adam Clayton Powell*.
    Washington, DC: Public Broadcasting System.
Scott, M. (1973). Recipe for Racial Greatness. *The gospel for
    the ghetto*. Nashville, TN: Broadman Press.
Smitherman, G. (1986). *Talkin and testifyin*. Detroit: Wayne
    State University Press.
Stewart, Sr., W. H. (1984). *Interpreting God's word in black
    preaching*. Valley Forge, PA: Judson Press.

15

Bone Beneath the Flesh: The Significance of the Oral Tradition in Louise Erdrich's *Love Medicine*

Patricia Riley
University of California, Berkeley

When studying contemporary Native American novels, it is imperative to bear in mind that there is no such thing as a "generic Indian" and no single, all-encompassing Native American culture. Native American cultures are plural, their world views are diverse, and this diversity must always be taken into account. Therefore, in order to better experience and appreciate the richness, depth, and complexity of a novel written by an author of Native American descent, it is helpful to not only place the work in its historical context, but to become grounded in the tribal-specific cultural matrix from which the work springs. Examination of the oral traditions of the author and of the author's subject(s) is one way of gaining additional insight.

Novels such as Leslie Marmon Silko's *Ceremony* and N. Scott Momaday's *House Made of Dawn* make open and obvious use of oral traditions. References to Laguna (Silko), Navajo, and Kiowa (Momaday) traditions are embedded within the text itself, cueing readers to take them into account. However, familiarizing oneself with the oral traditions of a given author and/or those of the novel's characters becomes even more crucial when their

use is less conspicuous. Failing to take these traditions into account, especially when studying mythologically subtle novels, at best leads to a fragmentary perception of the text and at worst may result in misguided interpretations and/or the re-enforcement of stereotypes.

Louise Erdrich's *Love Medicine*[1] is an excellent example of a novel that is mythologically subtle. The absence of an obvious employment of Chippewa[2] mythology has led at least one literary critic to decide that Erdrich's work is somehow less Native American than those texts whose mythological ancestry is more noticeable. According to Bo Scholer, "If the continuation of elements from traditional tales are taken as distinctive features of Native American long fiction, Erdrich's novels may be defined as 'marginally Native American,' although one would hesitate to make such absolute canonical statements" (p. 74). Indeed, one should. Erdrich's novel is firmly rooted in the Chippewa oral tradition and rich in its allusions. Scholer implies that, to be considered "Native American," a novel must be strewn with mythological, "in-your-face" references. It can be argued that such prescriptive criteria trivializes the artistry, depth, and complexity of works by Native American authors.

When students and scholars pick up a copy of Herman Melville's *Moby Dick*, a work to which, by the way, Erdrich also alludes, it is understood that they will have to work at comprehending it. Certainly, a student or scholar will need to become familiar with the Bible to develop a full appreciation of Melville's work, perhaps even delve into Gnosticism and Egyptian mysticism to glean finer interpretations. Melville's work deserves that kind of serious attention, as so does the work of Native American novelists.

A complete examination of references to Chippewa oral tradition in Erdrich's *Love Medicine*, as well as her strategic post-colonial employment of cross-cultural mythologies, would require more space than is available here. Therefore, I will confine my discussion to an analysis of the first and last chapters and in particular to certain aspects of the oral tradition and the Chippewa Midewiwin ceremony that structure and permeate the novel thematically.

To better understand Erdrich's use of Chippewa material, a brief overview of the Midewiwin is necessary. Bear in mind that what is offered here is in no way comprehensive. The Midewiwin is a ceremony of symbolic death and rebirth, the "most important collective religious ritual of the Chippewa" (Barnouw, p. 9), one of the oldest ceremonial societies (Johnston, *Ceremonies*, p. 95). The name itself has been translated by Basil Johnston as "The Society of Good-Hearted Ones" (Johnston *Cere- monies*, p. 95).

Johnston has noted that the Midewiwin came into being as a means to "attain inner peace by seeking for the good in life and so that they could perform rituals for the gift of good health" (Johnston, *Ceremonies*, p. 96). During the ceremony, a sym- bolic death occurs that is "real in a moral sense" (Johnston, *Heritage*, p. 92), and which is followed by a rebirth. The initiate emerges restored and possesses new powers (Johnston, *Heritage*, p. 91). To obtain full membership, a candidate must pass through four of eight possible degrees in the Mide society (Johnston, *Heritage*, p. 84). The afterworld is considered a Mide world populated by "earth initiated mide-persons"; therefore the uninitiated cannot gain entrance (Landes, p. 87). Johnston also asserts that one cannot enter the Land of Souls unless one possesses "peace of heart" (Johnston, *Ceremonies*, p. 96). To bring the uninitiated to "peace of heart" and assure a place for them in the afterworld, a Ghost Midewiwin could be held in which a relative, male or female, stands as proxy for the deceased, thereby assuring entrance into the afterworld for the loved one and gaining personal benefit for the relative (Landes, pp. 87-88). In this way, the soul of the deceased is strengthened and aided on its journey by the performance of the Ghost Mide (Landes, p. 52). According to Landes, the Midewiwin always begins with the story of the "Shell-Covered One," or "Shell," mourning over the coming of death into the world: "For the Indian was vulnerable to disease and death, since losing his enamel-armor [shell] and receiving Nenebushe's[3]

[the trickster's] gift of mortality." It continues with the journey to the Great Spirit to acquire the Mide ceremony that would bring rebirth (pp. 96-97). Barnouw states that the otter journeyed to the trickster, "who owned this earth," with the offer of a gift from the other spirits, so that Wenebojo would not destroy the world. The gifts that he was given were earth parents, and the Midewiwin ceremony (pp. 41-44).

The Mide theme of death, rebirth, transformation, and regeneration is central to Louise Erdrich's *Love Medicine* and illuminates the characterization of June Kashpaw and her unacknowledged son, Lipsha Morrissey. June dies, disillusioned and sick at heart, at the onset of the novel. It is her son Lipsha who undertakes a transformative journey towards identity and finally brings June's restless spirit home. The gifts gained by a first-degree initiate, "a new existence, a new life, greater in scope and depth" (Johnston, *Heritage*, p. 88), are exactly those which Lipsha receives at the novel's close. It is important to point out, however, that Erdrich's use of Chippewa oral tradition is not dogmatic or rigid. While drawing on various traditional elements, she does so with creative flexibility, inventing new twists, turns, and outcomes that, though they deviate from those of the oral traditional tales, serve to regenerate them contemporarily.

The first chapter, "The World's Greatest Fisher- man," tells the story of June Kashpaw's death which is brought about as a result of her own personal vulnerability. The action takes place in the Spring, when the Midewiwin usually takes place (Barnouw, p. 6). Specifically, the story begins on the "morning before Easter Sunday" (LM, p. 1), traditionally a time associated with death and rebirth in Christian and many pre-Christian religions as well. About to embark on what will ultimately be a journey to the afterworld, June waits in the noonday heat for the bus that will take her home, described as "killing time" (LM, p. 1), a clue that she has entered a mythic space where time is not fixed but fluid. Images of water and shells prolifer- ate. The window of the Rigger Bar is described as "watery glass" (LM, p. 1). June's eyes are "deeply watchful in their sea-blue flumes of shadow" (LM, p. 2). When she walked into the bar, "It was like going under water" (LM, p. 2), much as the otter went under water as he searched for Wenebojo. Indeed, June finds a trickster of sorts in the person of the mud engineer, Andy. Though Andy is "non-Indian," his occupation alludes to the Chippewa trickster, himself a mud engineer of sorts who recreated the world from a handful of mud following a flood (Barnouw, p. 66). June is wearing a "shell" which immediately associates her with the "Shell-Covered One" of the Mide ceremony. It is also significant that this shell is pink and "ripped across the stomach" (LM, p. 2), as it links her to the sacred megis shell, a variety of cowrie shell that is also pink and jagged across the middle (Dewdney, p. 71) and is used in the Mide ceremony to bring about the symbolic death of the initiate (Johnston, *Ceremonies*, p. 108). It was also a megis shell which floated in the sky, leading the Chippewa on their historic journey of migration (Johnston, *Heritage*, p. 88). Andy picks out an egg whose dyed shell matches the color of June's blouse/shell. He peels it and hands the "naked egg" (LM, p. 2) to June, in imitation of Nehnebushe's gift of mortality, and offers to peel her shell: "He said he would peel that for her, too, if she wanted . . ." (LM, p. 2). She accepts the peeled egg and eats not one, but several.

Taking a chance that Andy might be different from other men of her acquaintance, June decides to go barhopping with him. Driving down the street, she remembers another mud engineer she had known who had been killed by a pressurized hose "snaking up suddenly from its unseen nest," popping "suddenly through black earth with its killing breath" (LM, p. 3). The thought makes her "panicky" (LM, p. 3). When June accepted the peeled egg and Andy's invitation, she was, in a sense, dead already. Her fate was sealed. The significance of June's fear of the inanimate suddenly becoming animate lies in the obstacles that she must face as a soul on its journey to the afterworld. Entrance to the afterworld requires that four obstacles must be overcome along the road. The first obstacle is an

otter; the second, an owl. The third is two hills that the road runs between, which are actually fire-breathing snakes. The fourth is a river that must be crossed via a log bridge, in reality also a snake (Barnouw, p. 18). Anishinaabe author Gerald Vizenor says that the deceased's spirit "had to abide at least one year as a restless wanderer, doing penance for past transgressions during life" and that the bridge, which he calls "the bridge of destiny," would "become agitated to a degree equal to the sins the spirit was guilty of" (pp. 84-85). June's fear of the pressurized hose that suddenly springs to life is representative of her fear of the log bridge over which she must travel. It has the ability to spring to life and dislodge her journeying soul, thereby preventing her from gaining entrance to the afterworld and dooming her soul to wander, perhaps forever.

During the sexual encounter with Andy, June feels as if she is being swallowed up. The heater, inadvertently turned on in the heat of passion, is "open at her shoulder like a pair of jaws, blasting heat" (LM, p. 5), and she experiences "the momentary and voluptuous sensation that she was lying stretched out before a great, wide mouth" (LM, p. 5). The friction of Andy's vest against her body is "like being rubbed by an enormous tongue" (LM, p. 5). This scene re-enforces her encounter with the third obstacle to the spirit world, the fire-breathing snakes.

Following their sexual encounter, June frees herself from the now passed-out Andy in a scene filled with distinct images that signal her birth into the spirit world. Not unlike an infant in the birth canal, she feels enclosed and in danger of being crushed: "And then she knew that if she lay there any longer she would crack wide open, not in one place, but in many pieces . . ." (LM, p. 5). When the door springs open and she slips out, "It was a shock like being born" (LM, p. 5). June, misreading the weather forecast written on the wind, decides to walk home to the reservation and becomes caught in an unseasonal blizzard that is the direct cause of her death. But Erdrich writes that "the pure and naked part of her went on" (LM, p. 5). Her restless spirit continues its homeward trek and, though the "snow fell deeper that Easter than it had in forty years. . . June walked over it like water and came home" (LM, p. 5).

From this point on, though June is no longer physically present in the novel, her spirit nevertheless presides over it and makes its presence known. She is on everyone's mind throughout the novel and at one point her restless spirit shapeshifts and haunts her ex-husband Gordie, driving him towards madness in his grief and his guilt (LM, pp. 176-188). She has clearly walked back to her earthly home, since her unpeaceful heart prohibits her entrance into her new home in the Land of Souls (Johnston, *Ceremonies*, p. 96).

The title of the final chapter, "Crossing The Water," connects back to the close of Chapter One, which ended with June walking over the water, and echoes the final obstacle which must be overcome by the journeying spirit. Like the proxy initiate of the Ghost Mide carried out on behalf of the deceased, Lipsha ultimately acts on behalf of his mother's unpeaceful spirit, bringing peace to them both. One example of Erdrich's flexible and creative use of the Chippewa oral tradition is the way she utilizes the mythological figures of the trickster, Naanabozho, and his grandmother, Nookomis, to bring this about. Rather than creating one character to represent each of the mythological characters, Erdrich creates sets of characters who share their actions and characteristics. Marie Kashpaw and Lulu Lamartine share the role of grandmother, and Lipsha Morrissey and Gerry Nanapush share that of the trickster.

According to Johnston's version of the traditional story, the trickster is orphaned and grows up with his grandmother. It is from her that he learns of his mother's death and that his father, who is still alive, had something to do with her demise. He subsequently sets out to find his father and avenge his mother (Johnston, *Heritage*, p. 18).

Like Nanabush, Lipsha grows up in the foster care of Marie Kashpaw, whom he calls Grandma, while considering her as his mother. Just as the trickster learned of his parentage from his grandmother, Lipsha learns from his biological grandmother, Lulu Lamartine, that June is his real mother, and that "[s]he watched [him] from a distance and hoped [he] would forgive her some day" (LM, p. 244). Lulu also tells him that her son, Gerry Nanapush (another variant of Naanabozho), a "famous politicking hero, dangerous armed criminal, judo expert, escape artist, charismatic member of the American Indian Movement" (LM, p. 248) is his real father. Erdrich has assigned the nurturing role of Nookomis to Marie and the disclosing role to Lulu. Lulu's disclosure, that Lipsha is the son of one who bears a variant of the trickster's name, legitimatizes and solidifies Lipsha's own trickster aspect by right of inheritance. He, like his father, is "a Nanapush man" (LM, p. 244). Like the trickster, Lipsha receives a gift of new parents (Barnouw, p. 44) in that he now possesses the knowledge of his true parentage. However, unlike the traditional tale, Lipsha's father did not have a hand in June's death. Therefore, Lipsha does not go in search of his father to avenge June, but to "get down to the bottom of [his] heritage" (LM, p. 248).

Lipsha finally encounters his father in the apartment of June's acknowledged son, King, who Lipsha now realizes is his half-brother. Gerry has escaped from prison and comes to King's, as Lipsha knew he would, to settle a score since King had informed on him while they were in prison together. He asks to be dealt into King and Lipsha's card game. Lipsha suggests to King that they play for June's car: "Let's play for the Firebird you bought with June's insurance" (LM, p. 262). It is at this point that June's homeward journey recommences; Lipsha notes that the snow, which had killed her that Easter, "had resumed falling softly in this room" (LM, p. 262). Throughout the novel, "June's car" (LM, p. 262) has been treated as a kind of vessel for June's spirit and shortly becomes a means of escape for Gerry as well. Lipsha wins the car by dealing himself "a perfect family. A royal flush" (LM, p. 264).

When the police arrive at King's apartment to arrest Gerry, he escapes in true trickster fashion. Lipsha is convinced that Gerry must have "laid a finger beside his nose and went flying up the air shaft. That's the only thing possible" (LM, p. 265). With the car keys and registration for June's car in hand, Lipsha leaves "without a word" (LM, p. 266).

As he drives away from the city, Lipsha muses about his father's ability to escape. The shape-shifting abilities he attributes to his father both echo and contemporize those of the Chippewa trickster, Naanabozho, in oral traditional tales:

I knew my dad would get away. He could fly. He could strip and flee and change into shapes of swift release. Owls and bees, two-toned Ramblers, buzzards, cottontails, and motes of dust. These forms was interchangeable with his. He was the clouds scudding over the moon, the wings of ducks banging in the slough . . . (LM, p. 266)

As Lipsha "[waxes] eloquent in his mind" (LM, p. 266), he notices "knocking" (LM, p. 266) coming from the back end of the car and discovers that Gerry has in actuality taken refuge there to make good his escape. Lipsha subsequently frees him from the trunk and takes him to the Canadian border where his wife and daughter wait for him.

In the short time they are together, Lipsha not only comes to know his father better, but his mother as well. During their conversation, Lipsha begins to see a side of June that he never knew existed. Lulu's previous disclosure regarding June's secret watchfulness over him as he grew up, combined with his father's memories, erode the bitterness Lipsha has felt over what he had perceived as his mother's abandonment of him as a child. Gerry's reminiscence of his love for June makes it possible for Lipsha to begin to recapture the love she must have felt for him, and to come to some sort of philosophical reconciliation that allows him to recover from the wound inflicted by their separation. Just as the Ghost Mide benefits both the proxy participant and the spirit of the deceased, Lipsha's journey accomplishes the Mide's goals and brings spiritual healing and "peace of heart" for himself and for June.

After dropping his father at the border, Lipsha continues homeward towards the reservation. He stops the car on the bridge that crosses the "boundary river" (LM, p. 271) and thinks of June and realizes that she had done what was best for him. The novel closes with the lines, "A good road led on. So there was nothing to do but cross the water, and bring her home" (LM, p. 272). Lipsha's final act fulfills the objective of the Ghost Mide. Shielded by the car which carries her spirit and strengthened by her son's love, June's spirit is finally able to cross over the final obstacle of the bridge and enter her new home in the Land of Souls.

While the mythological approach is certainly not the only viable method for analyzing and interpreting novels written by Native American writers, Louise Erdrich's *Love Medicine* illustrates the additional cultural insights that can be gained from the attempt. Just as the oral traditions of Native American peoples contain different levels of meaning, stories within a story, so do many contemporary Native American novels. On the surface is one story, the readily accessible story, and within this story lies a multiplicity of other stories. All are available to the reader who is willing to work for them, to engage the story actively, and to participate in its unfoldment.

Conclusion

The study of contemporary Native American literature, fiction, autobiography, poetry, and drama can give students a beacon to follow that overturns stereotypes, gives voice to the silenced, and renders the invisible visible. It can offer an opportunity to celebrate other ways of seeing and being in the world, to explore the dynamics of cultures other than their own, and to come away from the experience informed of the struggles of Native American people for autonomy, justice, and religious freedom. Lastly, the study of Native American literature can act as a force for change. Too many people, if they consider Native Americans at all, only think of them in terms of the distant past.

NOTES

[1]All parenthetical references to this text will be abbreviated as LM and followed by a specific page number.

[2]The tribal name is actually *anishinaabeg*. However, since Erdrich refers to herself as Chippewa, I have used that word throughout the discussion.

[3]In anishinaabeg the word is spelled *Naanabozho*. Variant spellings such as Wenebojo, Nehnebushe, and Nanabush appear in the text in accordance with the source being used.

REFERENCES

Barnouw, V. (1977). *Wisconsin Chippewa myths & tales and their relation to Chippewa life*. Madison: University of Wisconsin Press.

Dewdney, S. (1975) *The sacred scrolls of the southern Ojibway*. Toronto: University of Toronto Press.

Erdrich, L. (1985). *Love medicine*. New York: Bantam.

Johnston, B. *Ojibwa ceremonies*. Lincoln: Bison.

_____. *Ojibwa heritage*. Lincoln: Bison.

Landes, R. *Ojibwa religion and the Midewiwin*. Madison: University of Wisconsin Press.

Melville, H. *Moby Dick*. New York: Penguin.

Momaday, N.S. (1968). *House made of dawn*. New York: Harper.

Scholer, B. (1989). Young and restless: The treatment of a statistical phenomenon in contemporary native American fiction. In L. Cotelli (Ed.), *In Native American Literatures*, Pisa, Italy: Servizio Editoriale Universitario.

Silko, L.M. (1977). *Ceremony*. New York: Viking.

Vizenor, G. (1981). *Summer in the spring: Ojibwe lyric poems and tribal stories*. Minneapolis: Nodin.

16

Mexican American Cultural Experiences with Mass-Mediated Communication

Diana I. Ríos
University of New Mexico

The U.S. mass audience is no longer homogenous white milk. It never really was homogenous or white, but Anglo Americans tried to fool themselves into thinking that everybody was going to jump into the pot and melt down. Thanks to the Civil Rights movement, the ethnicity and culture of mass audience members have been given increasing attention in media studies over the last few decades. These elements continue to gain importance, given the unprecedented growth of ethnic and racial groups in the United States. Today, those who identify themselves as belonging to non-white ethnic co-culture groups represent about twenty percent of the population (U.S. Bureau of the Census, 1991). Of particular interest among ethnic minority groups are Hispanics, also referred to as Latinos[1], who have experienced particularly large aggregate population increases (Ramos & Morales, 1985; Chapa, 1991). Conservative figures show that Latinos represented more than six percent of the population in 1980, about eight percent in 1988, and nine percent in 1990 (U.S. Bureau of the Census, CPR: 1989, 38; U.S. Bureau of the Census, 1991). Researchers have projected that Latino populations will continue their ascent in certain cities and regions as a result of net migration and natural increase (Ramos & Morales, 1985; Hayes-Bautista, Schink, & Chapa, 1988; Chapa, 1991).

From those among us who study demographic profiles of U.S. society and mass media audiences, I have seen Mexican Americans draw the lion's share of attention as the largest national Latino population group (U.S. Bureau of the Census, 1991). What mystifies mainstream society about Mexican Americans, or Chicanos[2], is that the population is not only mounting rapidly, but Chicanos have continued to exist as an identifiable ethnic and cultural group. Having defined expectations of the ultimate cultural homogenization, Mexican Americans simply refuse to melt down.

As a Chicana user of mass media, my ethnic identity, my cultural-based values and attitudes, and my social experiences with ethnic, class, and sex discrimination all come into play when I engage in mediated communication. My cultural and social characteristics and interests are not just self-consciously utilized; they are an ever-present part of who I am. Thus my expectations, cultural needs, and desires comprise my point of view when I am watching movies such as an "Alien" sequel, a television program such as "Star Trek: The Next Generation," Spanish-language international news on Univisión, or the Spanish-language soap opera "Guadalupe" on Telemundo, or when I am looking for familiar names in the Chicano newspapers of Austin, Texas. With mainstream media, I have always kept a vigilant eye for people who looked like me and for issues that pertained to the Mexican heritage of people like myself. Growing up in a professional, lower-middle income family in grape-picking Fresno, California in the early 1960s, I became dissatisfied with pink dolls with blue eyes and yellow hair who did not look like they could sing "Bendito Sea Díos" at a Mexican mass. So I learned to view the visual and print media from a discreet distance until I found someone or something with which to identify, picking and choosing with very discriminate brown eyes.

This essay is intended to explore the significance of ethnicity and culture in relationship to Chicanos' dual use of mass-mediated forms of communication.

I will focus on two bilateral functions in terms of how the media serve Mexican Americans: (1) their acculturation to mainstream values and norms, and (2) the preservation and fortification of their ethnicity and culture. Mass-media research on Chicanos, as well as personal insights, are presented in regard to media-audience functions, dual functions of the media, media use for acculturation, and media use for ethnic and cultural self-preservation.

Media-Audience Functions

Communication functions have been studied within the mass communication field for a number of years (Hsia, 1988). More recently, researchers have moved away from the consideration of what media does *to* individuals and have focused more intensively on what audiences do *with* media. Researchers now address more the mitigating impact of audience-member needs and goals in the selection of each medium and in its usage. When engaging with the media, audience members are viewed as "free agents" who are not constrained or so easily influenced by media messages (Lindlof & Meyer, 1987, 3). Researchers who support this view do not treat audiences as "lumps of passive clay ready to be molded by what they view, read, and hear" (Severin & Tankard, 1992, 269), but as people taking active roles in the way they select media and in the manner by which they decide which form of mass media is most useful for them. This "audience function" approach is especially empowering to Chicanos, because they are a powerful minority group.

An audience function focuses not on what a media form does *to* a person, but rather on what a person does *with* a media form. Consider, for example, how I viewed the sequel "Aliens" at a northern California theater and what I drew selectively from this film. A female Hispanic was introduced in the movie who was not stereotyped either as a virgin, whore, maid, or mother-saint. Pleasantly surprised to see such a strong supporting character, I was excited that this courageous and beautiful woman actually had olive skin and dark hair like myself. As her image appeared on the screen, my brother who accompanied me exclaimed, loud enough for other Chicano audience members to hear, "Hey, they put a Chicana in there!" Most of the Anglos in the audience did not seem to share our enthusiasm. The film character's lightly accented intonations reminded me of the working-class Latinas whom I had known in East Oakland, California, in the late 1960s. This image of a Latina leader was what I had long been missing in popular media. She projected a positive image which I could relate to as a female Latina. But then, amidst the action sequences, she was suddenly killed off. I had to settle with rooting for Sigourney Weaver's Anglo heroine—a brave woman but no Latina, and definitely not a Mexican American. Once the Hispanic character was gone, the film ceased to serve any affirming Chicana cultural function for me.

Dual Functions

Two media-centered functions merit attention because they underscore the special relationship Chicanos have with mass communication when the functions are thought of as audience centered. These are the functions of acculturation (or the more encompassing terms "socialization" or "assimilation") and ethnic and cultural self-preservation. Though there is a dearth of scholarly studies that address these functions for ethnics, especially Chicanos, selected works which have dealt with these kinds of relationships include Park (1922); Warshauer (1966); McCardell (1976); Gutiérrez and Schement (1979); Burgoon, Burgoon, Greenberg and Korzenny (1986); and Subervi-Vélez (1984; 1986). McCardell, Gutiérrez, and Schement, Burgoon et al., and Subervi-Vélez have focused on Chicano and Latino media functions, while Park and Warshauer have touched on Spanish-language communities.

The media function that has attracted attention from the government, because of institutionalized efforts toward societal homogenization, has been the socialization power of media. For example, Park (1922) examined the role of the press for U.S., European, and some "Spanish" communities early in this century. Park's study on the press was part of a collection of materials sponsored by the "Division of the Immigrant Press of Studies of Methods of Americanization" (Park, 1922, vi). Ethnic presses are described as serving as tools of adjustment and as expressing a group's values, heritage, and changing sense of identity" (Miller, 1987, xvi). What I perceive as a cultural fear still exhibited by xenophobic individuals, who push such initiatives as "English Only," is what Park describes as the self-preservation role of ethnic print media for ethnic communities. During Park's time, there was a concern that ethnic-oriented newspapers could act as bridges to ethnic homelands and offer access to foreign political ideologies through the dissemination of information from outside the U.S. This xenophobic concern has probably not diminished today but has most likely intensified, since ethnic minorities such as Chicanos have had a longer history within the U.S. and now use presses for self-preservation in a more efficient manner than ever before. Mexican American presses, such as those found in Austin, are supportive of a bicultural Amerian ethnic community which does not want to be considered as either culturally foreign or linguistically alien.

Chicano-targeted media such as community presses provide a certain content of which audiences can take advantage. However, there is always the concern that the positive role of Chicano media may be diminished by the promotion of consumerism, through advertising to the economically disenfranchised. Warshauer (1966), and Gutiérrez and Schement (1979), contend that the dual functions of broadcast media such as Spanish-language radio may provide linguistic support; however, this is incidental when the mother tongue is used on behalf of a commercialistic form of Americanization. While listening to commercial Spanish-language radio in Austin, I have found that "Tex-Mex" and Latino Caribbean music are available to me but hardly as a Chicano community service, given the deluge of car and furniture advertisements, pitched by native Spanish speakers, which I am forced to endure. I consider myself a selective listener, and yet I and others who listen to Spanish-language radio must be bombarded constantly by appeals to buy the American dream. Chicano and Latino radio music and news are culturally affirming; but, as Gutiérrez & Schement (1979) have warned, other parts of the broadcast package essentially perpetuate "the unequal and internally colonial relationships between Anglos and Chicanos in the United States" (p. 102). We, as Chicano listeners, should be especially aware of the culturally affirming limitations that exist in the offerings of our own media.

Arguably, this observation can be generalized as applicable to other ethnic broadcast media, since co-culture-oriented media is not typically designed for the sake of social service interests, but rather that of capital gain. One exception is public broadcast stations, which have historically preserved non-commercial ideologies. Not all public broadcast stations completely fulfill the goal of public service. I have listened to some Texas stations that seem to want to maintain a culturally high-brow Anglo image for potential foundation funds rather than cater adequately to Mexican and African American listeners with limited resources in their service area. However, public radio stations offer far more opportunities and responsibility for uplifting, non-mainstream co-cultures (q.v. the case study by González, 1989).

Media-centered research with Latinos and media in various U.S. cities support the idea that dual media functions, and the potential for purposive audience utilization, are simply not isolated phenomenon. Suber, media-Veléz' (1984) work, based on Cubans, Mexican Americans, and Puerto Ricans in the midwest, found that mass media exposure reflected dual functions for mainstream social integration, as well as for sustained ethnic differentiation. In McCardell's investigation of socialization factors in the Spanish-language newspaper *El Diario-La Prensa*, the author finds that the content serves to socialize the New York Latino audience to American mainstream society as well as support ethnic and cultural self-preservation by promoting socialization within "Spanish-speaking society."

Part of a study conducted by Burgoon et al. (1986) in the southwest describes the importance of a number of general media functions to Mexican

Americans. These include: information about local events; local vigilance and publicity; relaxation, escapism, and pleasure; cultural information, cultural pride, and identity; language acquisition (Spanish or English); and conversation topics (pp. 113-115). Such findings indicate that Chicanos use media for the purposes of self-preservation and acculturation, along with general uses.

Two main functions have been presented as having a special significance for Chicanos. In previous research on media and ethnics, there has been a tendency to focus on relationships which are media-centered rather than audience-centered. A media-centered approach provides only limited insight into audiences, because media users are perceived as subordinate to potential media effects. From a new view, audiences are less likely to be perceived as undiscerning dupes but rather as empowered, selective individuals.

Media Use for Acculturation

The aspect of media use for the goal of acculturation has been explored in a large body of work on ethnics and mass media. It has been argued that this research is rooted in the belief that media can be used as an agent to stamp out ethnic and cultural diversity in a society which prizes Euro-American culture over others. Acculturation, which involves changes in ethnic values, customs, and cultural elements toward a dominant norm, has been a highly promoted process in the U.S. Often researchers view Chicanos as caught in an uneasy bind between the cultural processes of self-preservation within their own community and outside acculturation. However, Chicanos have access to both Mexican American and mainstream media, having acquired the tastes and needs for both.

The use of media for acculturation is not inherently bad. One problem, however, is that some Chicanos accept the nativist philosophies of Anglo-Saxon cultural superiority[3] and, as a result, use mass media to exhibit an acceptance of these beliefs in ways that I consider to be self-defeating. For example, some individuals use mainstream media as part of a program of Americanization for themselves and children. I have observed Latino children watch large amounts of mainstream serials and "kiddie" television, then heard justifications from immigrant Latino parents that this is good for their children because it helps them to master English. While mass media may indeed help co-cultural members improve their knowledge of English, as well as U.S. society, some Chicano and Latino parents harbor the false perception that acculturation will offer such members automatic access to the economic social structure.

One of the myths of the American melting pot suggests that losing one's mother tongue "makes more room" for English. Another myth offers the illusion that learning how to be "American" by Euro-American standards is the golden key to opportunity in this country. I have often looked with ethnic pride upon children with hereditary tan complexions and jet black hair, who could communicate competently in Spanish and English by necessity, and who favored their mothers' tamales. And yet I found it such a shame that their own parents believed so adamantly that watching TV would help these children become white and successful like Batman, Perry Mason, or the oil barons J.R. and Bobby Ewing from "Dallas." They did not even stop to consider the discreet social barriers that people of color face because they do not "look" right or know the right kind of people on the Anglo side of town. The sad truth remains that, though numerous ethnics in the U.S. have acculturated, the "Anglo Saxon center" has largely refused entrance to non-white minorities (Novak, 1972; Glazer & Moynihan, 1963, 20).

It is important for Chicanos to realize that, because of their unique biculturalism, they have access to media outlets in addition to those of the mainstream population. For example, Chicanos who are Spanish-language dominant use mainstream media as a tool to help improve their English, while still retaining their cultural identity through ethnic-oriented media and interpersonal communication. The mass media, though distorted, does offer a window of sorts to the values, attitudes, and norms of American society.

Media Use for Self-Preservation

In my view, the function of media, for purposes of ethnic and cultural self-preservation, needs to be emphasized more positively in audience studies (Ríos, 1991). The number of media outlets for Chicano audiences has not been in fair proportion to the number of Chicanos in this country. Nevertheless, this does not preclude Chicanos from utilizing local media to strengthen their cultural foundation.

In the Texas capital of Austin, for example, Chicanos have access to at least two community-targeted newspapers which feature artistic, cultural, political, and business news relevant to Mexican Americans in the area. Chicanos have access to *Arriba*[4], a free periodical which is delivered to small grocery stores, restaurants, and other public locations. Mexican Americans also read *La Prensa*[5], a paper with a much wider circulation which caters to Mexican Americans residing in Austin and San Antonio. Ethnic group pride and solidarity are reinforced, as social activists, artists, and school-age children read stories about themselves and announcements about Chicano events. Though Chicanos do not often find themselves reflected in the mainstream media limelight, the Chicano-oriented print and broadcast media cover such events as Chicana and Chicano politicians running for local offices, community "Cinco de Mayo" and "Diez y Seis de Septiembre" celebrations, accomplishments by Chicano students, and works by local Chicano artists.

The media offerings for Chicanos in Austin are not as grand as in such cities with higher Hispanic population densities as San Antonio or El Paso, Texas, or Fresno and Los Angeles, California. However, Austin's Chicanos do have access to a myriad of Latino-oriented television and radio stations, newspapers, magazines, music recordings, and videos in Spanish, English or both—originating in the U.S. as well as in Mexico and other parts of Latin America.

The newspaper *Arriba* tends to print in English, while *La Prensa* is bilingual. Chicanos with continued ties to Mexico seek out both local or international news stories from either small newspapers or the Spanish-language television network Univisión, as well as access to mainstream broadcast and print media such as the *Austin American-Statesman*. Latino popular culture, such as found in music and film, often deal with contemporary issues and shared feelings among Chicanos and other Latinos (Padilla, 1989). To this end, for example, the large video rental store "Acapulco" in the Chicano section of Austin specializes in offering Spanish-language film videos. One can walk in, indulge in an iced fruit *agua fresca*, and select movies from Mexico's golden age of cinema or American-made films dubbed in Spanish. There are two main Spanish-language radio stations at the time of this writing. KELG (AM)[6] offers "Tropical" Latino music as well as news broadcasts in Spanish. KTXZ (AM)[7] is a bilingual "Tejano" station. Both these stations are popular among immigrants and the U.S. born, though community people have often complained that they need more Spanish language stations from which to choose (Ríos, 1993).

During my field work among Mexican Americans in Austin, I encountered two women who were particularly conscious of and labored hard to strengthen their biculturalism. One was "Lupita," an immigrant who described to me how she cut out English-language stories from the newspaper to figure out unfamiliar American words, trying to utilize both English and Spanish print media. She also carefully monitored her children's cable television viewing of shows in English and Spanish. In her cultural values and attitudes, Lupita was unequivocally "Mexicana" and strived to retain this even in her efforts to function well in her new society. Dedicated to promoting *la comunidad* (the community), she became one of a group of neighborhood organizers who networked with other Latinos to address burning demands with the city of Austin. The other woman was "Lorena," a longtime Texan Mexican who took advantage of mainstream media, particularly professional trade media, in order to keep up in her area of expertise. She competed well in the Anglo world, yet always maintained her cultural ties through Mexican American newspapers, her family, and other Chicanos she had grown up with in the neighborhood.

Concluding Remarks

Mexican Americans must rely on communication among themselves in order to fulfill the need for self-validation. As this essay has illustrated, mass-mediated communication can be attained by Chicanos so that they can exercise cultural maintenance, strengthen ethnic identity, and gain the socio-cultural tools necessary to function within the dominant co-culture. Even when Chicanos live in areas of high ethnic concentration, they must interact with a mainstream society that has limited tolerance for linguistic and cultural diversity. Cultural dualism has long been a process by which I and others of Mexican heritage, and other U.S. Latinos, have balanced the conforming agents of mainstream socialization, such as private and public educational institutions and government bodies. Ethnic-oriented media, selected mainstream media, Chicano-Latino churches, professional and social groups all help to advance our co-culture in America.

NOTES

[1]"Latino" is a preferred term of reference over the imposed "Hispanic" term (see Hayes-Bautista and Chapa: 1987, for discussion).

[2]The term "Chicano," most popular during the Civil Rights era, connotes a political and ethnic consciousness. (For a historical account, see Acuña, 1988.) "Chicano" will be used here interchangeably with "Mexican American" to avoid repetition, as well as draw attention to this group's continued struggle for social equality.

[3]Menchaca's (1989) case studies describe how nativistic philosophies are enforced within Chicano communities.

[4]Arriba was established in 1980 as a response to poor Chicano cultural events coverage by Austin's main city paper, the Austin American-Statesman. Interview with Arriba publisher and editor Romeo Rodriguez, February 21, 1992.

[5]La Prensa, founded in 1986, is a free weekly distributed to Chicano parts of the city and elsewhere. The publisher and editor is Catherine Vasquez-Revilla. The co-publisher is State Senator Gonzalo Barrientos.

[6]Founded by José Jaime García, Sr., in 1985, KELG is a family-owned and operated business which plays many types of Latino music. It is currently managed by José Jaime García, Jr. Interview with José Jaime García, Jr., February 24, 1992.

[7]This has been a bilingual "Tejano" music station since 1986, geared to Texan Mexicans who were born and raised in Texas as well as others of Mexican origin. It is owned by SCAN Communications. Interview with Douglas Raab, general manager, February 24, 1992.

REFERENCES

Acuña, R. (1988). *Occupied America: A history of Chicanos*, 3rd ed. New York: Harper and Row.

Burgoon, J. K., Burgoon, M., Greenberg, B. S., & Korzenny, F. (1986). Mass media use, preferences, and attitudes among adults. In B. S. Greenberg, J. K. Burgoon, M. Burgoon, and F. Korzenny (Eds.), *Mexican Americans and the mass media* (Norwoord, NJ: Ablex), 79-146.

Chapa, J. (1991). Special focus: Hispanic demographic and educational trends. In American Council on Education, *Ninth annual status report on minorities in higher education* (Washington, D.C.: Office of Minorities in Higher Educa tion).

Glazer, N. & Moynihan, D. P. (1963). *Beyond the melting pot: The Negroes, Puerto Ricans, Jews, Italians, and Irish of New York City.* Cambridge, MA: The MIT Press and Harvard University Press.

González, A. (1989). "Participation" at WMEX-FM: Interventional rhetoric of Ohio Mexican Americans. *Western Journal of Speech Communication, 53,* 398-410.

Gutiérrez, F. F. & Schement, J. R. (1979). *Spanish-language radio in the Southwestern United States.* Austin, TX: The University of Texas at Austin, Center for Mexican American Studies.

Hayes-Bautista, D. E. & Chapa, J. (1987). Latino terminology: Conceptual bases for standardized terminology. *American Journal of Public Health, 77,* 61-68.

Hayes-Bautista, D. E., Schink, W. O., & Chapa, J. (1988). *The burden of support.* Stanford, CA: Stanford University Press.

Hsia, H. J. (1988). *Mass communications research methods: A step-by-step approach.* Hillsdale, New Jersey: Lawrence.

Lindlof, T. R. & Meyer, T. P. (1987). Mediated communication as ways of seeing, acting, and constructing culture: The tools and foundations of qualitative research. In T. Lindlof (Ed.), *Natural audiences* (Norwood, NJ: Ablex), 1-30.

Menchaca, M. (1989). Chicano-Mexican cultural assimilation and Anglo-Saxon cultural dominance. *Hispanic Journal of Behavioral Sciences, 11,* 203-231.

McCardell, W. S. (1976). *Socialization factors in El Diario-La Prensa, the Spanish-language newspaper with the largest daily circulation in the United States.* Unpublished doctoral dissertation, University of Iowa.

Miller, S. M., ed. (1987). *The ethnic press in the United States: A historical analysis and handbook.* New York: Greenwood Press.

Novak, M. (1972). *The rise of the unmeltable ethnics: Politics and culture in the Seventies.* New York: Macmillan.

Padilla, F. M. (1989). Salsa music as a cultural expression of Latino consciousness and unity. *Hispanic Journal of Behavioral Sciences, 11,* 28-45.

Park, R. E. (1922). *The immigrant press and its control.* New York: Harper and Brothers.

Ramos, H. A. & Morales, M. M. (1985). U.S. immigration and the Hispanic community: An historical overview and sociological perspective. *Journal of Hispanic Politics, 1,* 1-17.

Ríos, D. I. (1991). *Processes of ethnic change and persistence: Mexican Americans, ethnicity and acculturation.* Paper presented at the annual meeting of the Speech Communication Association, Atlanta, Georgia, November 1991.

Ríos, D. I. (1993). *Mexican American audiences: A qualitative and quantitative study of ethnic subgroup uses for mass media.* Unpublished doctoral dissertation. University of Texas at Austin.

Severin, W. & Tankard, J., Jr. (1992). *Communication theories: Origins, methods and uses in the mass media,* 3rd ed. New York: Longman.

Subervi-Vélez, F. A. (1984). *Hispanics, the mass media, and politics: Assimilation versus pluralism.* Unpublished doctoral dissertation, University of Wisconsin-Madison.

Subervi-Vélez, F. A. (1986). The mass media and ethnic assimilation and pluralism: A review and research proposal with a special focus on Hispanics. *Communication Research, 13,* 71-96.

Traudt, P. J. (1986). Ethnic diversity and mass mediated experience. In S. Thomas and W. A. Evans (Eds.), *Communication and culture: Language, performance, technology, and media.* Norwood, N.J.: Ablex.

U. S. Bureau of the Census (1991). *Census and you.* Washington, D.C.: Government Printing Office.

U.S. Bureau of the Census (1989). *Current population reports: Population profile of the United States* (special studies series P-23, no. 159). Washington, D.C.: Government Printing Office.

Warshauer, M. E. (1966). Foreign language broadcasting. In J. Fishman, *Language loyalty in the United States* (London: Mouton).

◆ ◆

17

Native American Culture and Communication through Humor

Charmaine Shutiva
Isleta Elementary School
Isleta Pueblo, New Mexico

"One of the best ways to understand a people is to know what makes them laugh."

Vine Deloria, Custer Died for your Sins *(p. 146)*

Contrary to popular belief, Native Americans are not a stoic, quiet people (Deloria, 1969; Giago, 1990; Hill, 1943; Opler, 1938). They are generally a joyful people (Deloria, 1969; Hill, 1943; Miller, 1967; Obamsawin, 1983) who appreciate and dote upon humor. Although the role and function of humor have been components of the religious, social, and political lives of Native Americans, it has rarely been acknowledged (Deloria, 1969; Ortiz, 1984) or examined as an element of communication in social and interpersonal settings (Deloria, 1969; Ortiz, 1984).

This essay will explore Native American humor, its form and function, and its usefulness in interpersonal communication in various Native American secular and sacred social settings.

Native American Humor and Group Cohesiveness

In the lively world of the Native American, many religious, cultural, and social events are breeding grounds for humor. Humor permeates even the most serious tribal council meetings. Parliamentary procedures are repeated, but in the "Ini'n way"— which invariably involves much humor (Miller, 1967). The pace of meetings is often slow, with wandering topics, drawn-out discussions, and inevitable exchanges of humorous stories and asides.

Although each tribe is different and has traditions and ceremonies that are tribally specific, researchers (Eyster, 1980; Faas, 1982; Hanson and Esienbise, 1983; Miller and Garcia, 1974; Sanders, 1987; Supaka, 1972) have developed lists of values and beliefs that can be considered cross-tribal. The use of humor among Native Americans has aided in helping to maintain many of these values and, conversely, these values and beliefs have aided in helping to establish humor as an intrinsic component of Native American communication. Two of the cultural values that strongly influence this humor are perception of time and group orientation.

Native American Perception of Time

The Native American perception of time is different from the dominant Euro-American perception of time (Attneave, 1982; Faas, 1982; Hanson and Eisenbise, 1983; Sanders, 1987), which is linear and segmented. For the latter, punctual activities are the norm. In contrast, among the various tribal societies, the perception of time is circular and flexible. The predominant attitude is that the activities will commence "whenever people are ready; when everyone arrives" (Pepper, 1976). According to Garrison (1989), "[Native American] people see no need to control time or to let it control them. . .; the goal is not to limit the time, but to experience and enjoy time as it passes" (p. 122). This consideration of time symbolically reinforces the Native American religious belief of achievement and maintenance of harmony with nature because "nature is allowed to take its own course."

This somewhat "laid back" attitude about time has been jokingly referred to as "Indian time" (Anderson, Burd, Dodd & Kelker, 1980; Lockart,

1978; Marashio, 1982) and has contributed to the development and maintenance of humor in the Native American world. "Indian time" has provided Native Americans unstressed, unpressured time to teach younger generations the "proper way" to greet friends and relatives and to exchange stories and anecdotes. While patiently waiting for cultural festivities to begin, the individual is provided the opportunity to entertain the "audience with his/her talent and flair for the spoken word." For example, according to Steve "Raising" Kane, a Northern Pauite comic orator, a Native American operating on Indian time is an individual who is either early or not so early, but never late (Giago, 1990).

Native American Group Orientation

A second traditional Native American value that has had an impact on the use of humor is an emphasis on group and community rather than on individualism (Eyster, 1980; Faas, 1982; Garrison, 1989; Hanson and Eisenbise, 1983; Light and Martin, 1986; Miller, Garcia, 1974; Supaka, 1972). A harmonious balance with self, others, and nature is emphasized; cooperation with others is stressed. Competition is regarded with disdain by traditional Native Americans. Individual achievements are viewed as contributions to the group, not to personal glory (Pepper, 1967).

Attneave (1982) noted that when the needs or goals of a group conflict with individual decisions and preferences, the group will exert stronger influence, whether the group is understood as the tribe, a band of the tribe, the family, or any other coherent cluster of people. In Native American culture, to excel for personal fame is frowned upon because it sets one above and apart from the others. This disturbs the group's cohesiveness and the balance that tribal members endeavor to maintain. The solidarity of tribes and the group cohesiveness that Native Americans value have been supported and reinforced by the use of humor. It has been a significant and instrumental factor that has helped maintain unity and traditional cultural values.

Studies on humor conducted by McGhee (1970) have shown that humor can serve to facilitate social acceptance by producing an "in-group." The shared knowledge of in-groups is especially important in the Native American world, where humor functions to guide social situations when various tribal communities interact (Deloria, 1969; Giago, 1990).

Deloria (1969) has noted that "rather than embarrass members of the tribe publicly, people used to tease individuals they considered out of step with consensus of tribal opinion." (p. 147). "If someone is out of line, that person [is kidded to convey] that he's doing wrong, and that realization gives value to teasing. The one doing the teasing is not trying to be better than the person being teased but is trying to make a point" (Giago, 1990, p. 52). For example, the young Native American girl is teased about dragging her swal on the ground. "Are you trying to catch your supper?" she is asked (i.e., to collect bugs). The teenage boy is kidded about falling asleep while prayers are being recited in the kiva. "Your mouth was open so big we could have put a whole fried bread in it."

Deloria (1969) also noted that, when various tribal people get together for social and cultural functions (such as a pow-wow), "everything is up for grabs" (p. 163). Sioux tease Chippewas; Chippewas tease Pueblos; Pueblos tease Sioux, etc. Their ability to laugh, to take a tease, and to share jokes creates a bond and a "solid feeling of unity and purpose to the tribe" (Deloria, 1969, p. 147). For example, Pueblos tease Sioux that their hamburgers bark when they bite into them. (Sioux traditionally ate dogs.) Chippewas tease Pueblos that their outdoor ovens would make good bomb shelters.

Giago (1990) observed that the development of cross-tribal teasing may have gained increased popularity when Native Americans were sent away to attend Bureau of Indian Affairs boarding schools. The humor helped "to lighten the lonely feeling and harsh conditions at the schools" (Giago, 1990, p. 52). According to Giago (1990), the adaptability and tenacity of Native Americans, combined with their spiritual beliefs (of a harmonious balance with life and nature), have enabled them to survive centuries of orchestrated hardships and devastation. Humor, Giago notes, was vital because it created a link that connected Native American people.

Native American Humor

In addition to the rampant teasing, many other forms of humor are also prevalent: puns (Navajo, Arapaho, $50-a-night-ho), practical jokes (gluing high heels to the bottom of a pair of moccasins for an "evening look"), ribbing and sexual innuendo ("He just likes long-haired Native American girls so he can get all wrapped up in them." "Custer wore Arrow shirts." "It is a good thing Columbus was not looking for the country of Turkey or else we would be called Turkeys instead of Indians.") Many Native Americans are excellent mimics and mimes, with a superb sense of timing and climax (Giago, 1989; Hill, 1943).

The Sacred Clown

No better example of this humor is the role of the sacred clown in the various tribes' religious ceremonies (Giago, 1989). This religious yet entertaining figure facilitates group unification through humor that brings together all who are within sight and hearing. Heib (1984) stated that "the ritual clown is the embodiment and articulation of humor from a structural perspective . . . If it is to be fully understood [it] requires an understanding of a great complexity of structural relationships extending beyond the ritual process itself to the larger context of how [Native Americans] live" (p. 190).

During the religious ceremony, no one is exempt from the exaggerated, often embarrassing, acts and mimickings of the tenacious clowns. Governors and other tribal officials often become the target of each clown's jest and fun. The clown's obvious disregard for authority helps to unify the group.

Koestler (1964) refers to this social phenomenon as a participatory or self-transcending tendency in that "the self is experienced as being part of the larger whole" (p. 54). The sacred clown tests an individual's ability to take a joke and laugh at themselves and others. For example, the sacred clown will walk behind an elderly woman and mimic her slow, deliberate steps. This teaches the audience not only a great appreciation for humor and group solidarity, but the sacredness of humor

(Beck and Walters, 1977). While the majority of the sacred clown's actions are comical, there are lessons that the clown teaches about how Native Americans treat each other. For example, if two boys are caught fighting by the sacred clown, he and his fellow clown friends may mimic the boys' fighting and make the boys kiss each other to make up. By embarrassing the boys, he not only teaches them that it is wrong to fight, he teaches others observing the action that this type of conduct is inappropriate. Often, after people have observed this type of interaction, the adults will use this opportunity to admonish their children. "See what the clown did? You better behave yourself." Thus, the sacred clown functions not only to teach the lesson of not being too serious, but to protect and teach traditional values and beliefs that reinforce the tribal cohesiveness that is critical for tribal survival.

Pow-wows

Another avenue for the expression of humor in the Native American world occurs at social gatherings called "pow-wows" and "49'ers." Young and old participate and share in the pageantry, laughter, and merriment. Speakers noted for their colorful personalities and ability to captivate audiences are often asked to be the emcees at pow-wows (Giago, 1989). Their knowledge of ceremonialism and ritual is shared with the audience, along with their jokes, wisecracks, and puns. Humorous stories such as predicaments resulting from the Native Americans' unfamiliarity with some customs, mannerisms, and language patterns of the dominant Euro-American society are often the favorite topics of the pow-wow announcer. For example, one pow-wow announcer spoke about his recent experience on a plane. When he saw the flight attendant demonstrated the use of an oxygen mask, he thought it was a breath-analyzer and put his wine back in his boot.

49'ers

After the conclusion of the pow-wow ceremony, a "49'er" is often held. There is no simple way to describe what a 49er is, nor is there one accurate or authentic way to relate it to history. There are as many images associated with the 49'er as there are stories told about how "49'ing" first originated. It is a kind of "night capper" after a fine evening of pow-wow dancing and singing; an R-rated campfire sing-along that allows rookies, as well as master singers and drummers a chance to learn old songs and make up new ones using English and various tribal languages. Bystanders are free to enjoy the relaxed atmosphere and impromptu performances. The atmosphere is full of gaiety and laughter as Native Americans stand around the fire "milking" their jokes. Making up lyrics to each beat of the drum, the comedian receives continual reinforcement from cohorts. A special favorite at 49er's is a song entitled "One-eyed Ford." This is a song about a man taking home his "snag" after the 49'er has ended. There are various versions of "One-eyed Ford." One rendition is as follows:

When the dance is over, sweetheart
I will take you home
in my one-eyed Ford, one-eyed Ford.
Whay yah hi, whay yah hi, whay yah hi yooooo.
When I'm dry and sober, sweetheart
I will take you home
in my one-eyed Ford, one-eyed Ford.
Whay yah hi, whay yah hi, whay yah hi yooooo.

Storytelling

Another important element in the Native American world is its oral tradition and history. Among Native American circles, there has always been an orator or storyteller (Sando, 1976, Tafoya, 1982). Like the sacred clown of Native American religious ceremonies, storytellers have delighted young and old with their oratorical talents, using tales and myths, humorous in context and content, that are told and retold (Deloria, 1969). Their use of humor serves to captivate the audience, as well as to forcefully make points of social and cultural importance. For example, stories about Custer, Columbus, and the Pilgrims are given a different flair and unusual twist.

Conclusion

Humor plays an important role in helping to maintain and reinforce traditional Native American beliefs. Two cultural values, group cohesiveness orientation and circular time perception, are especially emphasized and have a great impact on the Native American's use of humor. To effectively communicate with Native Americans, an awareness of these two cultural values, plus an awareness of the Native American's spiritual belief of harmony with nature, must be acknowledged.

However, just because a Native American's choice of solving a problem may be humorous, this does not necessarily mean that he or she is not taking the task seriously. A supportive, non-judgmental, and accepting attitude is important in understanding how humor has served as a survival mechanism to help Native Americans deal with the complexity involved in living in two different worlds.

REFERENCES

Anderson, B., Burd, L., Dodd, J., & Kelker, K. (1980). A comparative study in estimating time. *Journal of American Indian Education, 19,* (3), 1-4.

Attneave, C. (1982). American Indians and Alaska Native families: emigrants in their own homeland. In M. McGodrick, J. K. Pearce, & J. Giordano (Eds.), *Ethnicity and family therapy* (pp. 55-83). New York: Guildford Press.

Beck, P. G., & Walters, A. L. (1977). *The sacred: Ways of knowledge sources of life.* Tsaile, AZ: Navajo Community College Press.

Deloria, V., Jr. (1969). *Custer died for your sins.* New York: Macmillan.

Exum, H. A., & Colangelo, N. (1981). Culturally diverse gifted: The need for ethnic identity development. *Roeper Review,* 15-17.

Eyster, I. (1980). *Culture through concepts: A teachers' guide.* Norman, OK: Southwest Center for Human Relations Studies. (ERIC Document Reproduction Services No., ED 176 928).

Faas, L. (1982). *Cultural and educational variables involved in identifying and educating gifted and talented American Indian children.* (ERIC Document Reproduction Service No. ED 255 010).

Garrison, L. (1989). Programming for the gifted American Indian student. In C. J. Maker & S. Schiever (Eds.), *Critical issues in gifted education: Defensible programs for cultural and ethnic minorities* (pp. 116-127). Austin, TX: Pro-Ed.

Giago, T., Jr. (1990). My laughter. *Native Peoples: The Arts and Lifeways, 3* (3), 52-56.

Hanson, W. D., & Eisenbise, M. D. (1983). *Human behavior and American Indians*. Rockville, MD: National Institute of Mental Health. (ERIC Document Reproduction Service No. ED 231 589).

Heib, L. A. (1984). Meaning and mismeaning: Toward an understanding of the ritual clown. In A. Ortiz (Ed.), *New perspectives of the Pueblos* (pp. 163-195). Albuquerque: University of New Mexico Press.

Hill, W. W. (1943). *Navajo humor*: Methods for identifying the gifted and talented American Indian student. *Journal for the Education of the Gifted, 11* (3), 53-63.

LeBrasseur, M. M., & Freark, E. S. (1982). Touch a child—They are my people: Ways to teach American Indian children. *Journal of American Indian Education, 21* (3), 6-13.

Light, H. K., & Martin, R. E. (1986). American Indian families. *Journal of American Indian Education, 26* (1), 1-5.

Little Soldier, L. (1985). To soar with the eagles: Enculturation and acculturation of Indian Children. *Childhood Education, 61*, 185-191.

Lockart, B. L. (1978). *Cultural conflict: The Indian child in the Non-Indian classroom*. (ERIC Document Reproduction Service No. ED 195 397).

Marashio, P. (1982). "Enlighten my mind" Examining the learning, process through Native American ways. *Journal of American Indian Education, 21* (2), 2-10.

McGhee, P. E. (1979). *Humor: Its origin and development*. San Francisco: W.H. Freeman.

Miller, D. L, & Garcia, A. (1974, May). *Mental issues among urban Indians: The myth of the savage-child*. Paper presented at the Annual Meeting of the American Psychological Association. (ERIC Document Reproduction Service No. 129 485 0).

Miller, F. C. (1967). Humor in a Chippewa tribal council. *Ethnology, 6* (3), 263-271.

Opler, M. E. (1938). Humor and wisdom of some American Indian tribes. *New Mexico Anthropologists, 3*, 3-10.

Ortiz, A. (Ed.) (1984). *New perspective on the Pueblos*. Albuquerque: University of New Mexico Press.

Pepper, F. C. (1976). Teaching the American Indian child in mainstream settings. In R. L. Jones (Ed.), *Mainstreaming and the minority child* (pp. 133-158). Minneapolis: Council for Exceptional Children.

Sanders, D. (1987). Cultural conflicts: An important factor in the academic failures of American Indian students. *Journal of Multicultural Counseling and Development, 15* (2), 81-90.

Sando, J. S. (1976). *The Pueblo Indians*. San Francisco: The Indian Historian Press.

Tafoya, T. (1982). Coyote's eyes: Native cognition styles. *Journal of American Indian Education, 21* (2), 21-33.

PART IV

TRAVERSING
CULTURAL PATHS

18

How We Know What We Know about Americans: Chinese Sojourners Account for Their Experience

Ling Chen
University of Oklahoma

In the last decade or so, there has been a steady influx of mainland Chinese visitors into the United States: students and scholars who have come to study, teach, or do research for an extended period of time. Unlike early Chinese immigrants who typically settled in Chinese communities, this group of sojourners are scattered all over the country in academic institutions. As adults fully socialized by their native culture, these people are competent communicators in Chinese culture. Like sojourners everywhere, they engage in intercultural interactions on a daily basis.

From the day they arrive, these Chinese find themselves on new terrain in more ways than one. The rules they are brought up with and are accustomed to follow do not apply anymore, though this comes as no real shock. Psychologically, these people are prepared for a big change in their lives. Aside from the academic and professional achievements to which they aspire, most of them are anxious to learn first-hand about America, a world different from China in almost every aspect—political, economic, historical, and cultural. Generally, their first perception of the U.S. is that of a highly industrialized, efficient, fast-paced, materialistic, and individualistic society. For many Chinese with fresh memories of the spiritually and materially impoverishing "Cultural Revolution," America represents what China is striving for: a democracy, a thriving economy, and a high living and educational standard. Based on information from media and hearsay, these sojourners feel they know what to expect in the U.S.

However, to know is never the same as to experience. Phenomenologically, these Chinese are removed from the familiar, in terms of time as well as space, as their routine is upset by the change of environment. They now share both time and space with the unfamiliar, where little can be taken for granted. It is a situation that calls for ingenuity, resourcefulness, and problem solving with heightened awareness.

The purpose of this essay is to explore the process of active sense-making among Chinese sojourners in the U.S. and the paradoxical imbalance between familiarity and reality. By definition, sense-making is activated by social interactions, either by direct experience or as reflection in hindsight (Blumer, 1969). The central question here is, "How do these Chinese interpret interactions they have with Americans, whether singly or with a group?" Throughout their stay in this country as foreign visitors, even if they decide to become residents, they are constantly confronted with the question "What should I make of this situation?"

From a cultural perspective, how these Chinese cope with living in America provides a specific example of the way in which people experience the phenomenon of intercultural communication. Though I have observed this phenomenon first-hand as a participant, the following accounts are related by selected Chinese friends and acquaintances who describe their experiences since arriving in this country. Specific attention will be focused on cases in which the participants become aware of their own sense-making efforts. These accounts were obtained through interviews with Chinese students in their mid-twenties and early thirties at two Midwestern universities. These interviews were spoken in Chinese, except where remarks were quoted, and then translated by this author. Each translation was verified by each interviewee to ensure accuracy. These accounts will demonstrate the conscious sense-making process: how the experience is triggered and brought into awareness, how it operates, and how it ends with tentative knowledge. Each stage will be discussed in three sections in that order.

Taking for Granted and Surprise

Chinese as cultural strangers in the U.S. face a situation in which little can be taken for granted. Though they may anticipate this and feel prepared for the unfamiliar, in practice true awareness only surfaces when something unexpected occurs. Until then, sojourners move about as if they knew the ropes, going about their business as if they were still in their native culture. They deal with matters in ways they always do, until that moment when they find themselves in a problematic situation. Only then are they surprised, realizing that too much has been taken for granted; only then do they begin trying to understand the situation, particularly the American with whom they interacted at the time. This process is reactivated every time a taken-for-granted situation results in a surprise. A student (Mr. An)* told me the following story about his first contact with an American on his way to the U.S.

> Mr. An: I was so excited about the trip and the opportunity to study here that I took the first flight available to the city where my school is. The flight would arrive at night which didn't bother me, as I figured I would find a way to get to school, although *I hadn't really thought about it*. I was sitting next to a woman named Alice, and we got into a conversation. I told her this was my first time visiting the U.S., and I was so excited about going to this school, etc. She asked me where I would be staying. I said I would probably be living in a student dormitory. She asked if I had made arrangements for the lodging and informed

* The names used are not real names.

the school of my arrival. I said no, but the school must have places. I would find out about it. She asked what I would do tonight. Offices would not be open until tomorrow. It was then I started to vaguely sense the situation I might be in. I said there must be a night guard post on campus where I could get directions to a school guest house or something. At this Alice said she could put me up for the night, that I could live in her house until I found a place, that I could use her son's room who was away. I was surprised but also very grateful. I now realized the seriousness of my mistake in not making any arrangements beforehand. . . .

This is a typical story among Chinese sojourners. As revealed by Mr. An's excitement, he anticipated something different; yet, his mode of thinking did not entirely incorporate this anticipation. When questioned, he justified his decision for not making housing arrangements with Chinese common sense: (1) schools in China have an obligation to allocate living quarters to students, be it in the guest house or a dormitory, and (2) there is always a security guard at the campus gate. Mr. An's story continues:

> Mr. An: The next day I visited the International Students' Office, assuming I would find a place to stay. A foreign student advisor who talked to me was very nice and tried to be helpful. She gave me a lot of information about a lot of things, one of which was housing. Instead of a place, I was given a list of rental offices and a local map. But I didn't know what to do with them. . . .

Obviously, Mr. An had not quite learned his lesson yet. His visit to the school was guided by the belief that he would find lodgings without a problem, again based on his past experience at home. So he was disappointed at the kind of help he got. Looking back, he now understands that the advisor had made an effort to be helpful in the American way, which was not taken as of much help at all at the time.

Similarly, a Ms. Bian remembered her surprise upon landing in the U.S.:

> Ms. Bian: I walked off the plane and followed the signs to the baggage claim. "This is really *convenient*," I remember thinking. I had two extra-large suitcases and a big carry-on bag. After picking up

the bags, I started to look around, trying to find someone to help me carry them. But not many people were around, and everyone had luggage of their own—only they all had wheels. I walked around and noticed there was a line of luggage trolleys on the far side of the hall. I was so relieved, thinking, "After all, it is America." Nothing is neglected. I walked over and immediately saw a sign: "Deposit One Dollar." My good mood was quickly replaced by a self-mocking thought: "You should have known better. This is America, after all." Somehow this first impression always stuck in my mind. Sometime later, I picked up an American saying, "No free lunch." It very vividly sums up my first experience in America. . . .

Ms. Bian seemed to be more aware of the change of environment than Mr. An. She was impressed by the convenient signs in the airport, which apparently were new to her. She was soon applying this new knowledge to the luggage carts, only to be disappointed by another surprise. Her self-mocking attitude indicated her awareness of her own assumption: in China, a (free) helping hand is always available in places like airports and train stations.

Reliance on familiar cultural schemes of behavior is also highlighted in the following two examples: (1) Mr. Cong's experience with marijuana, and (2) Ms. Dai's experience with her landlady.

Mr. Cong: The other day I came across Rod, a fellow student, outside the library. We started chatting. Somehow we brought up the topic of marijuana, and I said I knew about it but had never seen it. On this, Rod took out a pouch from a pocket and told me it was marijuana. He showed it to me, then put a pinch into a pipe and smoked it. I watched curiously. "You want to try it?" he asked as he demonstrated, offering me his pipe. I didn't expect such an offer, letting me share *his* pipe. I felt obliged to take the pipe and briefly tried it before handing it back to Rod, although I had no real interest. I guess I might have appeared to be too interested in it. Still, this was a novel experience. A couple of days later in the GTA office, several of us were around during the lunch hour, and naturally there was small talk. I remembered my experience with marijuana and told them about what happened without thinking about it. To my surprise, my story was met with an unusual reception. It seemed that these people were surprised by my telling this story and didn't know

how to respond. Nobody commented on it or said anything about it. . . .

Ms. Dai: I rented a room from Mrs. Robinson the first year I was here. The Robinsons also lived in the same house. The house had a back yard with laundry lines. Whenever I did laundry, I would hang my washing outside in the morning, and it would be dry by the time I returned from the school at the end of day. On one of those days, it rained shortly after lunch time. When I got home, I found the washing I had put out that morning sitting on the floor near the stairs. Everything was dry. I realized someone had brought it in before the rain. It had to be Mrs. Robinson, I realized, since she was at home all day. That was really *very kind of her*, I thought, and I was glad not to have to worry about wet clothes. Just then, Mrs. Robinson came out and, to my amazement, she started apologizing for removing my washing from the lines before I could thank her. For a while, I didn't know what to say. I assured her that she did just what I would have wanted her to do, that I must thank her for her kindness. I couldn't understand why she apologized for bringing in the wash for me. . . .

Both Mr. Cong and Ms. Dai had been in the U.S. for some time when these encounters occurred. Still they lived mostly by their cultural intuition. Mr. Cong was content with knowing what marijuana looked like and was surprised, not by the act of the offer but by the nature of the offer: the sharing of a pipe with a casual acquaintance. What was more interesting was his response. In spite of a lack of interest, and not without some reluctance, he accepted the offer. His sense of obligation to humor an offered kindness is reflective of the deeply rooted Asian tradition of "face-giving" (Goffman, 1967). Another surprise was in store for Mr. Cong when he shared his experience with other Americans "without thinking," another common practice among Chinese acquaintances. The unexpected reaction from his audience alerted him that something was wrong. He sensed that it might be the telling of the story but could not figure out the complete meaning of the reaction.

As for Ms. Dai, she rightly assumed Mrs. Robinson's kindness based on the fact that she was the only one home. Naturally she offered her thanks. But never would she have imagined that her landlady would apologize for her own act of kindness. Though Ms. Dai was left momentarily speechless, she quickly recovered and reciprocated with an assurance of no ill feelings. She instinctively enacted what seemed to be an appropriate response to an unexpected apology. Still, she couldn't understand it. From her Chinese perspective, it was a kind thing to keep her washing from being spoiled by rain. In China, it is common for room-mates to move around each other's possessions, an act no Chinese would normally consider unusual or imprudent.

So far, our analysis has posed the theoretical premise of the cultural stranger "who has to ques-tion nearly everything that seems to be unquestion-able to the members of the native cultural group (Schutz, 1964, p. 96), as illustrated by the true stories of these Chinese sojourners. Yet by and large, they still rely heavily on a knowledge of dealing with the world that they acquired in their home cultures.

The constant surprises in these people's new cultural environment no doubt reminded them that their old frame of reference was no longer valid here. This alone, however, was not sufficient to reorient their outlook. Their problem is rooted in a contradictory state associated with the status of being strangers—the paradox alluded to earli-er—that prevents them from identifying potential problems before they are experienced. The change in physical location does not axiomatically bring about a corresponding change in their social or cultural perspective. As a product of cultural development in a particular environment, one's social perspective constitutes one's reserve of knowledge, accumulated over time, that provides a frame of reference to make sense of the empirical world. Consequently, such a perspective cannot be replaced overnight without prior empirical knowl-edge, as there is nothing yet there to take its place. Inconsistency of position and viewpoint, therefore, is the dilemma facing all sojourners, which cannot be alleviated by simply acknowledging it. One may be fully aware of this dilemma but still be unable to

question anything one encounters in a foreign environment, despite subjective intent, because one cannot know the unknown or what to question. Questions can be asked only after situations are experienced as different from the expected.

Making Sense

Once unexpected surprises have brought the foreign environment to immediate attention, the sense-making process is activated. At this point, one does not automatically "know" just by being directly involved and must make efforts to "figure out and actively seek further explanation under the circum-stances. From Mr. An's account, not only did he not consider any possible lodging problems, he also gave no thought to his casual interaction with a helpful American. Once the conversation awakened him to his false assumptions, he could no longer take things for granted. Mr. An's account contin-ues:

Mr. An: I now realized the seriousness of my mistake by not having made any arrangements beforehand. It was very kind of Alice to ask, but what her offer also told me was that I might not be able to move into the dorm right away, which I was soon to find out. I was even more grateful to Alice. It turned out that, not only was there no guest house on campus, but the student dorms had to be booked beforehand. There was no place on campus that could have solved my immediate problem that night—nor even during the day. I felt fortunate to have met such a warm-hearted friend and was also glad to have someone to visit with later. . . .

Mr. An was wiser now. Alice's offer was inter-preted not just as kindness, the most common assessment the Chinese make in similar situations. It was taken also as a warning that there was likely to be a serious problem under the circumstances. Reality was beginning to sink in and other possibili-ties were emerging. He realized that she would not have invited him, a stranger, to her home if there had not been a real need on his part. Further, he took Alice's kindness as an offer of friendship. This type of situation is often the beginning of a friendship in China. The assumption that both persons will stay in touch is made without question, especially when they live in the same town. Once again Mr. An took a situation for granted, and his assumption later also proved to be wrong.

In the International Students' Office, an unexpected situation triggered a series of analytical questions to search for an explanation on the part of Mr. An.

Mr. An: From what my advisor Mrs. Hugh explained to me, I understood that I was to call people on the list and make arrangements. But how? I didn't have the faintest idea. On the map the city looked huge; even the campus area was too big to cross. I didn't know what to say when calling, because I had never done anything like this before. And I didn't know whom to call first; there were so many of them. I was painfully aware of being on my own. I had always been independent, but this was nothing like the independence I knew. I felt so alone, so much in the hands of the unknown. I had to try to do the best I could without knowing what would come out of it. On the other hand, I started to better understand the meaning of independence. I felt I really understood America now and was overjoyed when Mrs. Hugh told me there was a Chinese Student Association on campus. This meant that maybe I could get help from them. And I did. . . .

Confronted with this new problem of apartment hunting, Mr. An neatly assessed the situation. The city was big, and he had no transportation. He understood that he was facing a challenge, that he had to figure out a way to take it on. What had once been hearsay about being individualistic and independent in the U.S., was now a living experience for Mr. An; independence had taken on a new meaning. It meant not only his will to act, but also his responsibility and initiative, as well as the possibility of failure and its ramifications. Mr. An had come to grips with the reality he was facing.

Analogous to Mr. An's progress was Ms. Bian's experience, in which she had made a connection between what she knew indirectly about American materialism and what she had experienced firsthand—a charge for use of a luggage cart. In the world of business, she had realized, convenience

and services are provided as a business consideration rather than out of kindness. Here is how she came to that realization in a second interaction:

Ms. Bian: I was looking around in the lady's dress section of a department store, when a salesperson approached me. She appeared so *sincere* in wanting to help, so I told her what I wanted. She showed me a couple of items, but none of them appealed to me. So I thanked her and wandered into another area. Then at some other racks, she came up to me again, trying to help. Again I declined. As I didn't really have a particular thing in mind, I felt more efficient searching on my own. However, she was not discouraged. I felt maybe I *should* buy something. As soon as I found a sweater I liked, I bought it from her before continuing to look around. Sure enough, the lady didn't approach me again after that. "No free lunch." How very true. . . .

The first interpretation Ms. Bian made of the saleswoman's offer to assist was due to her sincerity, believing she wanted to help as one would help a fellow human being. Of course she realized the woman's role as a salesperson but felt she was only trying to help—a natural reflection of Ms. Bian's cultural intuition. Chinese culture emphasizes human relations as an integral part of human interactions. Thus, Ms. Bian acknowledged what she saw as good will from the salesperson by accepting the help and expressing her thanks, which was socially appropriate. We can see that Ms. Bian's initial understanding of the interaction was basically a social gesture, as opposed to business motive in the world of sales. What constituted the end of a social transaction to Ms. Bian was not regarded as such by the salesperson, who considered it the beginning of a possible financial transaction. Thus, she continued to interact with Ms. Bian until something was sold. Her persistence prompted Ms. Bian to reconsider their relationship and correctly reassess the offered assistance as a "Can I help you?" sales pitch.

Ms. Bian was in a similar situation as Ms. Dai: the immediate context of the situation provided each them with informational cues to make an alternative sense of the interaction; they then adjusted their own behaviors to accommodate the situation and take on the expected role. However, while Ms. Bian managed to grasp the situation for what it was, Ms. Dai was induced to make a seemingly appropriate response without understanding why.

Likewise, Mr. Cong, puzzled by the unexpected response he received from his story about marijuana, consciously tried to find an answer.

Mr. Cong: It could be that some people might not have attended to what I said. But the man I was talking to couldn't have missed it. Yet, his reaction was to just look at me with an expression that made me wonder what I had done wrong. . . .

Mr. Cong considered circumstantial explanations of the others' unresponsiveness during this interaction. He immediately ruled out that people had missed what he said—their expressions indicated otherwise. Moreover, the man's expression was unusual and odd under the circumstances. This assessment led Mr. Cong to suspect that he probably had done something he should not have, but still he could not figure out what that might be.

Sense-making is a process by which strangers reorient themselves. The change of environment brings about a two-fold separation of the sojourner's personal history, physically from that of the home culture and perceptually from that of the host culture. The surprise and the ensuing state of confusion are instrumental in solidifying the mismatch between physical standpoint and perceptual viewpoint. The abstract knowledge of differences has been activated by direct experience. In the struggle to come to grips with the here and now, the stranger is forced to cut ties to the past—slowly, a little at a time—and look for unfamiliar input from the immediate context to use in place of the old. As soon as old assumptions lose their relevance, the stranger stops taking things for granted and seeks new input. The questioning process initiates the perceptual, experiential, and psychological transition of the stranger into the new society.

Amidst all these questions, something fundamental remains unchallenged for these Chinese: the presumption of rationality and logic in the behavior of their American interactants. When confronted with the unexpected, they did not doubt for a moment the Americans' reasonableness in the Chinese's search for alternative interpretations.

Coming to Understand

The above interpretations of various accounts have demonstrated how these Chinese came to realize their own misconstrued perceptions of an interaction as different from that of the Americans, and how they constructed alternative readings of the situation from contextual cues. This new interpretation is certainly not taken as a complete understanding of the new cultural environment. Nevertheless, it is one step toward solving an immediate problem, though of course the process of sense-making does not end when the triggering episode is over. This new information is not treated as part of their reserve of intuitive knowledge (Schutz, 1964), but as subject to further verification the next time a similar situation is encountered. In the case of Ms. Dai, she was puzzled by Mrs. Robinson's apology. She accepted the apology, but a question mark remained in her mind. She continued to search for an explanation:

Ms. Dai: Later I learned that people here don't usually touch things that belong to others. I noticed in our office that my American colleagues would borrow each other's stationery only when the owner was present and after they had asked for permission. A student once told me that she and her roommate had a big fight, because the roommate had moved something that belonged to her without asking. Although she claimed that it was no big deal, I was impressed by the fact that it had caused such a quarrel. Now I know why my landlady apologized about the laundry: she didn't feel comfortable about moving my things while I was away, even for a good reason.

Ms. Dai considered various observations of what transpires when someone moves someone else's things, until she uncovered a recurring pattern that revealed an underlying cultural rule. This observation was then applied to her earlier experience for interpretation.

Mr. Cong's account of his story about marijuana also provided an explanation:

Mr. Cong: I didn't know what to make of it at the time, but later I learned that marijuana was an illegal drug. I probably shouldn't have told those people about my experience with an illegal substance, especially when it involved a third party, whom I referred to by name. I am glad that I didn't get anybody into trouble.

The knowledge of the legal complication of marijuana use solved the puzzle for him. Rightly or wrongly, it also shed a different light on the episode. Mr. Cong felt the weight of his fellow student's trust and his own carelessness.

Ms. Bian's understanding of American materialism was also achieved gradually. The first encounter in the airport gave her first-hand knowledge, which was verified by her later encounter in the department store. Accumulation of first-hand experience and verification finally led to understanding, as summarized by her repetition of the saying "No free lunch." For her, these words had acquired the status of a theory. On several occasions I have witnessed her using it at the conclusion of other stories and as a piece of advice for others.

Mr. An's account of his friendship with Alice is also of interest. It follows as such:

Mr. An: I stayed in Alice's house for four days until I found an apartment. For over half a year, I kept in touch with her, calling her a couple of times a month and visiting her. She came to visit me once after I just moved. Then I was too busy and called her less and less often. One day I realized I had not called Alice in a long time, then it occurred to me that she rarely called me; I was the one who usually made the calls. Since then, we haven't been in touch for about two years now. I just didn't get around to calling her again, but now I don't feel guilty about it. She didn't seem to mind one way or the other. I've learned that many Americans are ready to help others but never see them again afterwards. I have been helped several times by strangers when my car broke down. I also have seen it happen to others. People will jump-start your car or call for help, often before being asked. Sometimes, especially when there is snow, several people will stop and push your car, not even minding getting exhausted and dirty. Americans are really great.

Here Mr. An finally learns about American culture's emphasis on basic humanism. Understanding this phenomenon helped him to make sense of the friendship he thought he had with Alice: in actuality it was a momentary helping relationship built on a humanistic base, which is common in American society. Once the help was no longer needed, there was no reason to keep up the relationship. Mr. An reinterpreted Alice's friendliness as an appropriate gesture to help a stranger, with no intention of becoming friends, contrary to what Mr. An originally felt obliged to do. His experience with his stalled car again showed him that people were ready to help when others were in trouble, which brought him greater understanding of his experience with Alice and reinforced this new understanding. Now he no longer feels guilty for not being concerned about a "friendship" that is not mutual. Instead, he has acquired a new frame of reference.

Coming to a tentative understanding is the last stage in a cycle of sense-making. At this stage, the sojourner has solved the problem of a misplaced perspective and temporarily regained some balance. One can now see eye to eye with the American interactant and know how to deal with each situation. In the long run, however, this new perspective will never be completely fulfilled by one's accumulation of knowledge about various different situations within the host culture; hence, there is always the likelihood of further such learning cycles for the sojourner.

Summary and Conclusion

The sense-making process discussed in this essay is one whereby we begin to understand a new cultural environment by uncovering its implicit cultural rules. It is a process by which certain adjustments must be made to bring about a unity between physical proximity and perceptual familiarity. This is a slow and gradual process, barely noticeable at first, just like children growing up. Unlike growing children, however, the Chinese adults described above are more conscious and ready to make associations and inferences. They do so with the assumption that what they are learning must be reasonable, as it is part of the native common sense. It also becomes knowledge for these Chinese sojourners. Once verified, the knowledge they acquired will add to their own stockpile of information and be applied without question, until the next surprise comes around. The cycle of taking things for granted, surprises, and searching for and discovering meaning, will be repeated often in the process of sense-making. Over time, there will be fewer surprises as the sojourners come to better understand and are assimilated into their environment. When this happens, they will no longer be strangers.

REFERENCES

Blumer, H. (1969). *Symbolic interactionism.* Englewood Cliffs, NJ: Prince Hall.

Garfinkel, H. (1967). *Studies in ethnomethodology.* Englewood Cliffs, NJ: Prince Hall.

Goffman, E. (1967). *Interaction ritual.* New York: Anchor Books.

Merleau-Ponty, M. (1959). *Phenomenology of perception.* London: Routledge.

Schutz, A. (1964). *Collected papers II: Studies in social theory.* The Hague: Martinus Nijhoff.

Wieder, D. L., & Pratt, S. (1990). On being a recognizable Indian among Indians. In D. Carbough (Ed.), *Cultural communication and intercultural contact* (pp. 45-64). Hillsdale, NJ: Lawrence Erlbaum.

19

When Black Women Talk with White Women: Why Dialogues are Difficult

Marsha Houston
Tulane University

My conversations with white women of equal social status involve much competition, aggression, and mutual lack of trust, intimacy, and equality. However, there are exceptions.
—*A black woman graduate student*

Gender and communication researchers have demonstrated that women's conversations with each other are different from their conversations with men. For example, they are more egalitarian and mutually supportive. Certainly, many conversations between African Americans[1] and white women are of this sort. Yet I, and nearly every other African American woman I know, can recall many conversations with white women that were neither egalitarian nor supportive, conversations that we would describe as stressful, insensitive, and in some cases even racist. Like the graduate student quoted above, many African American women are likely to consider such "difficult dialogues"[2] with white peers to be the rule and open, satisfying conversations the exception.

The difficulties in black and white women's interracial conversations are the focus of this essay.

I do not intend to give a definitive or an exhaustive analysis of women's interracial talk, but to explore two reasons why black women so often find conversations with white women unsatisfying and to suggest three statements to avoid in interracial conversation. I write from an African American woman's perspective, from within my ethnic cultural group, but I hope this essay will spark dialogue about both the differences and commonalities between black and white women speakers.

A History of Suspicion and Distrust

Wed., Sept. 12, 1855. . . I have met [white] girls in the schoolroom—they have been thoroughly kind and cordial to me—perhaps the next day met them on the street—they feared to recognize me; these I can but regard now with scorn and contempt. . . . Others give the most distant recognition possible— I, of course, acknowledge no such recognition, and they soon cease entirely. These are but trifles, certainly, to the great public wrongs which we [black people] . . . are obliged to endure. But to those who experience them, these apparent trifles are most wearing and discouraging; even to a child's mind they reveal volumes of deceit and heartlessness, and early teach a lesson of suspicion and distrust.[3]

This quotation is taken from the girlhood diary of Charlotte Forten, who was born into an affluent, free, black Philadelphia family in 1838. Like many modern communication scholars, Forten saw her everyday conversations as microcosms of the larger social and political relationships of her time. To her, the "trifles" which defined her relationship to her white schoolmates were a reflection of the "great public wrongs" of slavery that defined the relationship of African Americans to U.S. society during her youth. Her words remind us that even a life of social and economic privilege does not protect African Americans from racist encounters.

Charlotte Forten's words are also a reminder of the long history of "wearing and discouraging" conversations between black and white women. Her experience with her white classmates is an example of what Philomena Essed has termed "everyday racism," that is, racism that is expressed by a range of acts that may appear to be "trivial" or "normal" to whites, but are a constant source of stress for African Americans.[4] Essed points out that everyday racism results in a communication climate in which blacks can never take for granted that whites will respect them, treat them with courtesy, judge them fairly, or take them seriously. In her study of African American professional women of the 1920s and 1930s, Gwendolyn Etter-Lewis reports an act of everyday racism that was told to her by a successful composer and music teacher:

> I can think of things that happened to me in high school. For example. . . a young white girl, whom I thought of as being my friend and she considered me a friend. But I remember how I felt one day when going up the broad steps of City High School. There were only ten black people at City High at that time. She spoke to me and smiled as she was passing me. . . as she always did. And her friend must have said something to her about speaking to me like why did you speak to that black person. And I heard my friend say, 'Well, she can't help it because she's black.' And that jarred me. . .[5]

This woman was so taken aback when her high school friend spoke about her color as if it were an affliction, that she never forgot the encounter and recounted it for Etter-Lewis at the age of seventy-five.

Although not every contemporary conversation between black and white women is stressful, uncomfortable, or unpleasant, much talk between black and white women takes place against a backdrop of long-standing suspicion and distrust. This often unspoken distrust is illustrated by the contrasting attitudes of black women interviewed by Essed in the Netherlands and the United States. Most of her interviewees in the Netherlands were recent immigrants from Suriname who were surprised when Dutch whites treated them with duplicity or hostility; but *every one* of her African American interviewees mentioned that as a girl she was "ingrained" with the expectation of encountering insensitive or racist communication from whites and with defenses against it.[6] African American women's defenses against everyday racist talk may not consist of verbal retorts but rather an attitude of

imperviousness to racial insensitivity, that is, cognitive skill in dismissing insensitive discourse, perhaps by thinking, "That's just the way *they* (whites) are." Some interracial conversations between women may appear untroubled because black women have learned to mask or ignore their dissatisfaction and distrust, rather than because white women have learned to be more sensitive than they were in Charlotte Forten's day.

In one research project, I attempted to probe beneath black women's defenses, to lift their mask a bit by asking comparable groups of black and white women to describe their own communication style and that of the opposite group. Their most frequent descriptions are summarized below. They suggest that one reason women's interracial dialogues are difficult is that black and white women pay attention to different features of talk.

Mutual Negative Stereotypes

A basic concept of contemporary communication theory is that a speaker does not merely respond to the manifest content of a message, but to his or her interpretation of the speaker's intention or meaning. In other words, I respond to what I *think* you *meant* by what you said. Such factors as the setting and occasion, the language variety or dialect, and the interpersonal relationship between speaker and listener influence message interpretation and response.

In addition, some understandings of talk are influenced by a speaker's gender or ethnicity. For example, researchers have found that when the same message is delivered in much the same manner by a woman or by a man, listeners interpret it quite differently, in part because they expect women and men to use different styles of talk and to have knowledge of different subjects[7]. Thomas Kochman has pointed out how the different nonverbal vocal cues that working-class African Americans and middle-class whites use to express the same emotion (e.g., sincerity or anger) can create diametrically opposed attributions regarding a speaker's intentions.[8] Each ethnic cultural group has come to expect the expression of various emotions or attitudes to sound a certain way. Thus, sincerity, when uttered in a high-keyed, dynamic, working-class black style, may sound like anger to middle-class whites. And when uttered in a low-keyed, non-dynamic, middle-class white style, it may sound like disinterest or deceit to working-class blacks. Because expectations for talk are culturally learned and seldom violated by speakers *within* a cultural group, they appear to be natural or normal to the members of that group. Misunderstanding and conflict can result when cultural expectations for how to express specific attitudes and emotions are violated.

By asking African American women to describe their communication style ("black women's talk" or "talking like a black woman") as well as that of white women ("white women's talk" or "talking like a white woman"), I endeavored to discover some of their expectations for talk.[9] Below are examples of these African American women's most frequent responses:

Black women's talk is:

- Standing behind what you say, not being afraid to speak your mind
- speaking with a strong sense of self-esteem
- speaking out; talking about what's on your mind
- getting down to the heart of the matter
- speaking with authority, intelligence, and common sense
- being very sure of oneself
- being very distinguished and educated
- reflecting black experience as seen by a black woman in a white patriarchal society

White women's talk is:

- Friendly (with an air of phoniness)
- arrogant
- know-it-all
- talking as if they think they're better than the average person
- mainly dealing with trivia
- talking proper about nothing
- weak, "air-headish"

- silly but educated
- illustrating fragility; seemingly dependent and helpless
- passive, submissive, delicate

I asked a comparable group of white women to describe their talk and that of black women. Here are their most frequent responses:

Black women's talk is:

- using black dialect
- saying things like "young 'uns," "yous," "wif," and "wich you"
- using jive terms

White women's talk is:

- all kinds of speech patterns
- distinct pronunciation
- using the appropriate words for the appropriate situations
- talking in a typical British-American language with no necessary accent and limited to "acceptable" middle-class women's topics

The above suggests that African American and white women hear very different things. Not only does each list contain positive descriptions of the group's own talk and negative descriptions of the other group's talk, but each focuses on different features. African American women concentrate on both their own and white women's interpersonal skills, strategies, and attributes. They see themselves as open, forthright, intelligent speakers and white women as duplicitous, arrogant, and frivolous. White women, on the other hand, concentrate their descriptions on language style—vocabulary, grammar, pronunciation—describing themselves as standard or correct and African American women and nonstandard, incorrect, or deviant.

Because they concentrated on language style, white women described only those African American women who use African-based black English as "talking like a black woman." Their descriptions suggest that black women who use General American Speech, the prestige variety of language in the

U. S.[10], are "talking white" (or talking "normally"). In contrast, African American women described themselves as speaking in "black women's talk" whenever they used particular interpersonal strategies (e.g., "standing behind what you say"; "getting down to the heart of the matter"), communication that is independent of language variety.

One reason why African American women perceived "black women's talk" as independent of language variety may be that many of us are bistylistic (able to speak two language varieties) while most white women are relatively monostylistic. College-educated, middle-class women who grew up and learned to speak in predominantly African American communities usually have a command of both Black English and General American Speech. Those of us who are bistylistic speakers switch language varieties to some extent[11] according to situations and conversational partners, but we do not feel that we shed our ethnic cultural identity when we use General American Speech. Barbara Smith describes black women's perspective on their two speaking styles in this way:

> Now, I don't think this is about acting white in a white context. It's about one, a lack of inspiration. Because the way you act with black people is because they inspire the behavior. And I *do* mean inspire. . . [W]hen you are in a white context, you think, 'Well, why bother? Why waste your time?' if what you're trying to do is get things across and communicate and what-have-you, *you talk in your second language.*[12]

In describing their style, African American women were able to look beneath the surface features of language choice and concentrate on underlying interpersonal skills and strategies. White women, unfamiliar with how language and interpersonal interaction work in black communities, defined only that black women's talk most different from their own in vocabulary, pronunciation, and grammar as "black."

Perhaps African American women's greater awareness of differences in language and style accounts for the final difference in the lists above. White women tended to describe their own talk as normal or universal ("all kinds of speech patterns") and African American women's talk as deviant or limited. But African American women described both their own and white women's talk as particular speaking styles.

The attention to different aspects of talk may be one reason why mutually satisfying dialogue between the two groups is often difficult. For example, researchers have noted the high value African American women place on talk that is forthright, sincere, and authentic, as did the women who responded to my questionnaire (e.g., "not being afraid to speak your mind").[13] This may sometimes conflict with the high value white women have been taught to place on politeness and propriety in speech, as several white respondents to the questionnaire indicated (e.g., "using appropriate words for the. . . situation").[14] Thus, white women may sound "phony" to black women because they have learned to be more concerned about being proper and polite than "getting down to the heart of the matter."

However, There Are Exceptions

The picture of black and white women's conversations painted here may seem particularly gloomy. The unequal power relationships that generally define the places of blacks and whites in the U.S. social order continue to intrude on our everyday interpersonal encounters, much as they did in Charlotte Forten's time. Our perceptions of one another as communicators are often riddled with stereotypes and misattributions. And yet open, satisfying conversations between African American and white women do occur; many black and white women are amicable colleagues and close friends.[15] As an African American woman who has been a student or professor at predominantly white universities for almost 30 years, I have many white women colleagues whose conversation I enjoy and a few friends whom I can count on for good talk. Even the graduate student whose stinging criticism of conversations with white women peers is quoted at the beginning of this essay admitted that "there are exceptions."

What is the nature of those exceptions? What communicative acts enable African American women to perceive white women's talk as authentic rather than "phony"? This is a complex question for which there may be as many answers as there are black women speakers (or as there are black and white women conversational partners). I would like to briefly suggest a response gleaned from my own interracial relationships and those of the members of my large network of African American women friends, relatives, students, and acquaintances.[16] I have chosen to phrase my response by offering three statements that a white woman who wants to treat black women with respect and friendship should never utter: (1) "I never even notice that you're black"; (2) "You're different from most black people"; (3) "I understand what you're going through as a black woman, because. . . ."

(1) 'I Never Even Notice. . . .'

The first statement sometimes comes as "We're all the same, really—just people." It expresses what I have come to call "the myth of generically packaged people." It is based on the incorrect assumption that cultural, sexual, or generational differences do not result in different social experiences and different interpretations of shared experiences.

Although intended to be nonracist, Statement 1 actually denies the uniqueness of black women's history and contemporary experiences. It suggests that the speaker regards blackness as something negative, a problem that one "can't help" and, therefore, as something that one's white friends should overlook. It denies the possibility that blackness could be something to be valued, even celebrated. Yet many black women view our blackness as a source of pride, not only because of the many accomplished African American women and men who have overcome racism to make significant contributions, but also because of our knowledge of how our personal histories have been influenced by our blackness.

In addition, as one white woman scholar has noted, when a white woman says, "We're all alike. . . . ," she usually means, "I can see how

you (a black woman) are like *me* (a white woman)"; she does not mean, "I can see how *I* am like *you*."[17] In other words, "just people" means "just *white* people"—that is, people who are culturally and behaviorally similar to me, just people who share my values and beliefs, just people who do not make me aware that they are culturally or historically different and who do not insist that I honor and respect their way of being human. It is an ethnocentric statement.

Despite the nonracist intentions of the white women whom I have heard utter ""I never even notice. . . ," I interpret it as blatantly racist. It erases my ethnic cultural experience (a part of who I am), redefines it in white women's terms.

(2) 'You're Different. . . .'

This statement is closely related to the first; I see it as an effort to subtract the blackness from the woman. Sometimes the statement precedes other negative or stereotypical statements about black people ("The black girls I went to high school with in South Georgia. . .", "Those black women on welfare. . ."). It indicates that the speaker perceives there to be "acceptable" and "unacceptable" black women or some groups of black women whom it is okay to hate.

Although I am anxious for white women to see that there is diversity among African American women, and although some African American women desire to separate themselves from elements of our community that they (and whites) perceive as undesirable, I believe that few of us fail to see the racism lurking behind this "divide and conquer" statement. I am different from the poor black woman on welfare; I have a different personal history, more education, the ability to provide a better lifestyle and better life-chances for my son. But I am also the same as her; we share an ethnic cultural history (in Africa and the U.S.), and we share a life-long struggle with both racism and sexism. When I hear "You're different. . . ", I always wonder, "If I can respect and accept white women's differences from me, why can't they respect and accept my differences from them?"

(3) 'I Understand Your Experience as a Black Woman Because. . . . '

I have heard this sentence completed in numerous, sometimes bizarre, ways, from "because sexism is just as bad as racism" to "because I watch 'The Cosby Show,'" to "because I'm also a member of a minority group. I'm Jewish. . . Italian. . . overweight. . . ."

The speaker here may intend to indicate her effort to gain knowledge of my cultural group or to share her own experiences with prejudice. I would never want to thwart her efforts or to trivialize such experiences. Yet I hear in such statements examples of the arrogance perceived by the black women who described "white women's talk" in the lists above. Similar experiences should not be confused with the same experience; my experience of prejudice is erased when you identify it as "the same" as yours. In addition, there are no shortcuts to interracial relationships, no vicarious ways to learn how to relate to the people of another culture (e.g., through reading or watching television). Only actual contact with individuals over an extended period of time begins to build interracial understanding.

I believe that "I understand your experience as a black woman because. . . " represents white women's attempt to express solidarity with African American women, perhaps motivated by the assumption that, before we can begin a friendship, we expect them to understand our life experiences in the way they understand their own. I make no such assumption about my white women friends, and I think they make no comparable assumption about me. There is much about white women's life experiences and perspectives that I may know about, but will never fully understand. Whether my friend is black or white, I do not presume to understand all, just to respect all.

The above three statements are words I have never heard from white women whom I count among my friends. Rather than treating our ethnic cultural differences as barriers to be feared or erased before true friendship can emerge, they embrace them as features that enrich and enliven our relationships.

NOTES

[1]In this chapter "black" and "African American" will be used synonymously.

[2]The phrase "difficult dialogues" was first used to describe talk between different social groups in Johnella Butler's "Difficult Dialogues," *Women's Review of Books* (February, 1989).

[3]Ray Allen Billington. (1953) ed., *The Journal of Charlotte L. Forten: A Young Black Woman's Reactions to the White World of the Civil War Era.* p. 74. New York: Norton. Charlotte Forten married the Reverend Francis J. Grimke in 1878; she was a prominent equal rights activist until her death in 1914.

[4]Philomena Essed. (1991). *Understanding Everyday Racism: An Interdisciplinary Theory.* Newbury Park, CA: Sage.

[5]Gwendolyn Etter-Lewis. (1991). Standing up and speaking out: African American women's narrative legacy, *Discourse and Society, II*, pp. 426-27.

[6]Essed, pp. 144.

[7]Barrie Thorne, Cheris Kramerae, & Nancy Henley. (1983). Language gender, and society: Opening a second decade of research," in their *Language, Gender, and Society*, pp. 7-24. Rowley, Mass.

[8]Thomas Kochman. (1981). Classroom Modalities in *Black and White: Styles in Conflict* Urbana: University of Illinois Press.

[9]One hundred thirty-five African American women (professionals, undergraduate, and graduate students) responded in writing to an open-ended questionnaire in which they freely described the talk of several social groups, including their own. A comparable group of 100 white women also responded to the questionnaire. Initial findings were reported in Marsha Houston (Stanback) and Carol Roach, "Sisters Under the skin: Southern black and White Women's Communication," and Marsha Houston, "Listening to ourselves: African-American women's perspectives on their communication style," both papers presented to the Southern States Communication Association, 1987 and 1992 respectively.

[10]The speaking style I refer to as "general American speech" others sometimes call "Standard English." I prefer the former term because it connotes the way of speaking (rather than writing) English that is accorded preference and prestige in the United States; thus, "General American Speech" is both a more communicatively and culturally accurate term than "Standard English."

[11]Some black women change only their intonation patterns, and not their grammar or vocabulary, when they "switch" to a more black style. See discussions of the "levels" of Black English speech in Mary R. Hoover. (1978). Community attitudes toward black English. *Language in Society*, 7, pp. 65-87.

[12]Barbara Smith and Beverly Smith. (1983). "Across the kitchen table: A sister to sister conversation. In *This Bridge Called My Back: Writings by Radical Women of Color*, p. 119. (eds.) Cherrie Moraga and Gloria Anzaldua. New York: Kitchen Table/Women of Color Press.

[13]Anita K. Foeman and Gary Pressley. (1989). Ethnic culture and corporate culture: Using black styles in organizations, *Communication Quarterly*, 33, 293-307; and Michael Hecht, Sidney Ribeau, and J. K. Alberts. (1989). An Afro-American perspective on interethnic communication, *Communication Monographs*, 56, pp. 385-410.

[14]Robin Lakoff. (1975). Why women are ladies in *Language and Woman's Place*. New York: Harper & Row.

[15]Mary McCullough, Women's Friendships Across Cultures: An Ethnographic Study (Unpublished Manuscript, Temple University, 1989).

[16]I admit that I chose these three statements in an "unscientific" manner, on the basis of their high experiential validity, rather than through any statistical sample. They are the statements that the women in my large network of black women friends, relatives, students, and acquaintances most often discuss as problematic in their conversations with white women; whenever I have shared my analysis of the statements with a group of black women whom I do not know (e.g., during a public speech for professional women or guest lecture at another university) they also have indicated that they hear them often and consider them insensitive.

[17]Elizabeth Spelman. (1988). *Inessential Woman: Problems of Exclusion in Feminist Thought*. Boston: Beacon Press.

20

The Cultural Experience of Space and Body: A Reading of Latin American and Anglo American Comportment in Public

Elizabeth Lozano
Loyola University of Chicago

This essay describes the cultural patterns of Latin American and Anglo American comportment in public space. It is grounded on my experience as a *Latinoamericana* (Latin American woman) who lives in the United States and as a researcher who studies matters of intercultural communication.

The essay is the result of a structural ethnography, an investigation that is based on lived experience, participant observation, interviewing, and extended descriptions of social settings and interactions. It focuses on the ways in which the body is understood and treated by Latin Americans and Anglo Americans, and the cultural differences that become apparent when these two cultural groups find themselves sharing a common space. It is also an opportunity to study the transformation and re-creation of social rules that take place when one becomes part of a new social setting, as is the case for the Latin Americans who now live in the United States.[1]

The need to address and understand the Latin American culture appears now more urgent than ever. The influence of this cultural heritage, which has been present in the United States for more than a century, is going to have an ever growing influence in the next few decades on the Anglo American scene, as Hispanics become the largest ethnic and linguistic minority in the United States. The more knowledge we gain from that which makes us culturally diverse, the more we will be able to appreciate what unifies us through the mixing and mutual exchanges of our cultures. Processes of transformation and adaptation are as important as tradition, historical roots, and language in understanding the nature of contemporary society.

The Territory of Cultural Differences

It has been argued that under the ethnic category "Hispanic" (which occasionally is used synonymously with "Latino"), a variety of cultural differences are disguised and overlooked (Bean & Tienda, 1987). "Hispanic" refers to any resident of the United States whose origin can be traced to a Spanish-speaking country. Such description is seen as both too general and too restrictive, for it bases ethnicity on the sole consideration of language. On one hand, the category seems to refer to a cultural tradition, the Latin American, but it excludes some of the Latin American countries (e.g., Brazil) whose language is not Spanish. On the other hand, the category includes Spain, a country whose cultural tradition, although very influential in Latin America, is distinctively *European*. Finally, not all Hispanic Americans speak Spanish. Some Chicanos (i.e., Mexican Americans) have been in the United States for over a century, and although they have ties with Mexico, they do not necessarily speak Spanish.

There are, in turn, important differences among the Latin American countries, from Brazil and Mexico, to Bolivia and Guatemala, to Cuba and the Dominican Republic. And yet, in spite of social and historical differences, there is a sense of cultural commonality among the societies of Central and South America, Mexico, and the Caribbean (see, for example, Neruda, 1991). The latter can be seen in aspects of social life as diverse as literature, music, television, political rhetoric, and oral storytelling (Martín-Barbero, 1988). In every case, the Latin American culture appears to be the common ground from which it is possible to examine national or regional differences (Lozano & Mickunas, 1992). In spite of social differences, in the realm of cultural practice Latin Americans recognize themselves as such.

A similar tension or ambiguity between commonality and difference can be seen in the case of the United States. Traditionally it has been assumed that the United States is a single culture. But recent critical reflections question the existence of this unified "American culture" in which everybody's cultural background "melts" into a mainstream that erases differences and makes us all equal. After all, ask the critics, what is *American* about the American culture? A nation formed by immigrants, the United States is a collection of differences. What is there in common among an African American, an Appalachian, a Midwesterner, or a Native American? What about the Germans, Irish, Scottish, Polish, Lithuanians, or Japanese that call themselves Americans? Where do we draw the line between similarity-in-difference and differences that assimilate?

The "melting pot" is not an adequate metaphor for a country which is comprised of a multiplicity of cultural backgrounds and traditions that affect one another and contribute to the creation of a distinctive, yet multi-faceted "American culture." Instead, suggests Reed (1991), we might better think of the United States in terms of a "cultural bouillabaisse" in which all ingredients conserve their unique flavor, while also transforming and being transformed by the adjacent textures and scents.

This does not imply, by any means, that the United States is a land in which diverse traditions have an equal share of power or influence. The white, Anglo-Saxon Protestant tradition constitutes the norm, the standard and the referent by which the United States defines its social mainstream and its "average" citizen. Nevertheless, such a standard and posited mainstream is continuously challenged by the presence of other cultural traditions (e.g., the African American, the Latin American, the Chinese, or the Japanese) which are neither dissolved within an Anglo mainstream nor relegated to the status of curiosity or extravaganza. Instead, cultural traditions survive within the United States as *transformed cultural practices*. Thus, the Latin American community of the United States is no longer purely Latin American or Anglo American, but an integration and transformation of both.[2] In fact, cultural traditions within the United States could be thought of as voices in a polyphonic chorus which is always struggling between dissonance and harmony, attraction and contradiction. To better understand the United States, one should examine the particular tensions and differences that appear when the "standard" voice—the Anglo-Saxon American —confronts a "marginal" voice—e.g., the Latino.

Although it is impossible to determine the limits or boundaries of a culture, we can recognize our own when we experience something that is shocking, unnatural and alien to us, but unnoticeable, normal and routine to others. Cultural shock can have a double edge: being alien to the familiar and finding the familiar alienating and out of place. Features, styles, voices, and cultural signatures appear that allow us to speak of an American culture as compared to that of the French, the Japanese, the Indian, or the English. The volatile features of the American culture—or of any culture, for that matter—which seem to defy definition and escape delimitations, become apparent in the contrasting light of another culture. That which is Latin American becomes apparent in the surprise and wonder that the Anglo American social space provokes in the Latin American newcomer. For the latter, the Anglo American social space and customs might seem as exotic, uncertain, or unnatural as Central or South America would appear to the Anglo American visitor.[3]

Contact with another culture is a form of *activating* one's own culture, of reflecting on it, making it visible and, therefore, "unnatural." It also allows one to understand the social and cultural ways in which diverse cultures intersect, overlap, and transform one another. Thus, what is Latin American will appear to be articulated differently, depending on whether the contrasting culture is Anglo-Saxon, Arabic, East European, or Japanese. Differences and similarities are held in simultaneous relief.[4]

Although Latin America is a mosaic of accents, racial mixtures, political traditions, and social customs, it remains *mosaic*—that is, a common pattern, a distinguishable design, a complex but characteristic texture. A common culture does not suppose the same accent or history, but a sense of recognition and understanding that is based on aesthetic grounds, myths, rituals, and social expressivity. In the same way that to speak of a Western Culture does not deny or contradict the idea of a French or a German culture, a Latin American culture exists and coexists with differences and similarities among countries, regions, classes, and ethnicities.

The U.S. Public Space

It is 6:00 p.m. The Bayfront, a shopping mall near the Miami marina, reverberates with the noise and movement of people coming and going, contemplating the lights of the bay, sampling exotic juice blends, savoring the not-so-exotic foods from Cuba, Nicaragua, or Mexico, and listening to the bands that here and there intone rock songs, blues, ballads, and, once in a while, something with a Hispanic flavor—"La Bamba," most likely, or "Guantanamera." The Bayfront is at once an outdoor and indoor space. It is a mall of homogenous halls, predictable stores, and casual window-shopping. It extends into a plaza that faces the sea and sky and invites one to contemplate the spectacle of people, sunsets, and boats.

The Bayfront provides an environment for the exercise of two different rituals: the Anglo American visit to the mall and the Latin American *paseo*, the visit to the outdoor spaces of the city—the plaza, the streets of the barrio, and the open cafes. The Bayfront is simultaneously a place for window-shoppers and a place to see and be seen, where display and consumption include the display of

oneself and the consumption of others. It is a place where one goes if one wants the company of Latinos and the sight of others.

Some of the people sitting in the plaza look insistently at me, making comments, laughing, whispering. Instead of feeling uneasy or surprised, I find myself looking back at them, entering this inquisitive game and asking myself some of the same questions they might be asking. Who are they, where are they from, what are they up to? I follow their gaze and I see it extend to other groups, the couples holding hands and kissing, the young women who have started dancing to the band, the children playing on the stairs. The gaze is returned by some in the crowd, so that a play of silent dialogue seems to grow amidst the anonymity of the crowd.

The crowd that participates in this complicity of wandering looks is not Anglo American. English is the language spoken; Anglo American, the architecture, the bands, the dress code, and the social rules. But the play of looks described above has a different "accent," a Hispanic accent, which reveals a different understanding of the plaza and its public space.

The Bicultural Dialogue

The Miami Bayfront is a place in which two cultural styles of body expressivity can be seen enacted simultaneously, interacting and overlapping. Although the Hispanic passers-by are strangers to one another, there is a sense of interaction among them. If I were to be addressed by anyone in this crowd, I would not be surprised, nor would I feel threatened. It would be no different from being addressed by someone in a crowded room. When I am walking by myself along the halls of a "Hispanic" mall, I am not *alone*. I do not expect, therefore, to be treated by others as if they were suddenly confronting me in a dark alley. I am in a crowd, with the crowd, and anyone there has access to my attention.

The Anglo American passers-by understand their vital space, their relationship with strangers, and their public interaction in a different manner. If I address them in the street, I better assume that I am confronting them in an alley. Pragmatically speaking, Anglo

Americans are alone (even in the middle of the crowd) if they choose to be, for they have a guaranteed cultural right to be "left alone" on their private way to and from anywhere.

To approach or touch someone without that person's consent is a violation of a fundamental right within the Anglo-Saxon, Protestant cultural tradition. This is the right to one's own body as private property. Within this tradition, touching is understood as an excursion into someone else's territory. It requires, as such, an explicit permission to "trespass" the spatial barriers that protect the perimeter of that physical property. The American remains in a private niche, the personal bubble, even when being in a public space.

It is understandable that, to the surprise of the Latin American newcomer, Anglo Americans excuse themselves not only when they accidentally touch someone, but even when there is the imminence of a touch. To accidentally penetrate someone else's boundary (especially if that person is a stranger) demands an apology and a willingness to repair the damage—by stepping back from the violated territory. This supposes an allegiance to the fundamental principles that the law dictates and protects (i.e., private property, autonomy, equality), as well as acceptance of the law as a universal mediator that guarantees the exercise of basic social rights. To excuse oneself, therefore, is to assure the other person that one recognizes and believes in the law and that no harm is intended.[5]

One can see how rude a Latin American might appear to an Anglo American when the former distractingly touches another person without apologizing or showing concern. Within the Latino and Mediterranean traditions (which are predominantly Catholic), the body is not understood as property. There is no formal distance between self and body, so that it is not possible to say "*I* own my body," as if it were something "I" have acquired somewhere. That is, the body is not understood as *belonging* to its owner. It does not belong to me or anyone else; it is, in principle, *public*. It is an expressive and sensual region open to the scrutiny, discipline, and sanction of the community; not to be regulated by universal law as property, but by the contextual rules of interaction.

It is, therefore, quite impossible to be "left alone" on the Latin American street. As long as one is there, one is a visible and accessible cipher, an enigma subject to interrogation. This implies that it is not possible to be neutral in the public space; it is sensually and erotically charged, a territory of mutual flirting and *seducción* that is expressed bodily in the ways of walking, moving, looking, smiling and—in the case of men—direct interpellation.[6]

In the United States, street flirting is understood basically as a form of harassment. In Latin America, street flirting has more ambiguous significations. Public forms of flirting (such as the *piropo*) are not only socially sanctioned but also welcomed—and expected—as expressions of a man's gallantry or *caballerosidad* regarding a woman's appeal or charm.[7] Piropos are *frases galantes*, courtly phrases that are meant to be celebrating, flattering, and appreciative of a woman's "graces." Piropos range from exclamations such as "adiós mamita," (*hi/bye, mama*), "qué buena que está" (*how good/delicious you look*), or "adiós cuñado" (*hi/bye, brother-in-law*, said to the man who accompanies a woman), to statements such as "si cocina como camina, me como hasta el pegado" (*if you cook like you walk, I'll eat the left-overs*), "bendita la madre que la trajo al mundo" (*blessed be the mother who brought you to the world*), or "benditos los ojos que la ven" (*blessed be the eyes that can see you*). But the distance between flattery and abuse grows very thin when a piropo progresses from "gallant" salutation to an appraisal of beauty to an explicit comment about somebody's anatomy. It may be that the only one flattered by the flattery is the one who volunteers it. Street flirting in Latin America can be play or provocation, cordiality or aggression, salutation or harassment.

While interrogating and examining others within the Latino public space is not a gender-exclusive privilege (i.e., both men and women participate), such activity is, nonetheless, *gendered*. That is, the forms of such public interpellation are defined along gender lines, their direct and most explicit forms being the male prerogative. While women might use piropos with men, men will "celebrate" women in the street, regardless of the latter's acknowledgement or approval. Both the Latin American and the Anglo American public spaces demand different attitudes by men and women—although this is more openly and clearly the case in Latin America.

Civility and Politeness

The U.S. public space is a homogeneous territory in which there is little ambiguity and options are clear and well-articulated. The struggle for non-ambiguity can be seen in the very architectural logic of the mall, a space in which everything is clearly identified, named, and defined in terms of purpose and function. It can also be seen in the logic of the fast-food purchase. When buying a hamburger at McDonald's, one knows precisely how the food is going to taste, how much it is going to cost, how long it is going to take before the order is ready, and how many options are offered. Every number corresponds to a different option, every name to a mass-produced, identical item. The space has been designed so that no time or energy is wasted, and no extra gestures, conversation, or interactions are required.

Walking the street in the United States is very much an anonymous activity to be performed in a field of unobstructive and invisible bodies. Since one is essentially carrying one's own space into the public sphere, no one is actually ever *in public*, exposed to the simultaneous and pervasive accessibility of others—unless that is one's specific function, as in the case of a public performer. Given that the public is private, no intimacy is granted in the public space, for its compartmentalization prevents any contact that lacks a specific and sanctioned function. Thus, while the Latin American public look is round, inquisitive, and wandering, the Anglo American is straight, non-obstructive, and neutral.

For Latin Americans, the access to others in a public space is not restricted by the "privacy" of their bodies. Thus, the Latin American does not find casual contact a form of property trespassing or a violation of rights. Civility requires the Anglo American to restrict looks, delimit gestures, and

orient movement; civility requires the Latin American to acknowledge looks, gestures, and movement and actively engage with them. For example, the Anglo American will respect the sorrow of another by remaining distant. He or she will likely intervene only if the other explicitly asks for help or consolation. On the other hand, the Latin American will approach the sorrowed one and offer consolation, even if it is not requested. For the Latin American, the unavoidable nature of a shared space is always a demand for attention and a request to participate.

An Anglo American considers "mind your own business" to be fair and civil. A Latin American might find this an ungranted restriction. What takes place in the public space is everybody's business by the very fact that it is taking place *in public*.

One can understand, in light of the above, the possible cultural misunderstandings between Anglo Americans and Latin Americans. If Anglo Americans protest the "impertinence" of Latin Americans as nosy and curious, Latin Americans protest the indifference and lack of concern of Anglo Americans. While Anglo Americans would defend their privacy above all, Latin Americans would take for granted their right to access in a communal space.

Conclusion

The scene in the Miami mall could happen just as easily in Los Angeles, Chicago, Philadelphia, or New York, cities in which Latin Americans comprise an important segment of the population. Latin Americans will not use the Anglo American public space as they would their own, but in the presence of other Latin Americans, they may choose to engage in the play of looks that transforms the anonymous crowd into a "community of strangers," so to speak. Although one might choose to remain a stranger and avoid personal contact, one cannot be anonymous, for one is recognized, addressed, and visually interpellated.

Alternately, one can make oneself more or less visible in a bicultural setting by changing the way of addressing and looking at others. Indeed, if I "look" like an American (in both senses of the word), I will be looked at in a similar way. I can use my "bilingual" knowledge as a Latin American in the U.S. to shift to a more Anglo American body language. I know, for example, that politeness and good manners require me to behave as if the Anglo American passers-by were not there. I also change my manners and bodily accent when I converse with American strangers. I will not look frantically at an Anglo American, and I will excuse myself if I accidentally touch her or him, avoiding any sign of intimacy that has not been explicitly called for.

Survival within a new cultural setting requires, as much as the acquisition of the language, an ability to perform according to the local rules of public interaction and to recognize patterns and rituals in daily encounters with others. This adaptation, however, is never a complete substitution of one style for another, but rather an interpretation and integration of two different languages which acquire its own, new features. Another style, a cultural, bilingual language, emerges from those who cannot consider themselves as Latin Americans any longer but are now Hispanic Americans: Hispanic citizens of the United States.

NOTES

[1] Estimates on the number of Latin Americans living in the United States vary greatly from source to source. (Some say 10 million, while others suggest 15 or 20 million). This is due, in part, to the fact that Latin Americans are usually considered a subgroup of a wider category, the "Hispanic." Thus, it is hard to find data that refers specifically to the Latin American. In this essay I focus on the Latin American, contrasting the Anglo and Latino traditions from which the Hispanic American emerges.

[2] I use the term Hispanic (in the absence of a better term) to name this new cultural practice that takes place "between" Latin American and Anglo American traditions and that, in turn, influences its two originating cultures. This term is not without its problems, for communities such as Chicanos (i.e., Mexican Americans) and Nuyoricans (i.e., Puerto Ricans born in the continental U.S.) resent its official use as a term that groups together anyone whose origin can be traced to a Spanish-speaking country.

[3] See, for example, the reflections of Paz (1987).

[4] For an interesting look at this cross-cultural dialogue and plurality, see Hall, 1982, Verburg, 1991.

[5] A gender difference still pervades what is supposed to be a gender-blind right to privacy. Although nobody has access to a man's or a woman's body without their consent in the Anglo American tradition, women find this right often violated in subtle (and not so subtle) ways. In spite of an equal right to privacy, the culture still assigns a higher value to the respect of "his" right. "No trespassing"" penalties are mich higher for the violation of a man's territory. Historically speaking, "her" rights are not as clearly defined or socially grounded as are "his."

[6] I am using the Spanish word, *seducción*, instead of its English translation, *seduction;* although they might appear to mean the same thing, they have very different implications. Indeed, the meaning here is closer to the French *seduisant* than to the English *seduction*. It does not imply a malicious abuse of an innocent, but a mix of personal atractiveness, sensuous appeal, and coquettish behavior.

[7] This does not mean, though, that women like piropos, but that it is very gentlemanly to speak in courteous and embellishing way to women. Most forms of gallantry and deference to women are well accepted and indeed expected from men.

REFERENCES

Bean, F. D., & Tienda, M. (1987). *The Hispanic population of the United States*. New York: Russell Sage Foundation.

Hall, E.T. (1982). *The hidden dimension*. New York: Doubleday.

Lozano, E., & Mickunas, A. (1992). Pedagogy as integral difference. In E.M. Kramer (Ed.), *Consciousness and culture: An introduction to the thought of Jean Gebser* (pp. 179-199). Westport, CT: Greenwood Press.

Martín-Barbero, J. (1988). Communication from culture: The crisis of the national and the emergence of the popular. *Media, Culture, and Society, 10*, 447-465.

Neruda, P. (1991). The word. In C. Verburg (Ed.), *Ourselves among others. Cross-cultural readings for writers* (pp. 478-479). Boston: Bedford Books. (Reprinted from Memoirs, 1977).

Reed, I. (1991). What's American about America? In C. Verburg (Ed.), *Ourselves among others. Cross-cultural readings for writers* (pp. 4-8). Boston: Bedford Books.

Paz, O. (1987). *Convergences: Essays on art and literature*. New York: Harcourt Brace Jovanovich.

Verburg, C. (Ed.). (1991). *Ourselves among others. Cross-cultural readings for writers*. Boston: Bedford Books.

21

Regionalism and Communication: Exploring Chinese Immigrant Perspectives

Casey Man Kong Lum
Adelphi University

A Cantonese immigrant in New York City once told me that getting lost in midtown Manhattan is an inconvenient and embarrassing experience. To him, however, the inconvenience does not stem from the fact that he cannot speak English. After all, it would never occur to him to ask an English-speaking person for directions. Finding a fellow Chinese in midtown Manhattan in the late 20th century is by no means a difficult task. Ironically, the source of his difficulty emerges when he *does* find another Chinese person. As he approaches his prospective rescuer, he always experiences anxiety: Will this person turn out to be a Chinese who speaks Cantonese, one with whom he can converse and feel at ease?

The experience of this Cantonese immigrant is not an uncommon one for Chinese immigrants in New York City. Immigrants have to adjust to all aspects of life in their host country, but facing uncertainties while interacting with their compatriots is not something they expect when they leave their homeland.

For example, Chinese immigrants from Hong Kong are members of a social majority in the British colony. Although many Hong Kong natives acquire a unique perspective about their ethnic identity, because of the colonial influences there,

they are raised in Chinese families that speak Cantonese, most of whom relate to themselves as definitively Chinese.

However, their sense of "Chineseness" is challenged when they immigrate to large overseas Chinese communities where they are no longer a clear majority, even within the Chinese population, and where they are constantly confronted by the different cultural sensitivities of Chinese from other regional backgrounds. Although Hong Kong immigrants represent a large percentage of the Chinese community in New York City, Chinese from other regions, such as various parts of the People's Republic of China, Taiwan, and Southeast Asia, are also represented economically, politically, and culturally. Many of these people do not speak or understand Cantonese, just as many Hong Kong Cantonese do not speak or understand Fujianese, Taiwanese, or Toishanese, or the many other regional dialects from Southern China. Because of the language barriers, many overseas Chinese tend to socialize only with people of regional background similar to their own.

Indeed, regionalism has long been an important element in facilitating and maintaining diversity in Chinese culture. In this essay, I will explore (1) the regional origins of Chinese immigrants in New York City and (2) the role that regionalism plays in the maintenance of these immigrants' culture, ethnicity, and communication. I will focus my exploration on the experience of the three dominant groups of contemporary Chinese immigrants in New York City: those from China, Hong Kong, and Taiwan.

Regional Origins of Chinese Immigrants in New York City

The region from which one originates is an important criterion in judging one's ethnicity (Isajiw, 1974; Keyes, 1976; Subervi-Velez, 1986). To acknowledge region as a basis of ethnicity, in turn, is to accept the assumption that the environment in which people are nurtured has a certain degree of influence on their cultural development and identification. China, Hong Kong, and Taiwan encompass a great variety of regions, which are defined by varying social, economic, and political arrangements as well as diverse language compositions.

Indigenous social, economic, and political arrangements play an important role in defining the regional characters of these immigrants. As a British colony for over a century and a half, for instance, Hong Kong has evolved from a tranquil fishing village in the Qing Dynasty (1644-1911) to one of the most vibrant financial centers in the world. As a result, many people in or from Hong Kong have long acquired the skills necessary to survive in a cosmopolitan world.

Although China lived under a rigid socialist economic and political system since 1949, the Chinese are very diverse in their regional outlooks. China's geography encompasses a complex typography and climate system that fosters a great variety of economic activities and lifestyles (Ginsburg, 1958, pp. 155-273; Sivin, 1988, pp. 36-37). Both this physical diversity and the uneven distribution of natural as well as social and political resources have affected the growth of China's various regions, resulting in varying degrees of economic sufficiency and modernization. As a result, people from the cities, such as Canton, Beijing, and Shanghai, tend to be more adaptive than those from the farming villages in Gansu Province or the western loess highlands to the pace of life in such modern urban centers as New York City.

Taiwan returned to the Republic of China in 1945 after 51 years of Japanese occupation.[1] In 1949, the Nationalist government regained complete political control over Taiwan, much to the dismay of many native Taiwanese.[2] However, with tremendous self-determination, a fierce, anti-Communist policy, and support from the United States, Taiwan has prospered and become a remarkable economic force. Because of their affluence and contact with the West, people in Taiwan today, especially those from the urban areas such as Taipei or Kaohsiung, have acquired a cosmopolitan outlook; while people from outside the cities still maintain a certain degree of provincialism.

The diversity of Chinese languages is another key contributing factor to the perpetuation of regionalism among many Chinese. There are seven major dialect groups in China, each with its own sub-groups (Sivin, 1988, p. 126; see also Sun, pp. 276-281). People in the northern regions of China generally speak "putonghua" ("common speech"), or what is known in Taiwan and the West as Mandarin. In regions south of the Yangtze River, the major dialect groups are Wu, Xiang, Gan, Hakka, Min, and Yue, under which there are numerous sub-groups.[3] Cantonese is but one sub-group of Yue spoken in and around the Canton area in southern Guangdong Province as well as in Hong Kong. In Taiwan, the two major languages are Mandarin and Taiwanese, while many other Chinese dialects are also spoken in families with ancestral links to the mainland.

Speakers of these regional dialects are generally incomprehensible to one another, not because their accent is too thick, but because the dialects they use employ different sounding systems and idiomatic usages.[4] Linguistically, these dialects are in fact distinct languages (Sivin, 1988, p. 126). While many Chinese are bilingual,[5] they remain divided into hundreds of language communities in which their regional identities are constantly reinforced by their respective dialects.

Regionalism and Social Interaction among Chinese Immigrants in New York City

Not only is regionalism a key element in the diversity of Chinese culture, it also plays a vital role in helping many Chinese maintain their sense of cultural continuity when they resettle as immigrants. In a study of Chinese immigrants in Southeast Asia between 1850 and 1940, for example, Hamilton (1977) examined how these early Chinese immigrants adapted among themselves and to indigenous people in host countries. He concluded that the ethnic identities of these Chinese immigrants were highly adaptive to their adopted societies, especially to conditions that "favored the continuation and even intensification of subethnic distinctions patterned after those made in China" (Hamilton, 1977, pp. 347-348). As Crissman (1967, p. 185) observed, the organizational patterns of overseas Chinese communities "derived from patterns indigenous to China itself" (cited in Hamilton, 1977, p. 338; see also Mark & Chih, 1982, pp. 45-59). Many early Chinese immigrants living in Southeast Asia organized among themselves strictly along regional lines, such as in the form of same-countryside or same-name associations modelled after similar organizations in their indigenous regions. Moreover, these overseas Chinese tended to maintain a double identity, i.e., an ethnic Chinese identification and a subethnic regional identification. That is to say, while it was essential for them to be acknowledged as being ethnically Chinese, it was equally important for them to retain their respective subethnic, regional origins for the maintenance of their social, economic, and cultural well-being.

Indeed, this "double ethnic identity" of early Chinese immigrants in Southeast Asia still persists and is manifested in many other Chinese immigrant communities today. While all Chinese immigrants in such communities acknowledge their ancestral origins in China (i.e., their ethnic roots), many would tend to associate with people from similar indigenous regions (i.e., their sub-ethnic identification and affiliation). At the level of language affiliation, for instance, the two Chinatowns in New York City provide an interesting illustration of this phenomenon of regional affiliation (or "separation").

New York's first Chinatown, located in the lower east side of Manhattan, is an established community with a history that goes back to the mid-1800s (Kwong, 1987; Lum, 1991; Wong, 1982; Zhou & Logan, 1991). The majority of Chinese residents in this neighborhood—most of whom came from Hong Kong and South China—speak Cantonese, Toishanese,[6] and increasingly Fujianese (from the Fujian Province). As all native Hong Kong Chinese are educated in both Chinese (Cantonese) and English, it is not uncommon for them to mix Chinese and English in their daily speech. For example, one may say "Kui ho handsome," which means "He is very handsome." Hong Kong Chi-

nese have also transliterated certain English words or expressions and have employed them as part of their daily vocabulary. For example, "sa lum" is used in the same way as the English "salute" from which it is derived. (One may say "Or yiu heung kui *sa lum*," which means "I have to *salute* that person.") By comparison, this linguistic habit is less apparent among Chinese immigrants from China or Taiwan.

The second Chinatown in the Flushing area of Queens evolved into being over the past two decades.[7] Many Chinese immigrants in this area are Mandarin- and Taiwanese-speaking Chinese from Taiwan. This Chinatown is also referred to by some as "New York's Taiwantown" (*Hsiang Hsun*, 1992, p. 2).

Although economic opportunities have brought Chinese from diverse regional backgrounds together in the Chinatown market places at large (Zhou & Logan, 1991), close regional affiliation still plays an important role in securing social and economic success among many Chinese immigrants in the area.[8] Most "old overseas Chinese" who came from Guangdong Province to New York City before 1965 (Wong, 1982, pp. 74-78) built very tight personal and business networks and close regional associations, because (1) they were ethnocentric and faithful to their indigenous culture; (2) they lacked the language skills to interact with the larger social environment; (3) the ethnic community offered more convenient economic opportunities; and (4) restrictive immigration laws did not allow most males to live a normal family life with a spouse and children, especially during the period of 1882 through 1943 (Wong, 1985, p. 234). These networks are exemplified by such organizations as same-surname associations and same-countryside clubs, or "Tongs." They provide their members with a variety of services: job referrals, the adjudication of disputes, financial assistance, and a context for leisurely social interaction. Of course, these organizations are also sources of regional or sub-ethnic rivalries in business, politics, and crime.

Similarly, thousands of illegal immigrants from Hong Kong, China, Taiwan, and Southeast Asia who stay away from the social mainstream for obvious legal reasons have also played a part in maintaining regionalism in the Chinese population of New York City. They often feel unwelcome by the larger society (Wong, 1982, p. 83)[9] and are therefore forced to remain in their subethnic groups for support and survival. I have a Chinese friend from Malaysia who will date only Chinese women from his home country. He has not been successful with non-Chinese Malaysian women, partially because his Southeast Asia Cantonese seems to have alienated him from Chinese women from regions other than Southeast Asia.

The regionalism of Chinese immigrants in New York City is also manifest in their cultural customs and practices. Although Chinese immigrants in New York City traditionally celebrate important festive occasions or Chinese holidays, such as the Lunar New Year, Dragon Boat Festival, and Mid-Autumn Festival, they differ along regional lines in how they celebrate.[10] While people from Hong Kong and the Canton area celebrate Mid-Autumn Festival with homemade or commercially available paper lanterns, people from Taiwan celebrate the occasion without lanterns. Food that people serve at home as part of any festive or significant celebration also differs according to regional culinary habits. During the Chinese New Year, for instance, pig's feet are popular food items among Hong Kong Cantonese because the Cantonese pronunciation of pig's feet ("chu sau") resembles the pronunciation of another term ("chou sau"), which means "easy" or "without trouble." Put in the proper context, eating pig's feet during the New Year is part of a ritual to bring in easy wealth all year round. During the Chinese New Year, the act of serving a friend pig's feet is an offering of good luck used to win friendship or make a good impression. Among Taiwanese, on the other hand, pig's feet are served with noodles to symbolize longevity at a birthday celebration rather than at Chinese New Year.

The Chinese immigrant media are another cultural arena where regionalism is evident. In reporting news from or about China, Chinese newspapers published in the U.S. report on events that occurred in their respective backers' places of origin.[11] In an informal survey of typical groups of Chinese immigrants, I came to realize that many of them feel more comfortable with papers published by their "own people" (e.g., Hong Kong Chinese identify with *Sing Tao Jih Pao*, a Hong Kong-affiliated paper; Taiwanese Chinese identify with *World Journal*, a paper published by people from Taiwan). The broadening of regional coverage, and the fact that written Chinese has long been standardized, have brought about a mixed readership. But that does not necessarily entail a cross-identification among Chinese from the various regions, social and economic strata, or political groups.

Regionalism is even more pronounced in the Chinese immigrant electronic media. These media are mostly targeted at audiences representing specific regional language groups: Mandarin and Taiwanese radio programs for Chinese from Taiwan, and Cantonese cable TV services for Hong Kong immigrants (Lum, 1991, pp. 94-95). These services capture a sizable immigrant audience, especially among those who lack the English skill to enjoy mainstream media for information and entertainment. More importantly, they offer all Chinese immigrants in New York City familiar media content relating to their cultural life before they were uprooted. In short, these media, along with social organizations and personal networks, furnish Chinese immigrants in New York City with a means to help maintain their ethnic and sub-ethnic culture and identification.

Nevertheless, it is obvious that this regional culture cannot exist without any influence from the new social environment. After all, these immigrants and their offspring must adapt to the larger American social and cultural environment. Culture evolves through its interactions with external forces. An American Chinatown is the result of cultural evolution in a North American context, which produces new practices that may look deceptively "Chinese" at first glance. Eating rice from a plate with chopsticks instead of from a bowl, or receiving enigmatic advice from a fortune cookie, have become common practice in American Chinese restaurants, even though these customs seem awkward to newly-arrived Chinese immigrants. New vocabulary also comes into being. For example, many long-time Toishanese and Cantonese in Chinatown use the Cantonese word "*par mun*" for the English word "apartment," as opposed to "*lau*" (as an apartment is called by Chinese from Hong Kong) or "*kung yu*" (the word used by Chinese from Taiwan). "*Par mun*," in its written version (with two characters that are phonetically close to two of "apartment's" syllables), is often used as an accepted term in the rental section of Chinese newspapers published in New York City, including those published by Taiwanese. New immigrants from China, Hong Kong, and Taiwan would certainly find this term unusual.

Conclusion

Chinese immigrants in New York City come from a great diversity of linguistic, social, economic, and political regions. As a result, regionalism has become a key component in defining the ethnic and sub-ethnic identity and affiliation of these immigrants. It also plays an important role in helping Chinese immigrants in New York City maintain a sense of cultural continuity. The regionalism among Chinese immigrants is manifested in how they interact among themselves, including social and economic associations, the maintenance of cultural customs or practices, media consumptions, and the dialects or languages they use.

However, while the Cantonese immigrant who is afraid of getting lost in midtown Manhattan, like many other Chinese immigrants, would hold dear his indigenous regional culture and identity, others may have different attitudes. Chinese immigrants who have higher levels of academic, professional, social, or economic achievement have much less difficulty in becoming an active part of the larger American social and cultural environment. Similarly, as foreign-born children of Chinese immigrants are better prepared to assimilate into American society, they may have less desire and very little need to cling to their parents' ethnic or regional networks. The same could be said even more emphatically for immigrants' children who are born in the U.S. as Chinese Americans. After all, the

U.S. *is* their country now, even though they may be confronted by racism and discrimination as well as questions surrounding their blend of "double identity."

NOTES

[1]Japan gained cession of Taiwan in 1895 after its military victory over china (Qing Dynasty)—although it met with strong resistance from the local populace. Many of the parents, grandparents, and great grandparents of the post-World War II genration of native Taiwanese were educated by the Japanese.

[2]There was a long period of mutual suspicion between native Taiwanese and Chinese from the Mainland, although the social tension between them (especially between those who were born after World War II) has subsided considerably. Intermarriage between Mainland Chinese and native Taiwanese, for example, is not uncommon nowadays. However, the tension between native Taiwanese politicians or political parties and the Nationalist-controlled givernment remains intense.

[3]In addition, there are 52 officially recognized minority languages in China (Sivin, 1988, p. 100), including Mongolian, Manchurian, and a variety of other dialects of Indo-European origins.

[4]Although there are many regional dialects in China, there is only one official writing system in the country that every school child is taught to use. However, a number of regional dialects still maintain their localized writings. For example, in New York City, one has the choice to take a Cantonese version of the written test for a driver's license. Parts of many Chinese newspapers in New York's Chinatown, such as entertainment news from Hong Kong, are written partially in Cantonese (i.e., Cantonese writing or "Guangdong mun," as it is called by some Chinese immigrants in New York).

[5]Although the government of China and Taiwan have promoted Mandarin as the official language, many people who were born and raised in families with a regional dialect still use their own regional dialect whenever necessary.

[6]Toishanese (or Toysanese) was the lingua franca for the New York's Chinese community in the pre-1965 period because the majority of Chinese immigrants in the area then originated from Toishan in Guangdong Province. Now, the standard Cantonese spoken in Canton in Guangdong and its vicinities (including Hong Kong and Macau) has taken the place of Toishanese as the predominant dialect in New York's Chinatown (Wong, 1955, p. 232).

[7]Chen (1992) argued that the characterization of Flushing as a new Chinatown is inappropriate. He contended that Chinatown is normally referred to as "a compact homogeneous Chinese settlement, with a core of Chinese businesses" and that this traditional conception of a Chinatown does not fit the characteristics of "the Queens Chinese communities in the mixed neighborhood of Flushing and Elmhurst" (p. x). However the Chinese

community in Flushing is called, the fact that this community is prominently represented by Chinese immigrants from Taiwan, a fact that is amply examined by Chen (1992) himself, illustrates the sub-ethnic, regional distinction between the Chinese immigrant communities in the lower east side of Manhattan and Flushing.

[8]Building personal networks consisting of people with family or regional ties in order to achieve social and economic success is a common practice among Chinese. See Chang and Holt (1991) for a recent study of how certain Chinese in Taiwan construct and maintain their social networks.

[9]Many of these illegal immigrants are discriminated against by both the larger society and the more established Chinese businesses to the extent that they cannot enjoy any social benefit and, because of their illegal status, they often have to take jobs with sub-standard financial returns or protection.

[10]Because all Chinese holidays or festivals are based on the Chinese lunar calendar, it becomes unlikely for many Chinese immigrants to participate in public celebrations, such as joining the New Year parade with firecrackers and dragon and lion dance in Chinatown. After work, however, many of these immigrants would celebrate privately at home.

[11]Historically, Chinese newspapers have tended to be more openly partisan than their American counterparts. It is not uncommon for newspapers in China, Hong Kong, Taiwan, and overseas Chinese immigrant communities to have an overt editorial identification with a given political party, cause, or government (see Chan & Lee, 1988; Merrill, 1991, pp. 224-230).

REFERENCES

Chan, J. M., & Lee, C-C. (1988). Shifting journalistic paradigms: Editorial stance and political transition in Hong Kong. Paper presented at the annual meeting of the Association for Education in Journalism and Mass Communication.

Chang, H.-C., & Holt, G. R. (1991). More than relationship: Chinese interaction and the principle of Kuan-Hsi. *Communication Quarterly, 39*(3), 251-271.

Chen, H-S. (1992). *Chinatown no more: Taiwan immigrants in contemporary New York*. Ithaca, NY: Cornell University Press.

Crissman, L. W. (1967). The segmentary structure of urban overseas Chinese communities. *Man, 2*, 185-204.

Ginsburg, N. (Ed.). (1958). *The pattern of Asia*. Englewood Cliffs, NJ: Prentice-Hall.

Hamilton, G. G. (1977). Ethnicity and regionalism: Some factors influencing Chinese identities in Southeast Asia. *Ethnicity, 4*, 337-351.

Hsiang Hsun [in Chinese]. (March 1992). Taiwanese Association of America Greater New York Chapter.

Isajiw, W. W. (1974). Definitions of ethnicity. *Ethnicity, 1*, 111-124.

Keyes, C. F. (1976). Towards a new formulation of the concept of ethnic group. *Ethnicity, 3*, 202-23.

Kwong, P. (1987). *The new Chinatown*. New York: Hill & Wang.

Lum, C. M. K. (1991). Communication and cultural insularity: The Chinese immigrant experience. *Critical Studies in Mass Communication, 8*(1), 91-101.

Mark, D. M. L., & Chih, G. (1982). *A place called Chinese America*. Dubuque, IA: Kendall/Hunt.

Merrill, J. C. (1991). *Global journalism: Survey of international communication* (2nd ed.). New York: Longman.

Sun, R. F. (Ed. in Chief). (1990). *Zhongguo shao shuo min zi jiao yu xue* [in Chinese] [*An introduction to pedagogy for ethnic minorities in China*]. Beijing: China Labor Publishing Company.

Sivin, N. (Consulting Ed.). (1988). *The contemporary atlas of China*. Boston: Houghton Mifflin Company.

Subervi-Velez, F. A. (1986). The mass media and ethnic assimilation and pluralism: A review and research proposal with special focus on Hispanics. *Communication Research, 13*(1), 71-96.

Wong, B. P. (1982). *Chinatown: Economic adaptation and ethnic identity of the Chinese*. New York: Holt, Rinehart and Winston.

Wong, B. (1985). Family, kinship, and ethnic identity of the Chinese in New York City, with comparative remarks on the Chinese in Lima, Peru and Manila, Philippines. *Journal of Comparative Family Studies, 16*(2), 231-254.

Zhou, M., & Logan, J. R. (1991). In and out of Chinatown: Residential mobility and segregation of New York City's Chinese. *Social Forces, 70*(2), 387-407.

22

Individualism and Collectivism in American and Chinese Societies

Changsheng Xi
Iowa State University

In the study of intercultural communication, semantic dimensions can be used to characterize cross-cultural differences. For example, Hofstede (1984) proposes several bi-polar dimensions, such as "masculine" and "feminine," and "individualistic" and "collectivist." He claims that Japan, Australia, Venezuela, Switzerland, Mexico, Ireland, Great Britain, and Germany are masculine cultures; while Sweden, Norway, the Netherlands, Denmark, Finland, Chile, Portugal, and Thailand are feminine cultures. Similarly, he asserts that the United States, Australia, Great Britain, Canada, the Netherlands, New Zealand, Italy, Belgium, and Denmark are individualistic cultures; while Columbia, Venezuela, Pakistan, Peru, Taiwan, Thailand, Singapore, China, and Hong Kong are collectivist cultures.

While Hofstede's approach may be useful in considering cultural differences, we should not deceive ourselves into thinking that there is no collectivism in American society, or that there is no individualism in China. In my view, polarization of various cultures into a Cartesian format of either/or is unproductive in discerning rich cultural differences. Instead, I contend that collectivism goes hand in hand with individualism and that they cannot be so neatly polarized.

With respect to American culture, a relevant question may be asked: can a highly individualistic American society exist without collectivity in social life? The answer is clearly no, as the term "society" necessarily entails some form of collectivism. Carbaugh (1988) argues that, for American individualism to work, it must be collectively celebrated. Varenne (1977) points out that "individualism implies community" (p. 40).

With respect to Chinese culture, a different question can be posed: Is collectivist Chinese society totally devoid of individualistic pursuit? I do not think so; otherwise, we would not be able to understand why the notorious Chinese Cultural Revolution failed, the goal of which was to eradicate the so-called evils of capitalism and individualism in China. Nor would we be able to understand why there have been anti-establishment student movements in China in recent years. The rise of the democratic movement in China suggests that individualism is indeed fomenting in China.

Thus, in my view the cultural dimensions of individualism and collectivism should be used, not to polarize cultures according to nationalities, but rather to compare them in specific social contexts. The rest of this essay represents my effort to examine American and Chinese cultural differences contextually within the semantic dimension of collectivism and individualism.

Collectivism

In a certain sense, American society has more rigorous social rules to follow than Chinese society. On the road, for instance, there is a myriad of traffic laws and regulations for the driver of an automobile to follow. To sight a police car in the rear-view mirror while driving is an unnerving experience for anyone. In a large institution, the first thing a new employee has to learn is a set of written rules and regulations. This person may be confronted with an incredible number of papers and forms that have to be read, filled out, and signed before he or she begins to work. And college students must follow rules and policies stipulated by the instructor in order to proceed in the course.

In addition to written rules, informal rules are regarded as equally or perhaps even more important in maintaining social structure. Following those implicit or informal rules enables a person to get along successfully with others. It seems that Americans view success not as much in terms of money as by the measure of a person's popularity. A loner who is not accepted by anyone seems to be regarded by Americans as a loser in society, no matter rich he or she might be. Thus, the ability to handle interpersonal relationships is crucial to survival in the U.S. Being an insider within a cultural or social group seems to be almost every American's ultimate goal.

In this regard, Bell's (1984) work is relevant. According to Bell, people use various strategies to seek affinity from each other in order to satisfy what Schutz (1966) calls interpersonal needs. Bell lists 25 affinity-seeking strategies used by Americans. Of these 25, the nine most frequently used are conversational rule-keeping, self-concept confirmation, eliciting others' disclosures, nonverbal immediacy, self-inclusion, listening, facilitating enjoyment, openness, and altruism (p. 100). The strategy of keeping informal conversational rules is the most frequently used and the most important strategy in the affinity-seeking process.

In contrast, Chinese society places more emphasis on altruistic acts or behaviors than on conventional rules in order to seek mutual affinity. For a Chinese, whether or not you are my friend does not depend on how well we converse with each other, but rather whether we can count on each other in times of need. Thus, altruism as a strategy is more frequently used and more important than conversation rule-keeping. If my analysis is correct, this may explain why Chinese often have a catch-phrase on their lips when they talk to each other as friends, namely, "ban shi" (do things). For example, it is not uncommon to hear two Chinese friends part from each other in the following manner:

A: you shi ma? (Do you have anything for me to do?)

B: mei shi. (I do not have anything for you to do.)

A: you shi shuo hua. (If you have anything for me to do, tell me.)

B: mei wenti. (No problem.)

A: zaijian. (Good-bye.)

B: zaijian. (Good-bye.)

As the above conversation indicates, in Chinese culture, whether two persons in relationship can "ban shi" or not for the benefit of each other is a touchstone for a long-term and close friendship. As for how well they carry on their conversation, it is secondary to whether they can "ban shi" to each other.

It can be argued that Americans are also more constrained than Chinese in emotional expression. Potter (1988) maintains that Americans are not free to express their emotions because doing so affects the maintenance or destruction of the social order and hence has serious social consequences. Thus, according to Potter's interpretation, Americans emotionally burden themselves in order to keep social order and achieve personal success. By contrast, Chinese seem to show no restraint in revealing their emotions because they consider emotional expression to be of no significance in shaping or changing the social order.

As a Chinese native, I feel that Potter's theses need qualification. In my view, American and Chinese cultures contrast in emotional expression, not because Americans recognize the possible impact of emotional expression on the existing social structure, but because Americans adopt a negative attitude towards that impact, treating it as dangerous and irrational; while Chinese adopt a positive attitude towards it, regarding it as helpful and sometimes effective in resolving social conflicts. For a Chinese, society is not just an amalgamation of individuals, out of touch with each other's feelings, but rather members of a larger family whose emotions and feelings are intertwined and influence the work they do together. Thus, as Potter rightly observed, Chinese have a difficult time separating emotion from behavior or work. By contrast, many Americans subject themselves to strong social pressure to suppress emotional expression. In this sense, Americans are not as free as Chinese.

American conformity also finds its expression in people's attitude towards their jobs. It seems that the most valuable asset for an American is a good job. It is not uncommon to find an American holding two or even three jobs. But what makes an individual succeed on the job? The overwhelming answer, given by a class of college students that I taught, was conforming to the rules and regulations of the institution with which one is affiliated.

American conformity on the job, however, does not seem to have anything to do with loyalty to the company or institution where one works. In my opinion, there is no such loyalty at all. Americans follow company or institutional rules not out of loyalty but because they must. Sometimes Americans work for one employer to acquire the skills and experiences needed to seek out a second job. Quitting one job for another is so common in the United States that it seems to encompass factory workers, sales clerks, secretaries, doctors, attorneys, teachers, professors, deans, university presidents— almost any worker at any stratum of American society. Clearly, the American culture does not instill loyalty in the relationship between employees and employers. What it does instill is a strong sense of individualism associated with an equally strong commitment to conformity.

Chinese students who visit the U.S. to pursue a scholarship often misunderstand American individualism. Initially, they are jubilant in the sense of liberation from a socialist country. Thinking that they can do anything they want in the U.S., they are sometimes petulant and argumentative with their supervisors or bosses. I have witnessed some Chinese students in the United States quarrelling with their supervisors for a promotion or a raise. It takes time for these Chinese to realize that Americans are more obedient to their superiors than Chinese—all in order to achieve their own personal goals and dreams.

Obedience as a form of conformity is most reflected in the decision-making process in corporate America. Decision making is almost always the business of top management in an American

company. Departments at lower levels have no choice but to execute the decision. This top-down decision-making process is not found in China, where decision making usually comes from the bottom up; workers at the lower level form a consensus which they convey to management, who will most likely accept it out of respect for its subordinates. If top-down decision making reflects collectivism, then corporate America is certainly more collectivist than its Chinese counterpart.

An analogy may be useful here for conceptual clarification. The relationship between individualism and collectivism in society parallels that between action and reaction in physics. Where there is an action, there must be a reaction. The stronger the action, the stronger the reaction. Action and reaction cannot be polarized or separated into two different entities. By the same token, where there is individualism in a society, there must be collectivism. The stronger the individualism, the stronger the collectivism will be. The two are just as inseparable.

Certainly, Americans are proud of their cultural inheritance of rugged individualism and freedom. Yet, as far as culture is concerned, Americans seem to make more effort to pull society together. As noted by Varenne (1977), these efforts are often made on a rhetorical level. For example, Americans often use the word "everybody" in their daily conversation without truly meaning it semantically or logically. I once asked an American friend whether exceeding the speed limit by ten miles an hour is okay when I find myself in fast traffic. He answered: "Of course. Everybody does that." But can you imagine how many times I could have been caught speeding if I had followed my friend's advice? Certainly, the use of "everybody" by my friend is not to be interpreted literally. Rather, it relates to a cultural need, at least on a rhetorical level, to view Americans as together.

Carbaugh (1988) uses "The Donahue Show" to illustrate how Americans try to solve social problems collectively via the rhetoric of individualism. Varenne (1977) studies how middle-class Americans work, fall in love, perform religious services, and enact other social activities together. Mechling

(1980) characterizes how American boys collectively celebrate their individuality through the tradition of the Boy Scout campfire. One fundamental point these authors all make is that American individualism cannot be separated from collectivism. On the contrary, they are intimately linked. If American culture is the most individualistic society in the world, perhaps it is also the most collectivist.

Let me discuss how self is collectively celebrated in the United States. There are three important areas of self studies: self-disclosure, self-presentation, and self-identification. Generally speaking, Americans tend to see self-disclosure as very important in interpersonal relationship development (Gilbert, 1976). Self-disclosure is used as a strategy by Americans to develop interpersonal relationships. By contrast, Chinese culture takes a conservative stand on self-disclosure. For a Chinese, a self-centered speech would be considered boastful and pretentious. Chinese tend to scorn those who often talk about themselves and doubt their motives when they do so. Chinese seem to prefer talking about external matters, such as world events. For Americans, self-disclosure is a strategy to make various types of relationships work; for Chinese, it is a gift shared only with the most intimate relatives and friends.

In the area of self-presentation, the American saying that one should put one's best foot forward conveys an important American ethos: the self is worth being celebrated, so there is nothing to be ashamed of in talking about one's achievements. In contrast, Chinese are taught to minimize the importance of one's accomplishments. Rather, a Chinese is conditioned to acknowledge the help of parents, teachers, and institutions that lead to one's personal success.

The Chinese mind-set on self-disclosure and self-presentation is also reflected in the arts. In music, for example, Chinese often sing praises of the sun, the mountain, the sea, their hometown, hoeing the fields, harvesting the crops—always something external to their lives that does not revolve around the self.

The more positive and open attitude about the self in American society presumes that Americans respect the self. Thereby, I would speculate that there must be a correlation between the social practice of self-disclosure, self-presentation, and cultural individualism. The more individualistic a society, the more positive the attitude that people adopt towards self-disclosure and self-presentation. Conversely, the more such practices are used in society, the more collective efforts people have to make to reaffirm the value of the self and individualism. The more collective celebration of the self calls for more collective efforts to understand the boundaries between the self and society, consequentially creating more laws and regulations to constrain the self. This development in the relationship between the self and society, or between individualism and collectivism, exists not only in the U.S. but in China and, for that matter, any human society.

Consider how an identity crisis is handled in American and Chinese societies respectively. A relevant question might be: who would you go to for help in the U.S. if you have a self-identity crisis? When I posed this question to my American students, most replied that they would see a psychoanalyst or a therapist to get counseling about their problem. A social program of mental health rehabilitation would be also be a viable option. Although Americans might discuss their personal problems with their parents or friends, generally speaking, this would not be their first choice. Therefore, there seems to be a cultural ordering of alternative resources for seeking help to handle and resolve one's identity crisis. In the U.S., such an ordering would not find parents or close relatives at the top of the list. If this is true, I would suggest that American society has made a collective effort to solve identity problems, because help is sought at the level of society rather than the family.

By contrast, Chinese collectivism is very weak in this respect. If a Chinese has an identity crisis, he or she usually goes to the immediate family for help first. As the Chinese saying goes, do not let people outside your family know that there is a skeleton in the closet. But if the individual fails to get help from family members, he or she might decide to seek external help, such as from friends, neighbors, or even an employer. While American employers rarely bother with the personal affairs of their employees, Chinese employers are sometimes willing to help with their employees' personal problems. One explanation of this phenomenon is that there are few social services or therapeutic programs in China to treat psychological problems.

Hence lies the inherent difference: although American society is highly individualistic, it is the most collective in its maintenance of contact with individuals through various sorts of social services and programs to help solve individual problems. Although Chinese culture is known to be highly collective, Chinese society maintains only indirect contact with individuals through intermediatory institutions such as families and neighborhood committees. Given this twisted contrast between two cultures, there seems to be a disparity between what things are on the symbolic level and what they are in reality.

Individualism

How do American and Chinese cultures contrast in individualism? If we understand individualism as a doctrine that upholds the principle that a person can do whatever one's free will dictates, we realize that there are different areas of individualism in both American and Chinese societies. For example, as already discussed, Americans are freer in self-presentation, while Chinese are freer in emotional expression. There are many other aspects of life that can be explored regarding the extent to which individualism permeates both American and Chinese societies.

In my view, Americans seem to be more individualistic than Chinese in the political arena, in the sense that they directly elect their public servants. This direct vote represents an expression of free will without any interference from society. It must be noted, though, that the free will of an individual is only exercised in the act of casting the vote. After the election, personal free will is supplanted by the will of the majority.

Perhaps the area of life in which Americans are most individualistic is ideology. People in the U.S. can talk about anything they want without ideologi-cal constraints. In China, on the other hand, any ideological discussion can have a significant impact on social structure and order; if it is not done appropriately, it can destroy interpersonal relationships and jeopardize one's employment. In the U.S., the government does not interfere with ideological exchange; Americans can adhere to any social and ideological value that they want to uphold in their lives. They can even debate openly over opposing social values, and heated debate is not subject to persecution. In principle, freedom of speech governs the American ideological life.

But it must be noted that freedom of speech is not without limits in the United States. For example, you cannot use speech to harass other people psychologically. To use an obvious case in point, it is against the law to shout "Fire!" in a crowded theater unless there is actually a fire. Therefore, logically speaking, freedom of speech as exercised in the United States is not absolute individualism, but rather a compromise between individualism and collectivism. Every personal freedom seems to be a necessary compromise between individualism and community. For example, smoking as a right in many U.S. institutions has been limited to areas outside public buildings. On the one hand, American smokers have the right to smoke; on the other, they cannot always smoke in public buildings, not even in the hallways. Thus, smokers' freedom to smoke has been interfered with by the non-smokers' right to be free from unhealthy smoke hazards. As a result of negotiation between smokers and non-smokers, limits have been set as to how free smokers can be. This simple example shows that, like the relationship between individualism and collectivism, freedom and social responsibilities are inseparable. As soon as anyone claims their inalienable right to freedom of speech, they are immediately subject to such social responsibilities as interdictions against harassment or causing undesirable and uncivil infringements against others.

Negotiation of the limits of freedom of speech seems to be a constant phenomenon in the United States. Just recently, CNN reported that some Californians will have to apply for a license from the police department to do poetry readings in coffee houses. Reading poetry in a public place would seem to fall perfectly in line with the American principle of freedom of speech. But according to the report, the police department is concerned with public safety when groups of people gather in coffee houses to read poetry. If there is a grain of truth in the police department's argument, it would seem to be due to the conceptual link between the freedom of individuals and their social responsibilities.

However, the judgment of whether or not a particular speech is socially responsible is not an easy task and always subject to debate. For example, one hotly contested issue on American campuses is whether a university's computer service should allow publicly accessible files in its electronic mail system for the transmission of pornographic stories written by students on the campus. Some argue that the use of such files is not compatible with the academic environment in the university. Others counter that freedom of speech should not be impinged upon by any means or under any circumstances.

The success of American freedom of speech supports the argument that the benefits from perfecting one's skills of expression to make one's voice heard is more important than trying to enforce censorship under any pretext. Perhaps this is the reason why "fundamentals of public speaking" has become a basic course on many American campuses, in contrast to Chinese colleges where it is virtually nonexistent in the curriculum.

The principle of freedom of speech produces a public speech environment in which people are less concerned about the moral values of a speech than the quality of its delivery. In this respect, Adolph Hitler's 1934 Nazi Party Congress speech has been rated as great oratory along with the speeches of Martin Luther King, Jr., and Franklin D. Roosevelt. Students in my public speaking class select topics such as prostitution, PMS, and the use of condoms. The predominant goal of a public speaking course here is to sharpen people's speaking skills rather than to advocate any moral point of view. Students are taught how to devise an ingenious attention-getter, how to use emotional triggers to achieve some persuasive effect, how to use metaphors, contrast, gestures, and visual aids to enhance the force and credibility of the speech. But since freedom of speech cannot be detached from social responsibility, social values have to be included and negotiated through speech. Lack of attention to social values in public speaking may in the long run destroy the relationship between individualism and the community.

Beyond political and ideological communication in the U.S., there is also strong embodiment of individualism in cultural communication. As discussed above, American cultural emphasis on the self instills more individualism than in China. In support of this claim are several pertinent facts. First, it seems to me that American students are more individualistic in their behavior in the classroom. Though they seem to enjoy and actively engage in class discussions, they seem to have no qualms about leaving the classroom any time they want to, without explanation. The respect given teachers in the Chinese community doesn't seem to exist in the American classroom. Also, American and Chinese students have different interpretations as to whether or not eye contact constitutes respect for the teacher. In America, students in elementary schools are reprimanded by the teacher if they look away; while in China, their counterparts are expected to look away.

Americans are so self-assertive that they often greet each other by querying about each other's feelings. It is not uncommon to hear an American ask, "How do you feel today?" From the Chinese perspective, such a query about one's feelings in greeting would only cause confusion and be considered rude and intrusive.

Americans are also more self-assertive in saying "I love you" than Chinese. We hear American lovers say "I love you" perhaps every time they meet or part. We also find that "I love you" is often repeated between American parents and their children. One summer I spent most of my days working at a library. I noticed that the librarian called her children at home once every day, just to check up on them. Before hanging up, she would always say "I love you." In addition to this rhetorical necessity of repeating "I love you" in maintaining intimate relationships, Americans sometimes use the word "love" as a complimentary closure when writing to friends. By contrast, this open and repetitive use of "I love you" is, by and large, restricted from in Chinese culture. Chinese say "I love you" and use the word "love" very sparingly.

As is clear from the above, Americans seem to rely more on rhetorical means to maintain emotional ties between each other than do Chinese. American self-assertiveness, though an indicator of individualism, is perhaps generated out of a cultural necessity to move from individualism to community.

It is also evident to me that in nonverbal communication Americans are more self-assertive than Chinese. For example, when Americans knock at the door of another's house or apartment, they rap with their knuckles. By contrast, Chinese usually use one finger to tap at the door. In my interpretation, different ways of knocking connote different cultural premises. Americans are brought up to be very assertive; therefore, when they knock, they want to make sure they are heard. However, in Chinese culture, people are taught to be self-effacing rather than self-assertive; therefore, when they knock, they do so lightly in order not to disturb anyone or trigger a false emergency. It could be argued that this cultural contrast shows that Americans are more self-oriented while Chinese are more other-oriented in social interactions, verbally as well as nonverbally.

Conclusion

In this essay, I have taken my own Chinese perspective to explain some of the cultural differences between the United States and China by comparing individualism and collectivism. Instead of conceptualizing the dimension of individualism and collectivism as two separate elements of polarity, I interpreted them in a contextual and holistic way. Contextually, I have looked at various cultural practices in American and Chinese societies and described how those cultural practices embody individualism and collectivism respectively. Holistically, I would view both as two fundamental elements of a culture that are instinctively linked. They cannot be separated from each other in society.

REFERENCES

Bell, R. A., & Daly, J.A. (1984). The affinity-seeking function of communication. *Communication Monographs, 51*, 91-115.

Carbaugh, D. (1988). *Talking American: Cultural discourses on Donahue.* Norwood, NJ: Ablex.

Dodd, C. H. (1991). *Dynamics of intercultural communication* (3rd ed.). Dubuque, IA: Wm. C. Brown Publishers.

Gilbert, S. J. (1976). Empirical and theoretical extensions of self-disclosure. In Miller, G. R. (Ed.), *Explorations in interpersonal communication* (pp. 197-215). Newbury Park, CA: Sage.

Hofstede, G. (1984). *Culture's consequences.* Beverly Hills, CA: Sage.

Mechling, J. (1980). The magic of the boy scout campfire. *Journal of American Folklore, 93*, 35-56.

Potter, S. H. (1988). The cultural construction of emotion in rural Chinese social life. *Ethos, 16*, 181-207.

Samovar, L. A., & Porter, R.E. (1991). *Communication between cultures.* Belmont, CA: Wadsworth.

Schutz, W.C. (1966). *The interpersonal underworld.* Palo Alto, CA: Science and Behavior Books.

Varenne, H. (1977). *Americans together: Structured diversity in a midwestern town.* New York, NY: Teachers' College Press.

APPENDICES

Suggested Questions
for Discussion

Supplementary Readings

SUGGESTED QUESTIONS
FOR DISCUSSION

Part I:

1. In what ways is naming and defining one's ethnicity a political activity?

2. In the U.S., what institutions have the authority to name ethnic populations?

3. What are some arguments for cultural participants/communities naming themselves?

4. What are some characteristics that you associate with the term "American?"

5. What are some arguments for and against populations using the generic term "American?"

6. Why would a political figure choose to accentuate his/her race or ethnicity? What is the strategic value of this naming?

7. What are some strengths and weaknesses of cultural distinctiveness and cultural uniformity? How does each belief affect the process of communication?

Part II:

1. Identify prescriptions for "proper" male communication in cultures that you are familiar with.

2. Identify prescriptions for "proper" female communication in these same cultures.

3. In what ways has Eurocentric patriarchy shaped our view toward men and women of color in the U.S.?

4. What cultural beliefs underlie opposition in the U.S. military to women flying combat missions?

5. What cultural beliefs underlie opposition to ending the ban on gays in the U.S. military?

6. What cultural assumptions about men and women lie behind actions in the Navy Tailhook scandal?

7. Is talk between any male and any female an intercultural interaction?

Part III:

1. Some students have described their cultural origins as so distant or forgotten that they are essentially "without a culture". Support or counter this statement.

2. How does your way of speaking reflect a distinct cultural community?

3. How can a mass media outlet, such as radio or TV, maintain and recreate cultural knowledge?

4. Identify a joke or humorous narrative from a cultural community other than your own and provide a cultural explanation for the (understood) premises of this humor.

5. Rent the 1993 film *Posse,* starring Mario Van Peebles. Using *Posse* as an example, how can film be used to represent cultural knowledge?

6. What are some salient cultural themes in American media?

7. Cultural values and practices can be self-contradictory. Discuss some contradictions that you have observed in U.S. society.

Part IV:

1. In what contexts are the following terms used in ordinary conversation: *foreigner, alien, immigrant, naturalized* citizen? What are some assumptions associated with each term?

2. What expectations do you have when speaking to someone of a different race or culture? Where do these expectations come from?

3. Describe an interaction you have had with someone of a different race or culture.

4. Interpret and discuss the notion of "cultural differences".

5. Define the term "tourist." What is the relationship between the tourist and the cultural native?

6. Research the following topic: Exactly what information was given to U.S. military personnel about the Middle East during the Gulf War. How did this information facilitate or hinder intercultural communication?

7. Research the information given to U.S. military personnel about Somalia during recent relief efforts there. Compare this information with that given about the Middle East. Account for the differences in approach.

SUPPLEMENTARY READINGS

Part I: Naming Ourselves

Anzaldúa, G. (1987). *Borderlands/La Frontera: The new mestiza.* San Francisco: Spinsters/Aunt Lute.

Beck, P. V., & Walters, A. L. (1988). *The sacred: Ways of knowledge, sources of life.* Tsalie, AZ: Navajo Community College Press.

Chan, A. B. (1984). Born again Asian: The making of a new literature. *Journal of Ethnic Studies, 11,* 57-73.

Chan, S. (1991). *Asian Americans: An interpretive history.* Boston: Twayne Publishers.

Collins, C. A., & Clark, J. E. (1992). A structural narrative analysis of *Nightline's* 'This Week in the Holy Land.' *Critical Studies in Mass Communication, 9,* 25-43.

Daniels, R. (1988). *Asian America.* Seattle: University of Washington Press.

Fessler, L. W. (1985). *Chinese in America: Stereotyped past, changing present.* New York: Vantage Press.

Flores, J., & Yudice, G. (1990). Living borders/buscando America: Languages of Latino self-formation. *Social Text, 8,* 57-84.

González, A. (1990). Mexican 'otherness' in the rhetoric of Mexican Americans. *Southern Communication Journal, 55,* 276-291.

Hobson, G. (Ed.). (1979). *The remembered earth: An anthology of contemporary Native American literature.* Albuquerque: Red Earth Press.

Hoskins, L. A. (1992). Eurocentrism vs. Afrocentrism: A geopolitical linkage analysis. *Journal of Black Studies, 23,* 247-257.

Hourani, A. H. (1991). *A history of the Arab peoples.* Cambridge, MA: Harvard University Press.

Keefe, S. E., & Padilla, A. M. (1987). *Chicano ethnicity.* Albuquerque: University of New Mexico Press.

Lincoln, K. (1983). *Native American renaissance.* Berkeley: University of California Press.

Momaday, N. S. (1976). *The names: A memoir.* Tucson: University of Arizona Press.

Ogawa, D. (1971). *From Japs to Japanese: The evolution of Japanese-American stereotypes.* Berkeley: McCutchan.

Omi, M. & Winant, H. (1986). *Racial formation in the United States.* New York: Routledge & Kegan Paul.

Padilla, F. M. (1985). *Latino ethnic consciousness.* South Bend, IN: University of Notre Dame Press.

Riley, P. (1993). *Growing up Native American: An anthology.* New York: William Morrow.

Rotberg, R. I. (Ed.). (1978). *The mixing of peoples: Problems of identification and ethnicity.* New York: Greylock.

Sedano, M. V. (1980). Chicanismo: A rhetorical analysis of themes and images of selected poetry from the Chicano movement. *Western Journal of Speech Communication, 44,* 170-190.

Shorris, E. (1992). *Latinos: A biography of the people.* New York: W. W. Norton.

Takaki, R. (1989). *Strangers from a different shore*. Boston: Little, Brown and Company.

Trinh, T. M. (1989). *Woman, native, other*. Bloomington: Indiana University Press.

Tsai, S. H. (1986) *The Chinese experience in America*. Bloomington, IN: Indiana University Press.

West, B. A. (1992). Women's diaries as ethnographic resources. *Journal of Narrative and Life History*, *2*, 333-354.

Part II: Negotiating Sexuality and Gender

Allen, P. G. (1986). *The sacred hoop: Recovering the feminine in American Indian traditions*. Boston: Beacon Press.

Belenky, M. F., Clinchy, B. M., Goldberger, N. R., & Tarule, J. M. (1986). *Women's ways of knowing: The development of self, voice, and mind*. New York: Basic Books.

Bell-Scott, P., Guy-Sheftall, B., Jones-Royster, J., Sims-Wood, J., DeCosta-Willis, M., & Fultz, L. (1991). *Double stitch: Black women write about mothers and daughters*. Boston: Beacon Press.

Carter, K. (1992). Disrupting identity: Feminist reflections on women and difference(s). *World Communication*, *21*, 13-21.

Carter, K., & Spitzack, C. (1990). Formation and empowerment in gender and communication courses. *Women's Studies in Communication*, *13*, 92-110.

Cisneros, S. (1991). *Woman hollering creek and other stories*. New York: Random House.

Christian, B. (1985). *Black feminist criticism*. New York: Pergamon.

Doucet, S. A. (1989). Cajun music: Songs and psyche. *Journal of Popular Culture*, *23*, 89-99.

Fitch, K. L. (1991). The interplay of linguistic universals and cultural knowledge in personal address: Colombian *madre* terms. *Communication Monographs*, *58*, 254-272.

Foss, K. A., & Foss, S. J. (1991). *Women speak: The eloquence of women's lives*. Prospect Heights, IL: Waveland Press.

Gay Men's Oral History Group. (1989). *Walking after midnight: Gay men's life stories*. London: Routledge.

hooks, b. (1981). *Ain't I a woman: Black women and feminism*. Boston: South End Press.

hooks, b. (1990). *Yearning: Race, gender, and cultural politics*. Boston: South End Press.

Houston Stanback, M. (1985). Language and black women's place: Evidence from the black middle class. In P. A. Treichler, C., Kramarae, & B. Stafford (Eds.), *For alma mater: Theory and practice in feminist scholarship* (pp. 177-193). Urbana: University of Illinois Press.

Johnson, F. L. (1989). Women's culture and communication: An analytical perspective. In C. M. Lont & S. A. Friedley (Eds.), *Beyond boundaries: Sex and gender diversity in communication* (pp. 301-316). Fairfax, VA: George Mason University Press.

Lesbian Oral History Group. (1989). *Inventing ourselves: Lesbian life stories*. London: Routledge.

Lim, S. G., & Tsutakawa, M. (Eds.). (1989). *The forbidden stitch: An Asian American women's anthology*. Corvallis: Calyx Books.

Martin, E. (1987). *The woman in the body*. Boston: Beacon Press.

Perlmutter Bowen, S., & Wyatt, N. (1993). *Transforming visions: Feminist critiques in communication studies*. Cresskill, NJ: Hampton Press.

Pharr, S. (1988). *Homophobia: A weapon of sexism*. Little Rock: The Women's Project.

Steihm, E. (Ed.). (1984). *Women's views of the political world of men*. Dobbs Ferry, NY: Transnational Publishers.

Trujillo, N. (1991). Hegemonic masculinity on the mound: Media representations of Nolan Ryan and American sports culture. *Critical Studies in Mass Communication*, *8*, 290-308.

Part III: Representing Cultural Knowledge in Interpersonal and Mass Media Contexts

Allen, P. G. (Ed.). (1983). *Studies in American Indian literatures: Critical essays and course designs*. New York: Modern Language Association of America.

Asante, M. K. (1990). The tradition of advocacy in the Yoruba courts. *Southern Communication Journal, 55*, 250-259.

Basso, K. H. (1979). *Portraits of 'the whiteman': Linguistic play and cultural symbols among the Western Apache*. Cambridge: Cambridge University Press.

Chen, V. (1990/1991). 'Mien Tze' at the Chinese dinner table: A study of the interactional accomplishment of 'face.' *Research on Language and Social Interaction, 24*, 109-140.

Garfield, E. P. (1985). *Women's voices from Latin America: Interviews with six contemporary authors*. Detroit: Wayne State University Press.

González, A., & Bradley, C. (1990). Breaking into silence: Technology transfer and mythical knowledge among the Acomas of *Nuevo Mexico*. In M. J. Medhurst, A. González, & T. R. Peterson (Eds.), *Communication and the culture of technology* (pp. 63-76). Pullman, WA: Washington State University Press.

Gray, H. (1989). Television, Black Americans, and the American dream. *Critical Studies in Mass Communication, 6*, 376-386.

Katriel, T. (1986). *Talking straight: Dugri speech in Israeli Sabra culture*. Cambridge: Cambridge University Press.

Katriel, T. (1987). Rhetoric in flames: Fire inscriptions in Israeli youth movement ceremonials. *Quarterly Journal of Speech, 73*, 444-459.

Kim, M. S. (1992). A comparative analysis of nonverbal expressions as portrayed by Korean and American print-media advertising. *Howard Journal of Communications, 3*, 317-339.

Lake, R. A. (1991). Between myth and history: Enacting time in Native American protest rhetoric. *Quarterly Journal of Speech, 77*, 123-151.

Larson, J. F., McAnany, E. G., & Storey, J. D. (1986). News of Latin America on network television, 1972-1981: A northern perspective on the Southern Hemisphere. *Critical Studies in Mass Communication, 3*, 169-183.

Lewels, F. L., Jr. (1974). *The uses of the media by the Chicano movement: A study in minority access*. New York: Praeger.

Lopez, B. (1977). *Giving birth to thunder, sleeping with his daughter: Coyote builds North America*. New York: Avon Books.

Mayerle, J. (1987). A dream deferred: The failed fantasy of Norman Lear's *a.k.a. Pablo. Central States Speech Journal, 38*, 223-239.

Morris, R., & Wander, P. (1990). Native American rhetoric: Dancing in the shadows of the Ghost Dance. *Quarterly Journal of Speech, 76*, 164-191.

Mulvaney, B. M. (1990). Popular art as rhetorical artifact: The case of reggae music. In S. Thomas (Ed.), *Communication & culture: Language performance, technology, and media* (pp. 117-127). Norwood, NJ: Ablex.

Owens, L. (1992). *Other destinies: Understanding the American Indian novel*. Norman, OK: University of Oklahoma Press.

Ruoff, A. L. B. (1990). *American Indian literatures: An introduction, bibliographic review, and selected bibliography*. New York: Modern Language Association of America.

Trafzer, C. (1993). *Earth song, sky spirit: An anthology of Native American fiction*. New York: Doubleday.

Tucker, L. R. & Shah, H. (1992). Race and the transformation of culture: The making of the television miniseries *Roots*. *Critical Studies in Mass Communication*, *9*, 325-336.

Part IV: Traversing Cultural Paths

Alexander, A. F., Cronen, V. E., Kang, K-W., Tsou, B., & Banks, J. (1986). Patterns of topic sequencing and information gain: A comparative analysis of relationship development in Chinese and American cultures. *Communication Quarterly*, *34*, 66-78.

Althen, G. (1992). The Americans have to say everything. *Communication Quarterly*, *40*, 413-421.

Anderson, T. (1992). Comparative experience factor among black, asian, and hispanic Americans: Coalitions or conflicts? *Journal of Black Studies*, *23*, 27-38

Bruner, E. (Ed.). (1984). *Text, play, and story: The construction and reconstruction of self and society*. Washington, D. C.: American Ethnological Society.

Chesebro, J. W. (1982). Illness as a rhetorical act: A cross-cultural perspective. *Communication Quarterly*, *30*, 321-331.

Churchill. W. (1992). *Fantasies of the master race: Literature, cinema and the colonization of American Indians*. (M. A. Jaimes, Ed.). Monroe, ME: Common Courage Press.

Essed, P. (1991). *Understanding everyday racism: An interdisciplinary theory*. Newbury Park, CA: Sage.

González, A. (1989). 'Participation' at WMEX-FM: Interventional rhetoric of Ohio Mexican Americans. *Western Journal of Speech Communication*, *53*, 398-410.

Huang, S. (1991). Chinese traditional festivals. *Journal of Popular Culture*, *25*, 163-180.

Jaimes, M. A. (Ed.). (1992). *The state of Native America: Genocide, colonization, and resistance*. Boston: South End Press.

Kang, K-W., & Pearce, W. B. (1984). The place of transcultural concepts in communication theory and research, with a case study of reticence. *Communication*, *9*, 79-96.

Kim, E. H. (1982). *Asian American literature: An introduction to the writings and their social context*. Philadelphia: Temple University Press.

Leonard, R., & Locke D. C. (1993). Communication stereotypes: Is interracial communication possible? *Journal of Black Studies*, *23*, 332-343.

Leroux, N. (1991). Frederick Douglass and the attention shift. *Rhetoric Society Quarterly*, *21*, 36-46.

Marsella, A. J., DeVos, G., & Hsu, F. L. K. (Eds.). (1985). *Culture and self: Asian and Western perspectives*. New York: Tavistock.

Momaday, N. S. (1966). *House made of dawn*, New York: Harper & Row. (Reprint by Perennial Library, 1989).

Penfield, J., & Omstein-Garcia, J. L. (1985). *Chicano English: An ethnic contact dialect*. Philadelphia: John Benjamins.

Philips. S. U. (1983). *The invisible culture: Communication in classroom and community on the Warm Springs Indian Reservation*. Prospect Heights, IL: Waveland Press.

Philipsen, G. (1992). *Speaking culturally: Explorations in social communication*. Albany, NY: SUNY Press.

van Dijk, T. A. (1987). *Communicating racism: Ethnic prejudice in thought and talk*. Newbury Park, CA: Sage.

West, C. (1993). *Race matters*. Boston: Beacon Press.

Zaharna, R. S. (1991). The ontological function of interpersonal communication: A cross-cultural analysis of Americans and Palestinians. *Howard Journal of Communications*, *3*, 87-98.